A Question of Emphasis

Louise Fishman
Drawing

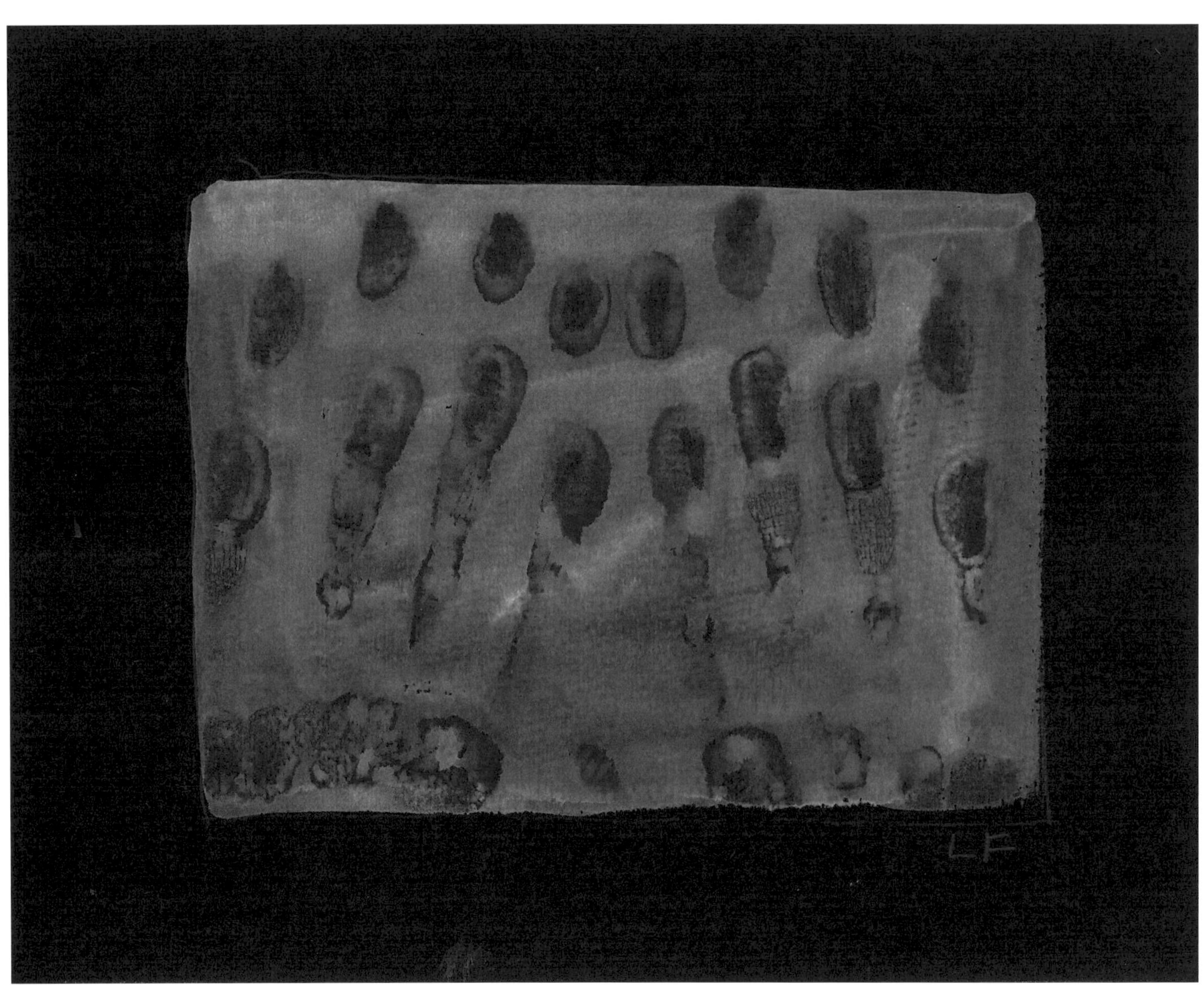

1

Untitled, 1991

Watercolor, charcoal, and graphite on paper
8 × 10⅜ inches

A Question of Emphasis
Louise Fishman Drawing

Amy L. Powell

CONTRIBUTORS

Jill H. Casid

Louise Fishman

Catherine Lord

Ulrike Müller

KRANNERT ART MUSEUM

University of Illinois Urbana-Champaign

This publication accompanies the exhibition *A Question of Emphasis: Louise Fishman Drawing*, organized by Krannert Art Museum, University of Illinois Urbana-Champaign, on view August 26, 2021–February 26, 2022.

Lead exhibition support is provided by the Henry Luce Foundation American Art Program.

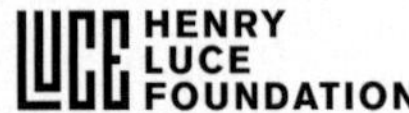

Additional funding is provided by the Rosann Gelvin Noel Fund for Krannert Art Museum; College of Fine and Applied Arts, University of Illinois Urbana-Champaign; Vielmetter Los Angeles; Sueyun Locks, the Locks Foundation; Karma, New York; and the Sandra L. Batzli Memorial Fund.

An initiative presented in association with the Feminist Art Coalition (FAC).

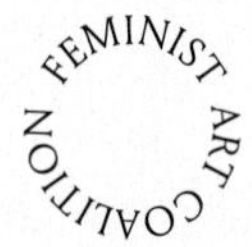

LIBRARY OF CONGRESS CONTROL NUMBER
2020918119
ISBN: 978-1-64657-017-1

PUBLISHED BY
Krannert Art Museum
University of Illinois Urbana-Champaign
College of Fine + Applied Arts
500 East Peabody Drive
Champaign, IL 61820 USA
kam.illinois.edu

DISTRIBUTED BY
ARTBOOK | D.A.P.
75 Broad Street, Suite 630
New York, NY 10004
artbook.com

PRODUCED BY
Lucia | Marquand, Seattle
luciamarquand.com

Curated by Amy L. Powell
Edited by Kristin Swan
Designed by Thomas Eykemans
Typeset by Tina Henderson
Color management by iocolor, Seattle
Printed and bound in China by Artron Art Printing
Typefaces: ITC Avant Garde, Silva
Note on the typography: The typefaces were selected to echo Louise Fishman's aesthetic philosophy and her historical context. Herb Lubalin and Tom Carnase designed Avant Garde in New York in the 1970s. Its geometric structure yields a spectacular *Q* letterform, which finds prominence in the main title and in the word *Queer*. Silva, designed by Daniel Sabino, has roots in calligraphy that introduce a humanistic and expressive counterpoint to the geometric display type. —Thomas Eykemans

Front Cover: Louise Fishman, *My Pigeon*, 1976 (detail). Oil and wax on paper. 30½ × 22½ inches. Collection of the artist, FS.38616. Back Cover: Louise Fishman, page from *Book of Abuse*, 1993–94. Acrylic, oil, oil stick, graphite, staples, and wire with aluminum and paper collage on paper; Japanese leporello binding. 6⅝ × 3⅝ × 1⅝ inches (closed). Collection of the artist, FS.35386.

Contents

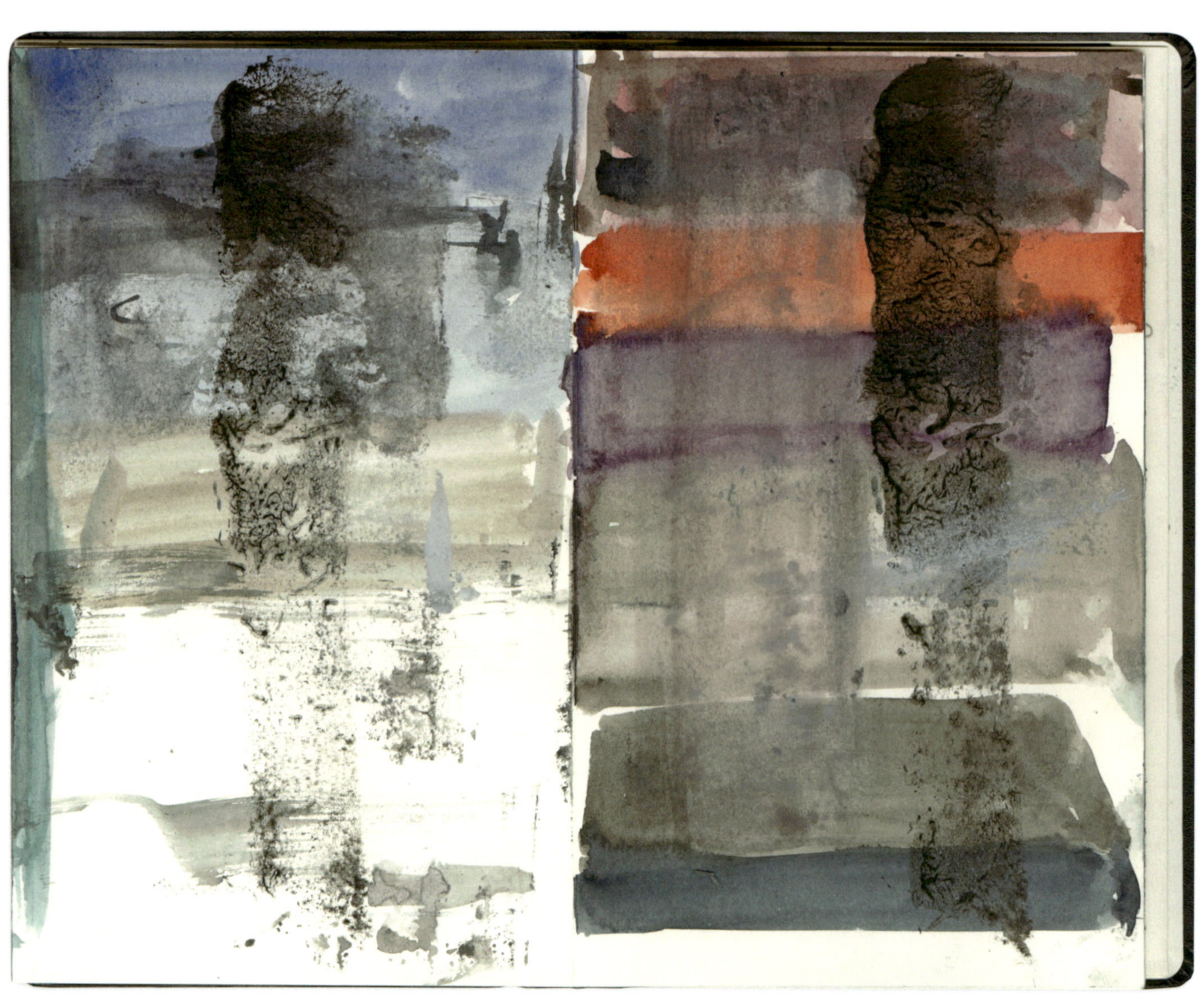

2

From **Vaporetto Leporello No. 2**, 2016

Watercolor and tempera on paper; leporello binding

5 × 8¼ × ¾ inches (closed)

Foreword

Krannert Art Museum is proud to present the first exhibition and publication on the subject of Louise Fishman's remarkable works on paper, an arc that begins in 1964 and runs to the present day. While Fishman's paintings have long been celebrated — even as their importance in the history of art still remains insufficiently appreciated — her drawings are a true revelation. The exhibition crests one hundred works, most of which come from the artist's archive and have never been exhibited, along with important loans from institutions and private collectors. Taken together, these works on paper present one of the most significant drawing practices of the late twentieth and early twenty-first centuries. Rather than preliminary studies for paintings, the drawings are independent statements, tied to Fishman's feminist and queer networks and addressing literary, historical, and artistic references of remarkable scope and fluency, a powerful and ongoing act of creative response to both the past and the conditions of the present moment.

We are immensely grateful to Amy L. Powell, Krannert Art Museum's curator of modern and contemporary art, for developing this exhibition and publication with intellectual rigor, a thoughtful sense of history, and the urgency to bring Fishman's drawings to the attention of a broad public. Jill H. Casid, Catherine Lord, and Ulrike Müller all contributed important new thinking in this catalogue, for which we express our appreciation. It would also be impossible to overestimate Ingrid Nyeboe's contribution to the project as archivist, collections manager, and intellectual partner. Her collaboration and commitment has been essential to the success of the book and exhibition.

And, of course, we cannot possibly express sufficient gratitude and admiration to Louise Fishman for opening up this staggeringly important body of work for presentation and exploration in this exhibition and book. We admire your long dedication to the craft of drawing, your cerebral approach to the medium, and your interrogation — and creation — of so many histories in startling, meaningful, and beautiful ways through your work.

Jon L. Seydl
DIRECTOR

3

Pin Up, 1991

Graphite on paper
5½ × 7½ inches, two sided

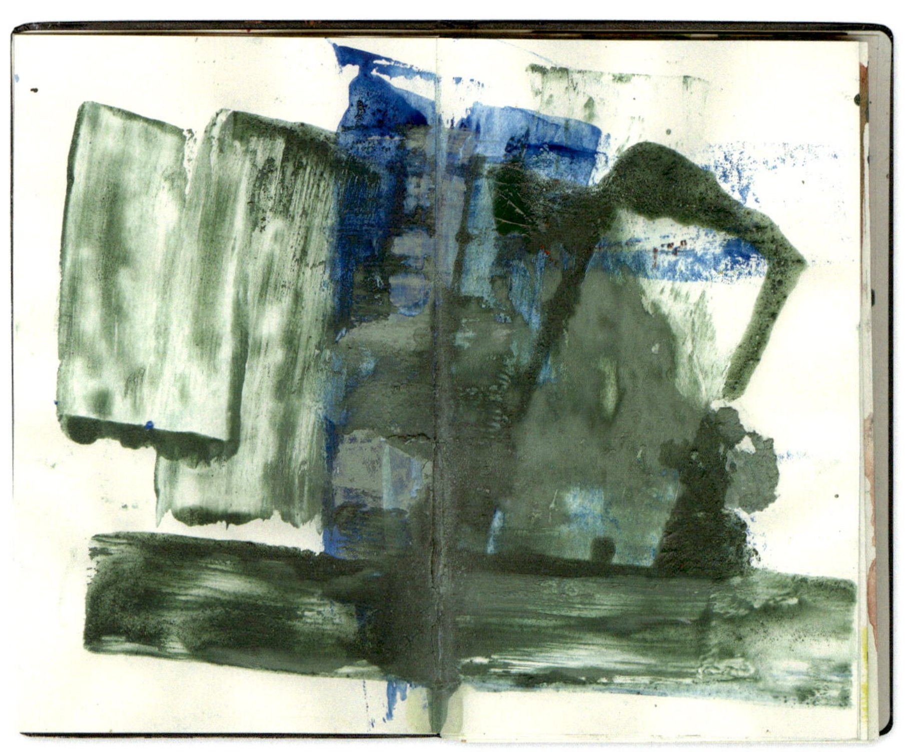

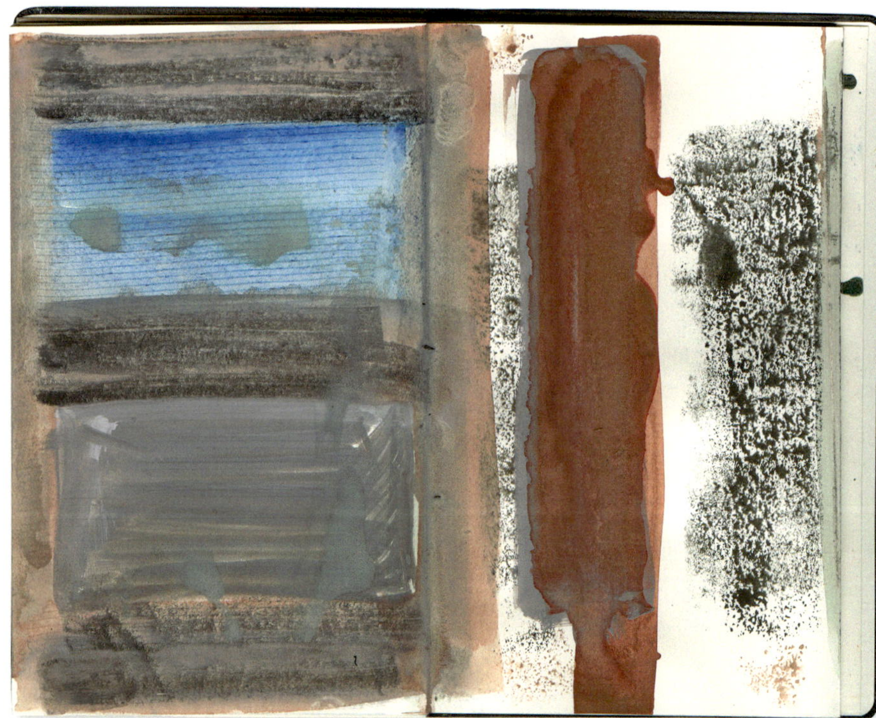

4

From **Vaporetto Leporello No. 4**, 2017

Watercolor and tempera on paper; leporello binding

8¼ × 5 × ¾ inches (closed)

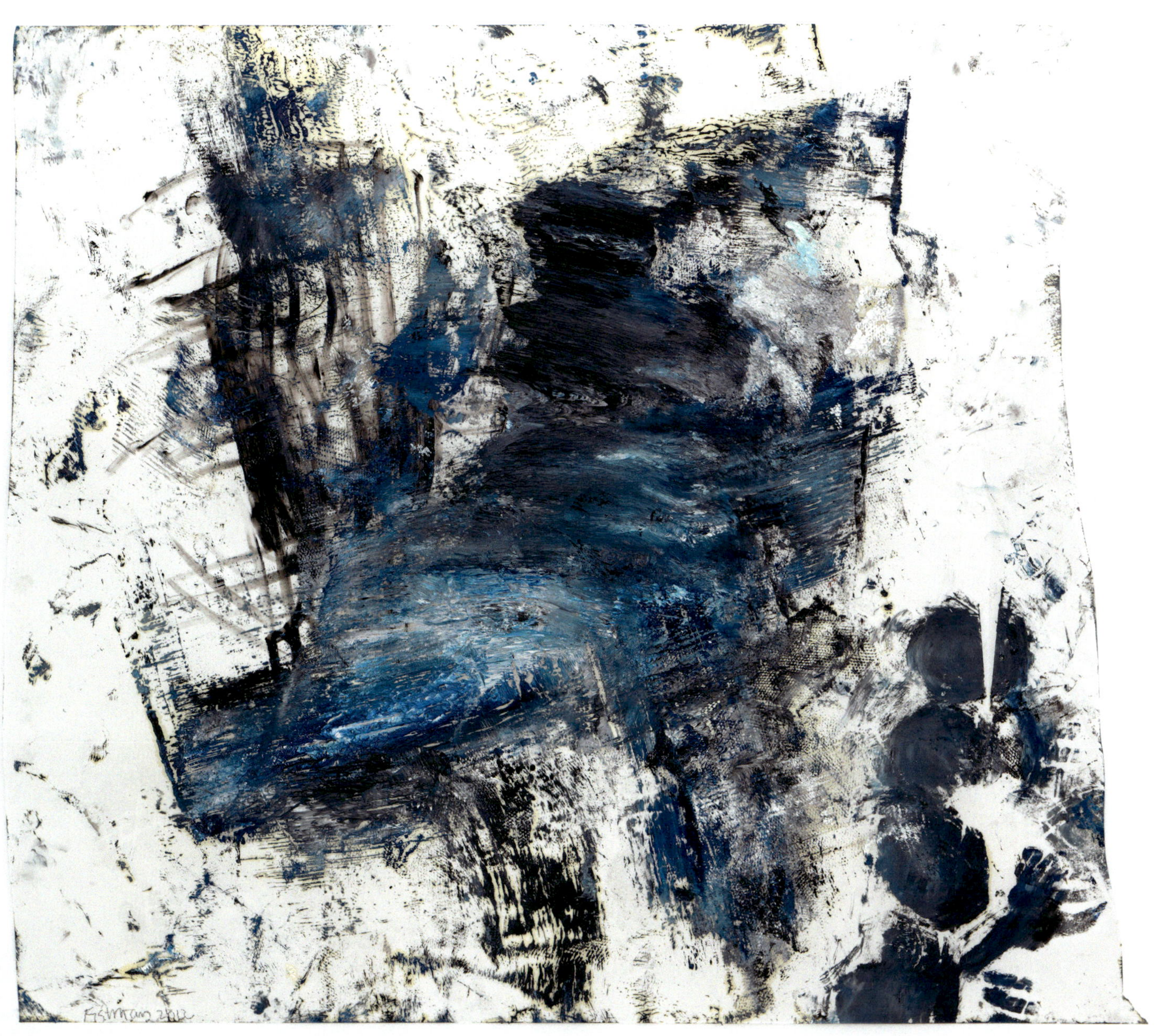

5

Untitled, 2012

Oil on tracing paper
41⅞ × 49½ inches

6

Untitled, 1993

Charcoal and sumi ink on paper
24 × 19 inches, two sided

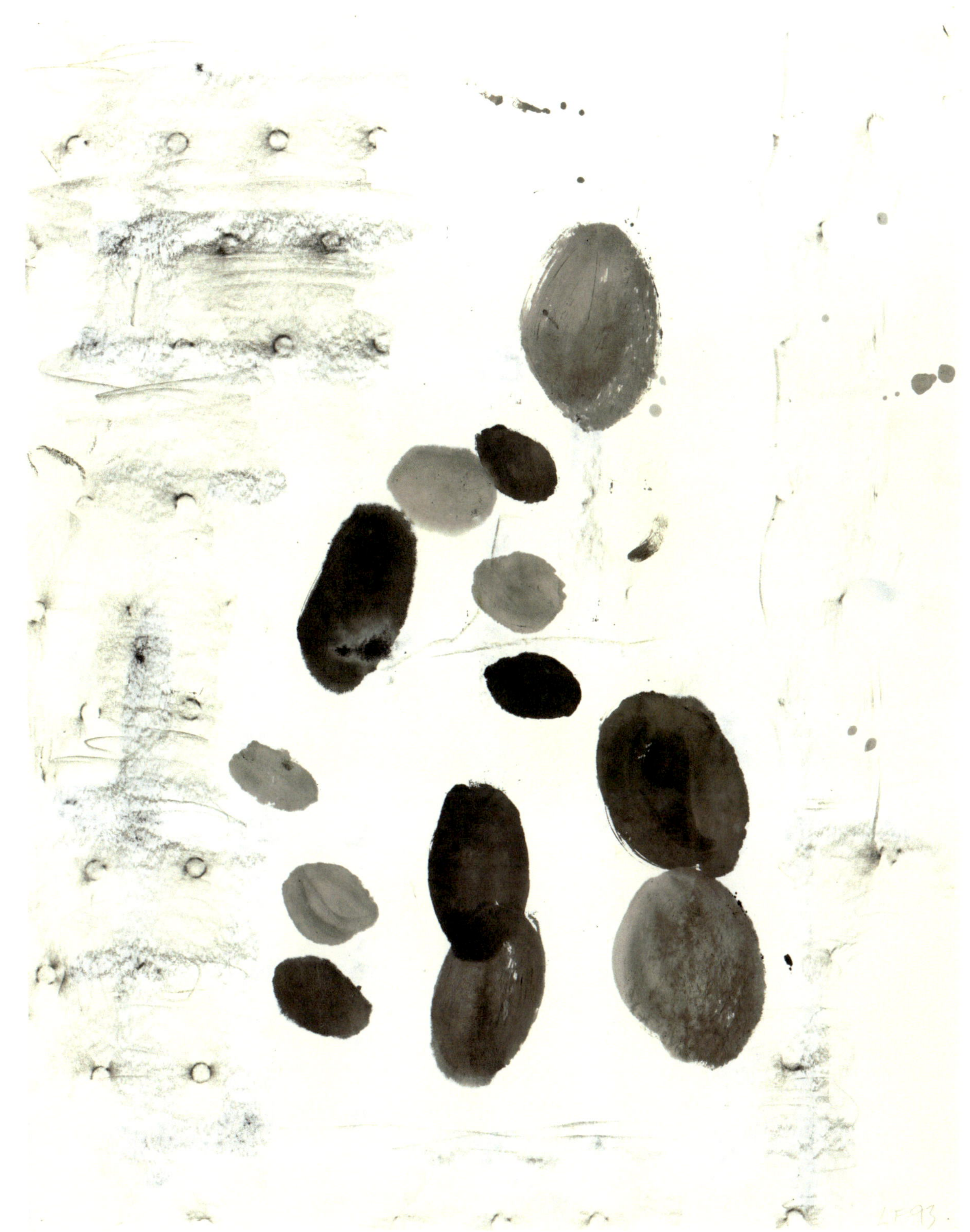

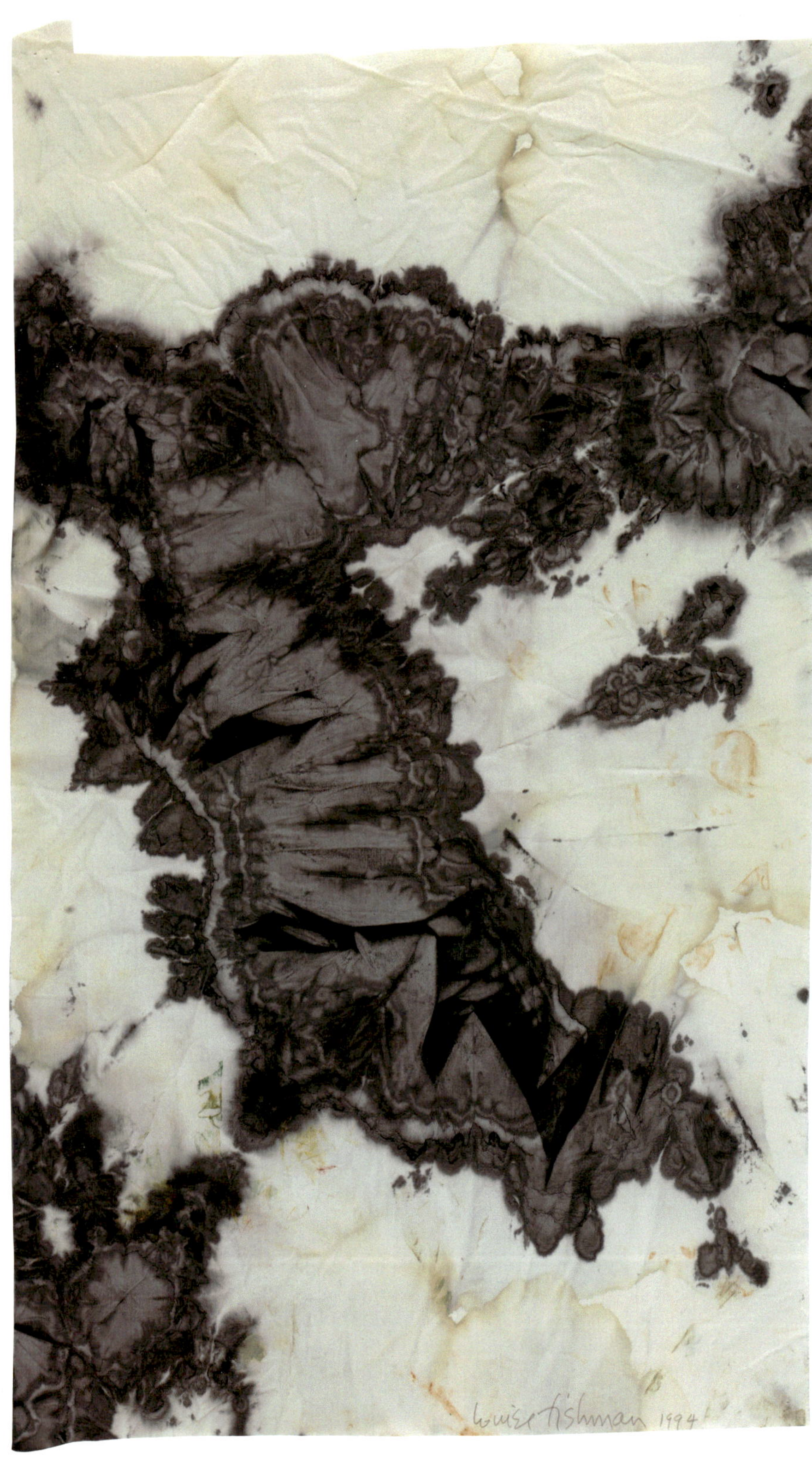

7
Untitled, 1994

Ink on cotton fabric
26 × 15 inches

8
Untitled, 2001

Acrylic on paper
30 × 22¼ inches

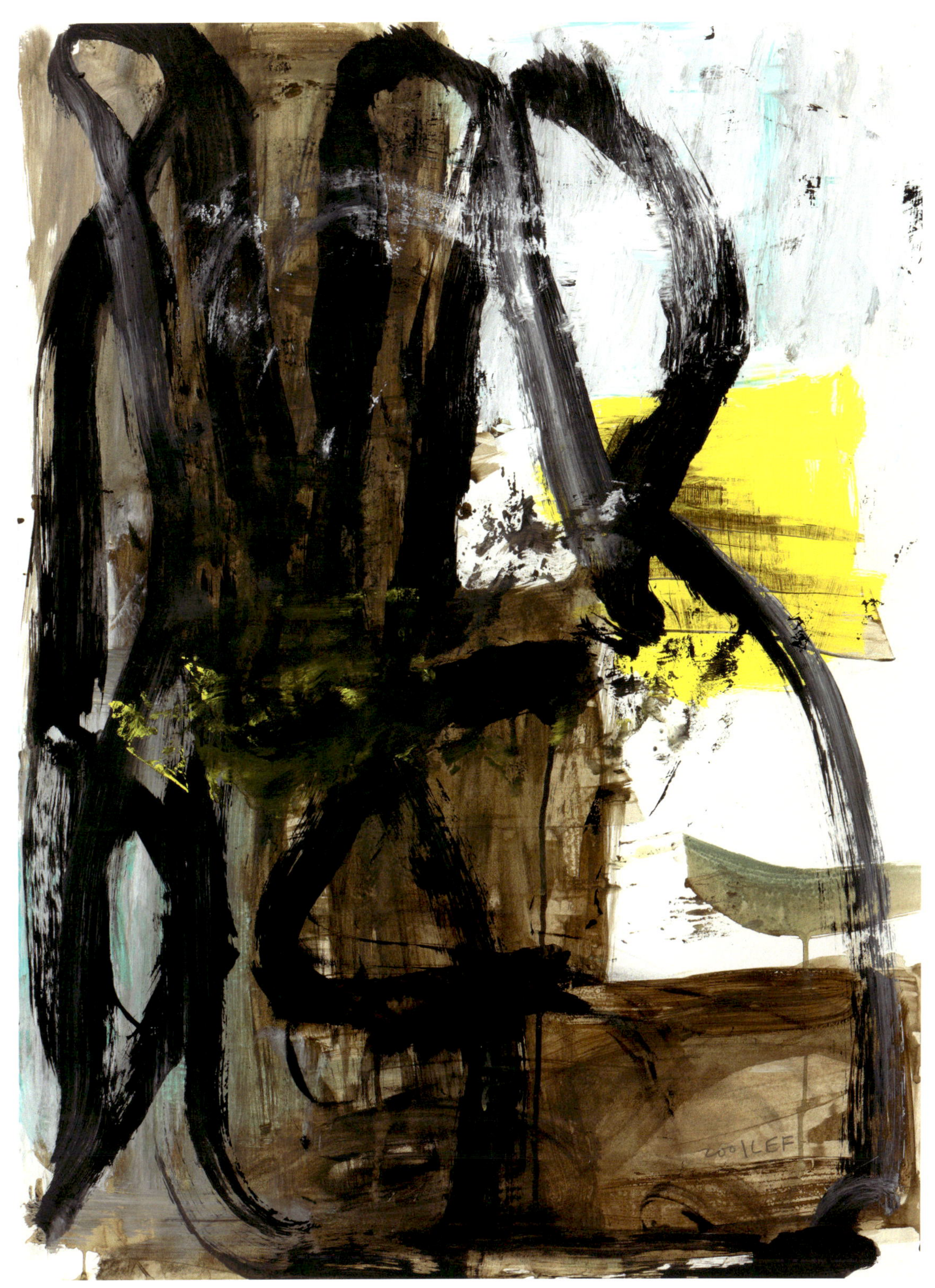

9

Untitled, 2013

Tempera, ink, and watercolor on paper
24 × 18 inches

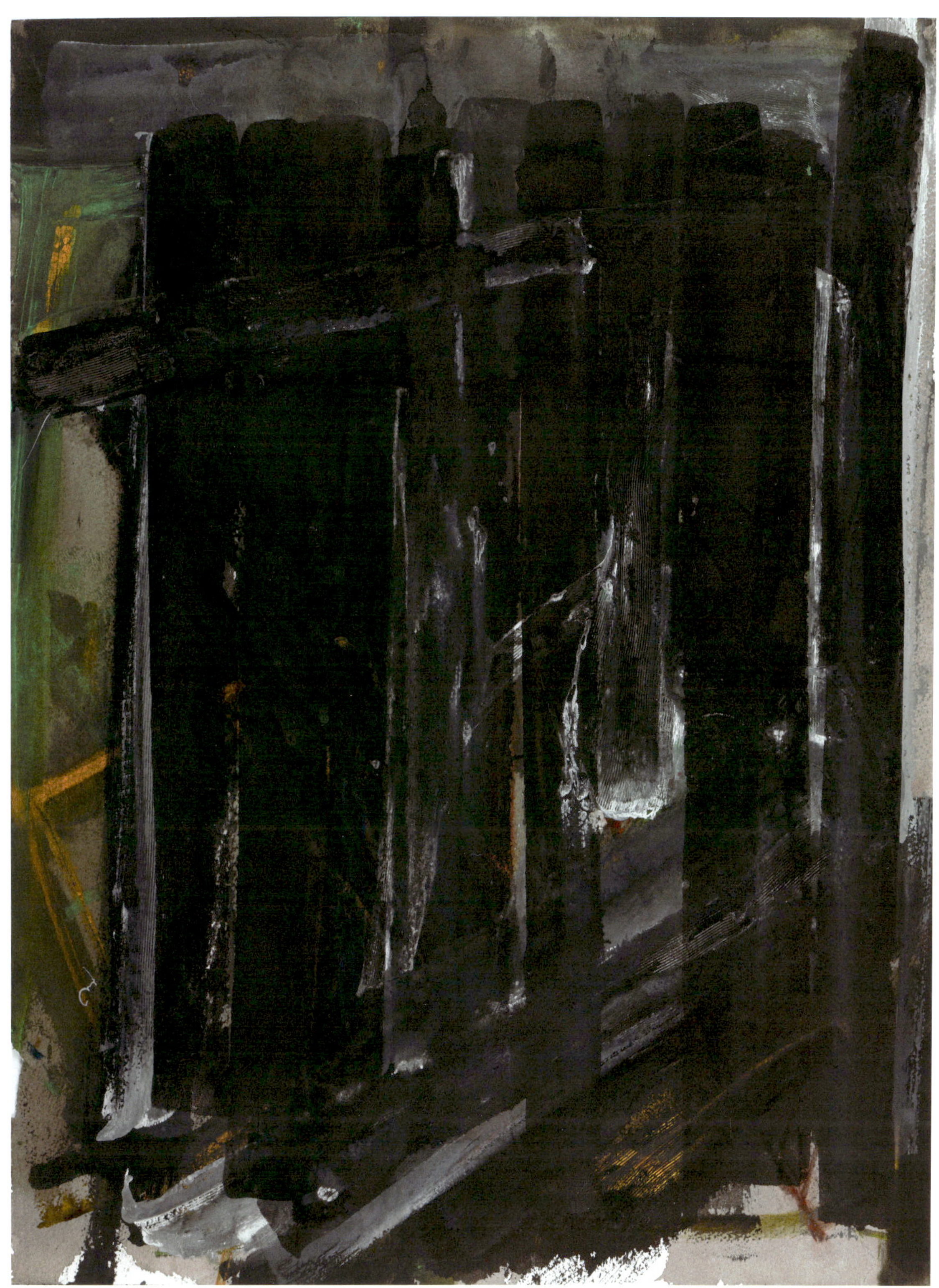

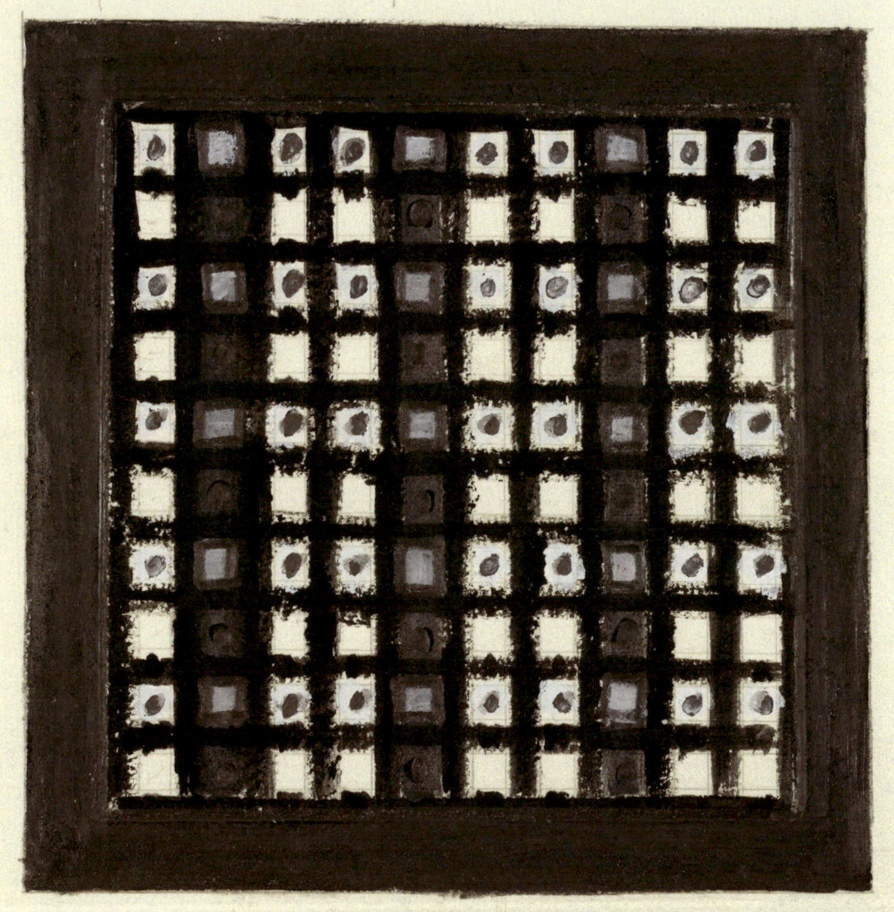

A GROGGER FOR EVA AND AGNES. 1992
BY LOUISE

Louise Fishman Drawing

Amy L. Powell

Fold, grid, staple, transfer, curve, dedicate. As descriptors of processes that animate Louise Fishman's drawings, these verbs call to mind the artist's hands manipulating paper. In works ranging from pocket sized to human scale and, at times, recalling the physicality and abundant energy of her paintings — the broad brushstrokes; scraping with trowels and other tools; bold, undiluted, and layered colors grappling with such enduring themes as post-Holocaust memory, feminist rage, and the power of abstraction (and expression, as we learn from Jill Casid's essay in this volume) — Fishman's emphasis on process envisions and enacts the world. In her drawings, she pieces together, she gives form. She convenes a gathering of artists and writers who have been her teachers, her lovers, her family members. For Fishman, as a lesbian feminist artist, worldmaking means surviving and thriving, in part through the discipline of painting and her lifelong commitment to her work. And it also means *doing*, building up through pigment and paper a sense of possibility for kinship and history.[1]

A Grogger for Eva and Agnes (1992, fig. 1.1), for example, is a small drawing of a grid in the collection of the Jewish Museum in New York. Each of the grid's one hundred squares is just large enough to contain a smaller gray square, a white square with a gray circle inscribed, or nothing at all. Each section of the grid has a logic, which in broader perspective reveals five white horizontal bands cut through by three dark vertical columns. All lines are drawn in thick black watercolor that is, for the most part, opaque. Set well within the boundaries of the off-white paper's irregular edges, a wide, thickly drawn square of silver graphite frames Fishman's grid. In art and in life, this drawing is a dedication to Eva Hesse and Agnes Martin (figs. 1.2 and 1.3), two artists whom Fishman knew and whose influences pervade her work. In this homage, her grid conveys repetition without rigidity, a breathable structure that Fishman learned from Martin. She has continuously reworked this structure, from her brief foray into minimal painting in the late 1960s and early 1970s through the implied grids in such significant canvases as *Blonde Ambition* (1995, plate 17) and *Bel Canto* (2014, fig. 1.4).[2] From Hesse, Fishman learned about the sheer variety and flexibility of materials available to an artist concerned with gender and with defying the canon of abstract painting and sculpture (both artists were educated in Bauhaus techniques of color and composition). Rubber, thread, vellum, and cellophane tape would form other grids in Fishman's works from the early 1970s (for example, *Untitled*, 1971, see fig. 2.2), during a period when she avoided using the things that she associated with male painting tradition.[3] Fishman made *A Grogger for Eva and Agnes*, along with another small drawing called *Grogger from Mesa Verde* (1992, fig. 1.5), for the Jewish holiday of Purim. The latter invokes the dynamic energy of the occasion's rattling noisemakers with colorful stacked architecture perched on an unrolled handle. Both drawings celebrate the artist's attachments: her teachers, her commitment to abstraction, her Jewish heritage. They exemplify how Fishman enlists process — in these works, the grid and dedication — as visual and tactile tools that make the world.

Fig. 1.1. *A Grogger for Eva and Agnes*, 1992. Watercolor and graphite on paper, 10 × 10 inches. The Jewish Museum, Gift of the artist, 1992-32.

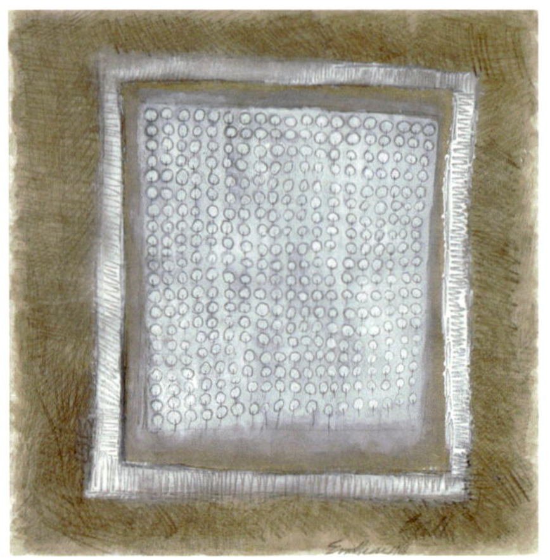

Fig. 1.2. Eva Hesse, No title, 1968. Graphite, brown wash, and gouache, 12⅛ × 12¹³⁄₁₆ inches. Saint Louis Art Museum, Gift of Dr. and Mrs. Edward Okun.

Fig. 1.3. Agnes Martin, *White Flower*, 1960. Oil on canvas, 72 × 72 inches. Solomon R. Guggenheim Museum, New York; Gift of Lenore Tawney, 1963.

Process in Fishman's work both prefigures and exemplifies queer theory's attention to epistemologies that move under the radar and unsettle, in what performance studies scholar José Esteban Muñoz underscored as "a sense of self-knowing, a mode of sociality and relationality."[4] Her aesthetic, at turns subtle and dramatic, entangles the viewer to tremendous effect.[5]

Fishman has made drawings throughout her career. Chronologically, they cluster in particular moments: in the early and mid-1970s when she participated in consciousness-raising groups and examined the relationship between shape and ground, in the mid-1980s as curves came into her work, in the 1990s as she reinvented her use of the grid, in 2001 as she completely deconstructed and rebuilt her relationship to gesture after September 11th, in 2007 during a residency at Dartmouth College when she renewed her attention to calligraphic marks, and since the mid-2010s in Venice with watercolor and handmade egg tempera in Japanese-bound leporello (accordion-style) books. Fishman's drawings — which also encompass collage, oil and wax, thread, acrylic, ink, charcoal, printmaking, and oil stick — have never been studies for her paintings on canvas. Instead, she has used drawing to think through physicality and materials on a different register: generally small- and medium-scale, often sculptural and tactile, and gesturing outward to encompass both the history of painting and her community of politically and artistically radical feminist lesbian writers and artists in New York.

A Question of Emphasis: Louise Fishman Drawing attempts to trace the artist's process to see where it may lead us, what worlds we can envision through her work, and why such an effort matters. This may entail reconsidering some basic

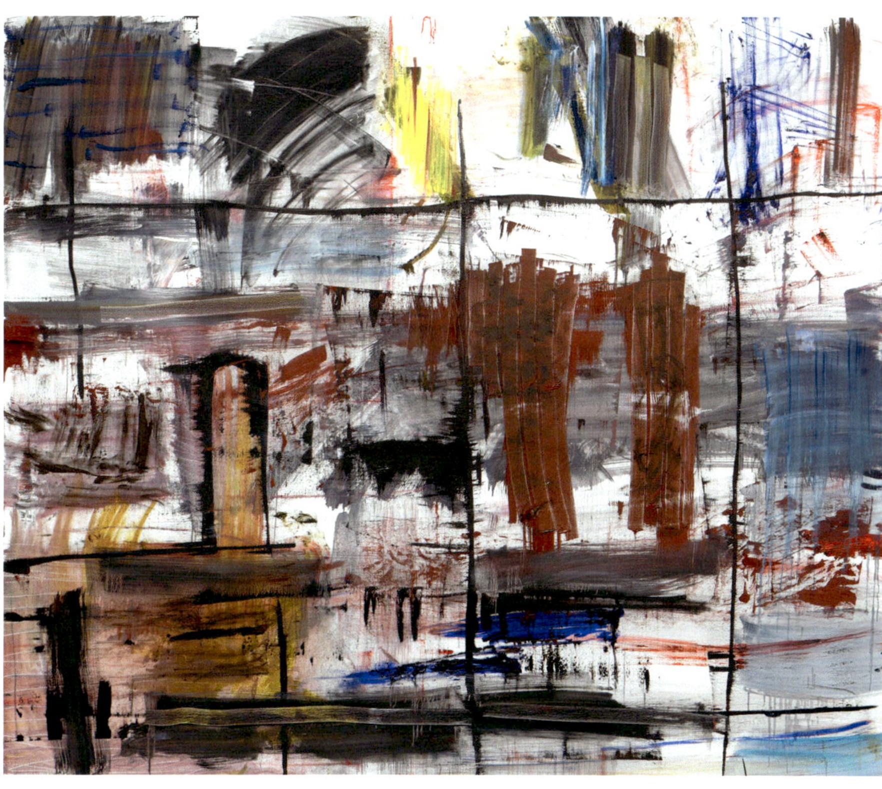

Fig. 1.4. *Bel Canto*, 2014. Oil on linen, 74 × 88 inches.

assumptions about drawing, especially drawings by a major painter. Instead of a window to the artist's interiority, a provisional key to her paintings, or a spontaneous activity that happens more readily than working on canvas, Fishman's drawings are expansive works that create their own meaning. Besides showing clear evidence of her thoughtfulness and labor, they offer a queer feminist case study for both their worldmaking potential and their challenge to narratives of genealogy and inheritance in abstract art in the United States. Artist and writer Catherine Lord offered such perspective in her essay on Fishman's most widely exhibited drawing series, *Angry Women* (1973, plates 23–27), for the 2007 exhibition catalogue *WACK! Art and the Feminist Revolution*.[6] The series comprises thirty works on paper, each pairing the word "angry" with a name — *Angry Yvonne*, *Angry Djuna*, *Angry Bertha*, *Angry Marilyn*, *Angry Jill*, *Angry Louise* — set within a scheme of acrylic brushwork, scrawled pencil marks, and bold colors. Fishman made the *Angry Women* during her involvement with consciousness-raising groups that included Women's International Terrorist Conspiracy from Hell (W.I.T.C.H.), Redstockings, and the collective of lesbian artists who edited the third issue of the feminist journal *Heresies*. Lord described the drawings as a shifting lesbian counter-archive, one that evidences the history of angry women (including those Fishman does not picture) while also forging their networks and modes of relating to one another.

Fishman's work requires that we square history and community with matters of form and process. Such a methodological and curatorial challenge is "a question of emphasis," to quote John Cage, another Fishman interlocutor, in his chance-determined mosaic diary response to the question "What is drawing?"[7]

The late critic Douglas Crimp's exhortation for scholarship attending to queer and cultural history remains relevant: this is the Fishman, and the drawing, that "we deserve."[8] Not because her work shores up lesbian feminist painting, but because it unsettles everything: art historical canons, what process can do, how categories of identity try and fail to cohere. *A Question of Emphasis* seeks to hold space for what happens between Fishman's work and the world, sometimes enacting queer meaning, as in Catherine Lord and Jill Casid's remarkable essays in this catalogue, and also by paying close attention to materials and process, as in the transcript of artist Ulrike Müller's conversation with the artist. In what follows, I describe moments in Fishman's work that are, for me, emblematic of their worldmaking potential. Like the exhibition, these are neither chronological nor comprehensive.

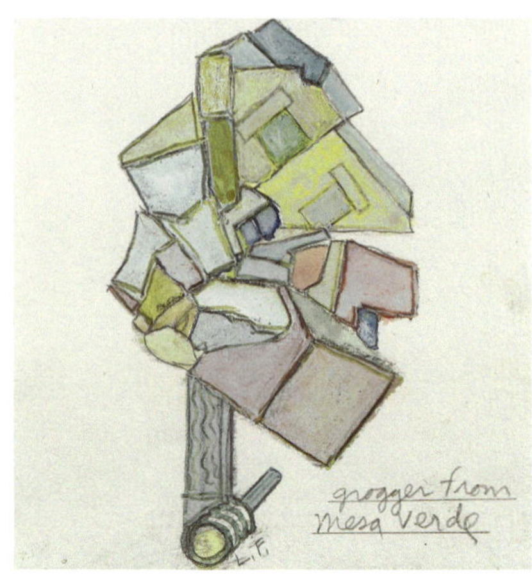

Fig. 1.5. *Grogger from Mesa Verde*, 1992. Watercolor and graphite on paper, 5½ × 5½ inches. The Jewish Museum, Gift of the artist, 1992-58.

Fishman began painting, drawing, stapling, and collaging in leporello books the same year that she made the grogger drawings, soon after her return from visiting Martin in New Mexico with then-partner Betsy Crowell. The binding of leporello books allows them to unfold like an accordion or scroll — the paper extends continuously outward from the book's spine. For her first books in 1972, Fishman cut pieces of canvas and drew grids on them. In subsequent leporellos, she treated each set of facing pages between folds as a discreet vignette; in *Ingrid* (2013, plate 30), the book becomes a continuous object with marks running onto adjacent unfolded pages.

Book of Abuse (1993–94, plate 14) could be a miniature survey of Fishman's work. The first three openings contain hand-drawn grids in pencil, less containers or established boundaries for color and more a complementary structure to the pages' varied brush marks and textures, including what may be thumbprints or residue from the transfer of another painted surface. In the third opening, each of two slender upright rectangles is split vertically; in both cases, the right side is filled with color and other side left blank. This simple drawing remains imprinted, if no longer clearly visible, in the openings that follow. An underpainting is nearly completely covered in black oil paint, which encrusts on top of the paper right up to the edges of the long vertical columns at the center of the page. The darkness and texture are profoundly dramatic, all the more so for the staples placed across the column as though to suture a wound. The leporello concludes with three openings where Fishman collaged both aluminum and paper, the latter torn and stapled and burned. Grids, grays, and pieces overlay one another, and it is difficult to discern what parts of the process may have come first or last. Key tools for Fishman at the time — a flexible grid, a preponderance of materials, the length of a line informing her decisions about a brushstroke or a particular color — trace the contours of relating to one another and explore the terrain of bare survival. Fishman made *Book of Abuse*, along with *Down and Dirty (A Book for Bertha Harris)* (1994, plate 29), with Harris in mind (the latter intended as a gift). Harris was a professor of women's studies and a writer; her landmark novel *Lover*, from 1976, was inspired by and dedicated to Fishman. Fishman and Harris had come back into contact in New York around this time, and a swirl of painful memories is manifest in this intimate object.[9]

Fishman credits Buddhist ritual, along with Cage's technique of burning drawings, with informing the production of her first leporellos.[10] She understood that the unfolding books (which she purchased in Chinatown) referred to meditative travelogues from China, a kind of passport in which a pilgrim would collect stamps from places where the Buddha had stopped along the path of enlightenment. She had seen an exhibition of Asian-influenced work that included Cage's drawings and Mark Tobey's all-over compositions.[11] The marks in *Down and Dirty* are more horizontal than vertical, with staples, overpainting, and trowel scrapes covering the small book, which measures less than five by four inches.[12] A drawing from three years prior, *Untitled* (1991, plate 1) shows Fishman's fingers spread onto the page and coated with graphite and charcoal. She describes this work, an index of the simplest mark of the self, as a reminder of her existence.[13] Such objects show Fishman pushing herself to make new and different marks, or to repeat old ones in new ways, and they are also laden with feeling and experience shared among women.

Transfers and the contact of paint between surfaces happen frequently in Fishman's drawings. She has made drawings on tracing paper, paper towels, or whatever else is in the studio by adhering them to and lifting pigment from her wet canvases (for example, *Untitled*, 2012, plate 5). She may leave these transferred images as she finds them — another instance of chance in her work — or she may continue painting and drawing on them until she feels they are resolved. The stunning series of seven *Vaporetto Leporello* books she has made in Venice since 2016 (see fig. 4.5; plates 2, 4, 19, 20, 37, 68), which incorporate watercolor and egg tempera, have at times been allowed to dry while closed, leaving imprints and marks from other pages. Such a direct material relationship between the pages of her books, and between her paintings and works on paper, contributes to the worldmaking capacity of her abstraction.

In 1977, Lyn Blumenthal and Kate Horsfield interviewed Fishman as part of their video series *On Art and Artists*, archived at Video Data Bank in Chicago (fig. 1.6).[14] *On Art and Artists* began as a feminist project dedicating time to women talking about their work. Blumenthal later described their format as "single fixed camera, tight focus on the subject, off camera interviewer," a straightforward formula that nonetheless yielded complex biographical documents.[15] Fishman's interview begins with a close-up shot of the lower half of her face. In a matter of seconds, the camera pans out to reveal the image as a live feedback monitor behind Fishman while she talks to Horsfield. The camera continues to pan out further, and by two and a half minutes it becomes clear that we have been watching live feedback all along. The interview continues for fifty-five minutes, with Fishman and Horsfield speaking continuously (except for Blumenthal changing the tape and one other moment toward the end, the interview is uncut and unedited), but the relationship between their conversation and the video image is unpredictable. Sometimes the live feedback monitor shows Horsfield, and sometimes Fishman moves out of frame. All three artists are well matched in their commitment to process.

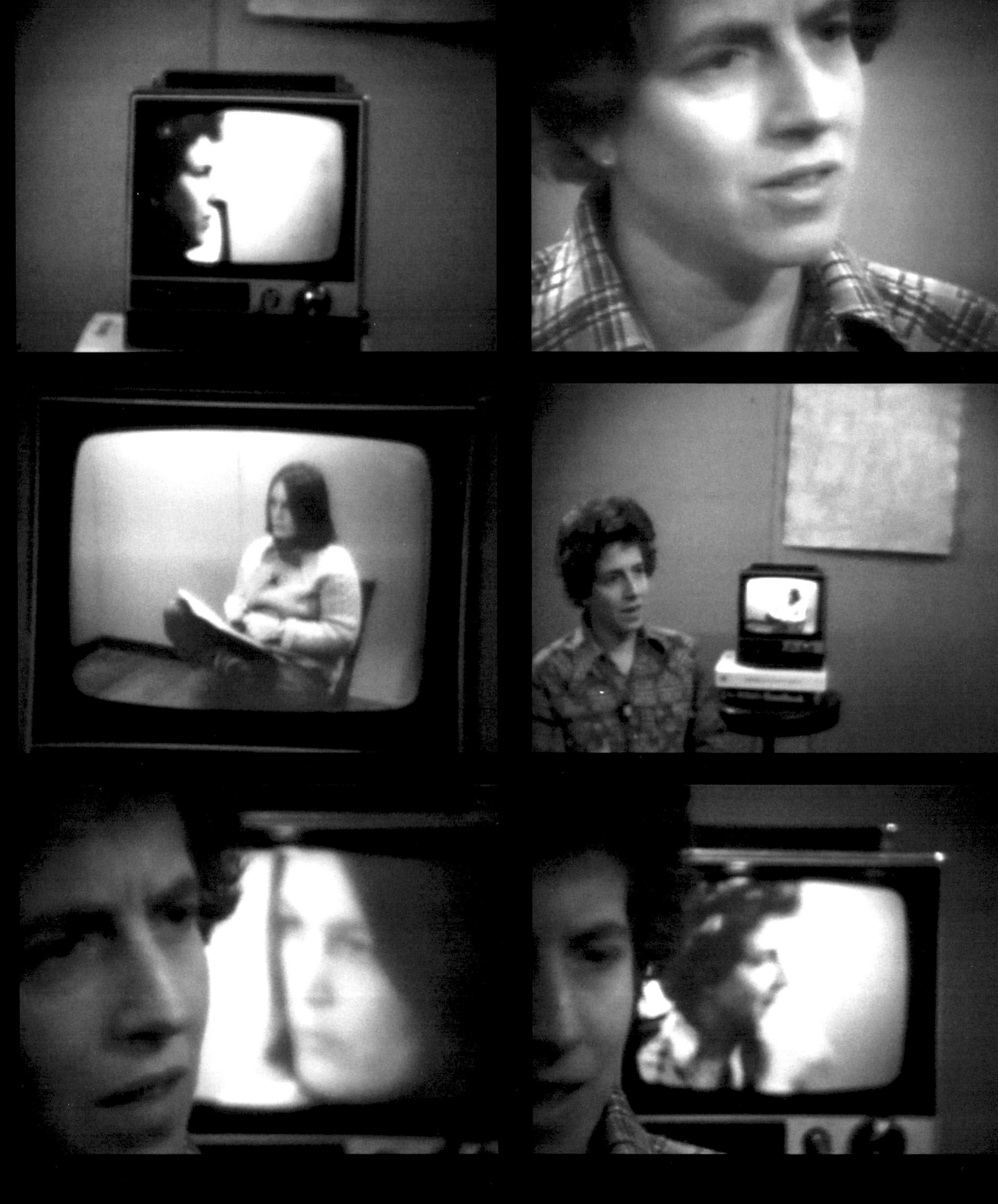

> FISHMAN: I'll come up with an image — it takes a certain amount of time for that image to come up. And then I'll destroy it because I want to go further with it. I very rarely let an image be there except if I'm confused about it and I want to look at it longer.
>
> HORSFIELD: There's a terrific amount of risk in working like that. How do you manage to keep your confidence as you go from step to step?
>
> FISHMAN: I have a lot of confidence. Which I think I've always had but I was really mystified by myself. I'm not too mystified by it now. I go through periods where I have great doubt. But I'm aware of those periods as part of the process rather than as being a real question about my validity.

In 1977, at the time of Blumenthal and Horsfield's interview, Fishman had spent several years examining shape, grid, texture, and ground in her drawings. *Leftover Colors* (1974, fig. 1.7) is a series of seven sequential drawings of circles at the center of each page, followed by a page of text. Selection and chance were then important to Fishman, and she began using Masonite circles she found on Canal Street in New York as either templates in her paintings or their actual ground (for example, *Mars and Jupiter*, 1974; *Jewish Star Painting*, 1973–74; and *Bianca's Repose*, 1973).[16] Likewise, *Leftover Colors* is made from the acrylic paint left on Fishman's palette. She must have been working on something incredibly varied in color, based on the range of pigments across seven circles. Despite the drawings' shared basic structure, they vary widely in technique, making Fishman's process their subject. Ever dependent on a grid, Fishman forced herself to resolve the circle's absence of corners and to apply Carl Jung's theories on the symbolism of the mandala, which she had been reading at the time.[17] An inscription at the bottom of each drawing frames a sensation of newness, texture, and the edges. "SIMPLE IDEA" comes first: a horizontally bisected circle, like a sunset landscape, is surrounded by four concentric circles and one half-circle in bold colors — red, blue, cream, and greenish-yellow. Inside the pencil outline of the circle, "NEW IDEA" is filled with rose and purple spiraling with intersecting lines at a blue center. "THINKING ABOUT THE EDGE OF THE CIRCLE" incorporates short brushstrokes that cover the left half arbitrarily with layered cream, browns, yellows, and green. "THINKING ABOUT SOUTINE AT BARNES" adapts the previous drawing's cream but makes it nearly monochrome, building up pigment and texture to mirror the twentieth-century Russian French painter Chaim Soutine's moody landscapes in the Barnes Foundation collection. Soutine was one of Fishman's most significant "teachers" while she was growing up in Philadelphia, where Barnes Foundation courses had provided the formal education of two other painters in the family, Fishman's paternal aunt Razel Kapustin and her mother, Gertrude Fisher-Fishman.[18] "TO PLEASE JENNY AND JEFF" (artists Jenny Snider and Jeff Way) is similar to Soutine, but

Fig. 1.6. Lyn Blumenthal and Kate Horsfield, *Louise Fishman: An Interview*, 1977. Video stills. ½-inch open-reel video, sound (black & white, mono, 4:3), 55:13 minutes. Courtesy of Video Data Bank.

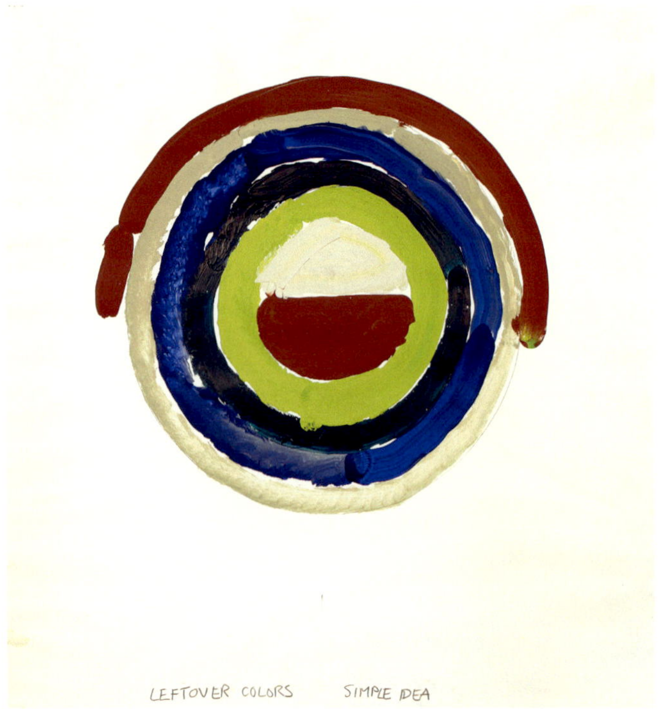

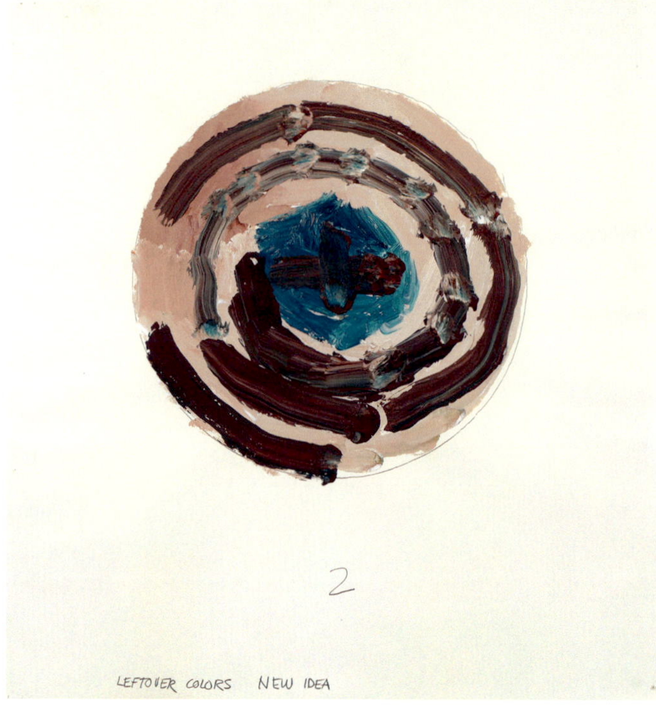

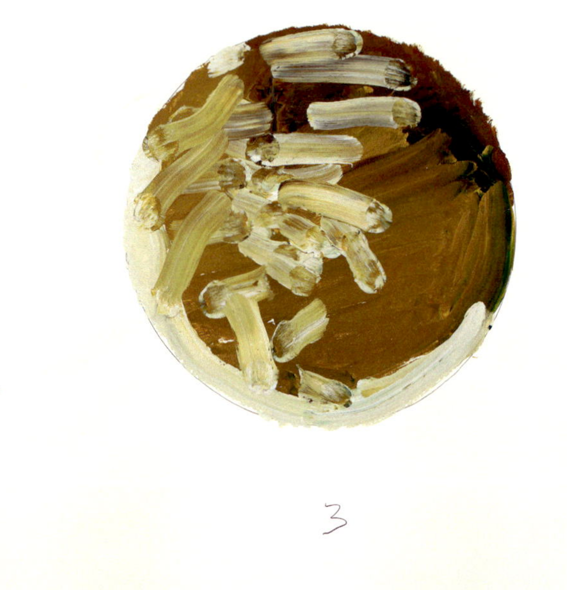

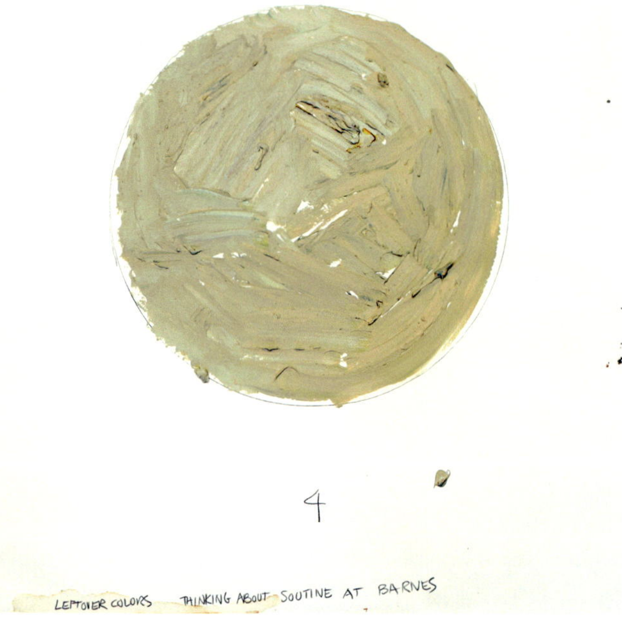

Fig. 1.7. *Leftover Colors*, 1974. Acrylic on paper, 18¾ × 20 inches.

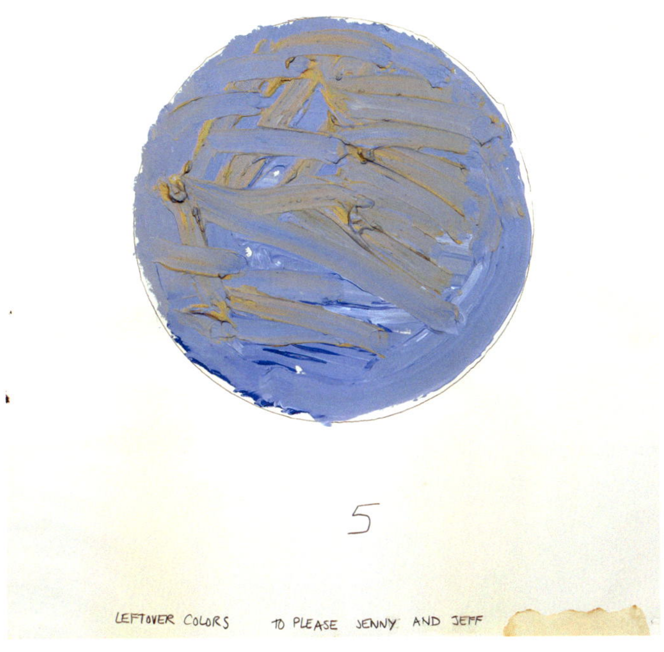

5

LEFTOVER COLORS TO PLEASE JENNY AND JEFF

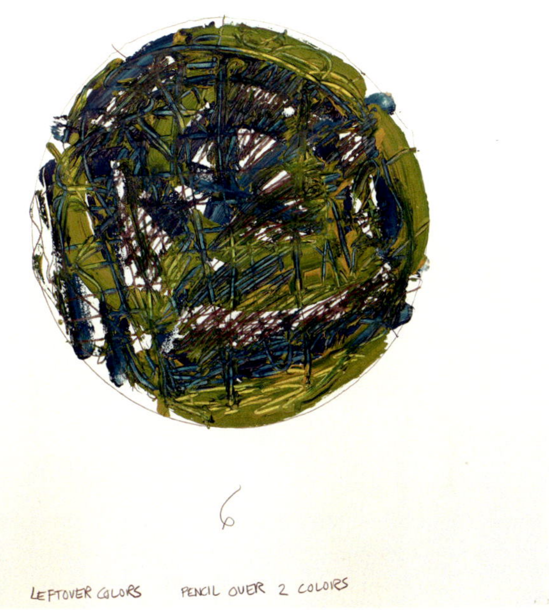

6

LEFTOVER COLORS PENCIL OVER 2 COLORS

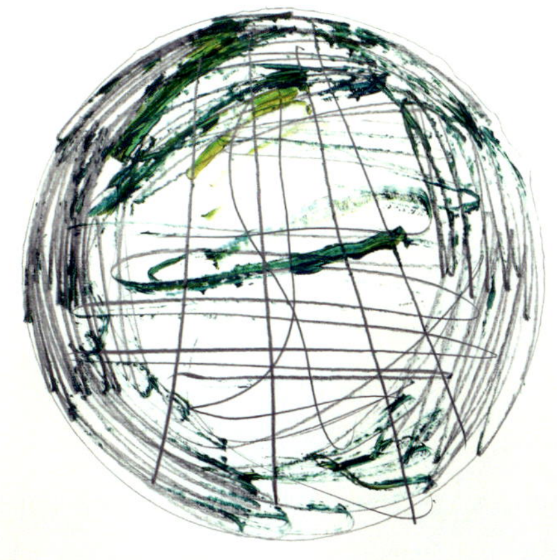

7

PENCIL FROM PREVIOUS DRAWING THINKING ABOUT THE AUDIENCE

AFTERWORD:

RUSH TO GET ESTHER TO SEE CIRCLE DRAWINGS. KNOWING ON THE WAY IT WOULD BE BETTER TO LOOK AT THEM FOR A WHILE MYSELF - BUT TOO INVOLVED ALREADY WITH HER LOOKING AT THEM. BUT ESTHER IS SLEEPING.

THINKING DURING EXECUTION THAT ANY MARK I MAKE IS WONDERFUL. A FLEETING THOUGHT BUT NECESSARY TO BEGIN WORK.

THINKING LATER HOW SLOPPY AND THOUGTLESS ARE THE PAINTINGS BUT CONTINUE TO LIKE THE IDEA OF TALKING WHILE PAINTING,

NO SECRETS

8

PAINTING TURNS TO JOURNAL.

in blue with orange-gray undertones. "PENCIL OVER 2 COLORS" inscribes a grid within the circle, where Fishman dragged the blueish purple and green-yellow paint around before it had a chance to dry. "PENCIL FROM PREVIOUS DRAWING THINKING ABOUT THE AUDIENCE" brings some green and yellow forward but is mostly a grid implied in pencil. The circle nearly becomes a sphere with dimensional receding lines at the top. Finally, "PAINTING TURNS TO JOURNAL" makes the series a rare surviving artifact of Fishman's (long-abandoned) attempt to combine her journal writing with her work. "AFTERWORD; RUSH TO GET ESTHER TO SEE CIRCLE DRAWINGS BUT ESTHER IS SLEEPING," the text begins, placing the series in the present tense. What Fishman tried to do with the drawings and how she processed them (and with whom, the anthropologist Esther Newton) becomes part of the work. Ostensibly an exercise at day's end — with what's left over, and on paper — Fishman's circle drawings make her world by speculating on an idea taking shape under considerations of influence, formal structure, and intimate relation.

Fishman's circles became folds morphing into angular multidimensional shapes at the center of the paper. *Al Dente* (1976, plate 56), *Dutch Blue* (1975), and *Interloper* (1976, plate 58), among several other drawings she made from 1975 to 1977, incorporate wax in the oil paint, allowing for dramatic play with texture. Shapes with sharp corners converge with heavier lines demarcating their edges, like a Rubik's cube or paper construction twisted and remade into different positions. Sometimes the ground behind each central shape is gray, as in *Interloper* and *To the Right* (1976, plate 61), and sometimes it is white. In each case, Fishman left visible marks through a halo of paint surrounding the central drama. Her formal choices — and that she could have made different ones — remain clear. In her video interview with Blumenthal and Horsfield, Fishman described how transitions occur when she finds new problems or realizes she is working arbitrarily. The shape drawings began to reach for the edges in different ways, a transition that ultimately culminated in Fishman moving on to something else.[19]

At turns subconscious, by chance, or with intention, Fishman's process lends both physicality and depth of memory to her work. The terrazzo floors of Venice, her hands imprinted to form an organic grid, the mark of her brush onto paper resting on the studio floor, her spouse Ingrid's hair painted into a book, and countless other stories locate us in Fishman's world, but they also give us tools for understanding and expanding our own. To be with these drawings is to convene with the writers and thinkers who shaped new forms of expression and culture after Stonewall. And it is also to be preoccupied with making, witness to a fearless experimentation that can leap off the page and, as painter Susan Frecon has described of Fishman's work, be in our space instead of something we merely look at.[20] Fishman's drawings result from her expressive experience and the methods she continues to develop in her studio. They unfurl in the world and refuse to be contained, performing and enacting queer meaning through process, both intimate and grand.

Notes

1. This exhibition's focus on process as an organizing principle is indebted to my early conversation with Jill Casid about Louise Fishman's work.
2. Fishman had long followed Martin's work, but her use of the grid transformed after visiting Martin in New Mexico in 1991. See Ingrid Schaffner, "Getting Small with Louise Fishman," in *Louise Fishman*, ed. Helaine Posner (Purchase, NY: Neuberger Museum of Art, and Philadelphia: Institute of Contemporary Art, 2016), 195.
3. See, for example, Fishman's conversation with Ulrike Müller in this volume; Holland Cotter, "Art after Stonewall: 12 Artists Interviewed," *Art in America* 8, no. 6 (June 1994): 56, 59–60; Helen Molesworth, *Dance/Draw* (Boston: Institute of Contemporary Art, 2011); and Nancy Princenthal, "Louise Fishman: Language Lessons," in Posner, *Louise Fishman*, 45–53.
4. José Esteban Muñoz, "Ephemera as Evidence: Introductory Notes to Queer Acts," *Women & Performance: A Journal of Feminist Theory* 8, no. 2 (1996): 6.
5. Reflecting on the worldmaking aspects of Fishman's work, I am taken with Kaelen Wilson-Goldie's description of Etel Adnan's paintings as "talismanic objects for contemporary times." She writes: "But with sustained attention, her paintings may actually change you. They may save a world you have known. They may protect a person you have loved. They are things to be believed in." Kaelen Wilson-Goldie, *Etel Adnan* (London: Lund Humphries, 2018), 26.
6. Catherine Lord, "Their Memory Is Playing Tricks on Her: Notes toward a Calligraphy of Rage," in *WACK! Art and the Feminist Revolution*, ed. Cornelia Butler (Los Angeles: Museum of Contemporary Art, and Cambridge, MA: MIT Press, 2007), 440–57. Fishman considers the series of thirty drawings a single work even though they can be shown separately.
7. "What is a drawing? / No one knows any longer. Something / that doesn't require that you wait / while you're making it for it to dry? / Something on paper? Museum director / said (Tobey, Schwitters), 'It's a / question of emphasis.'" John Cage, *Diary: How to Improve the World (You Will Only Make Matters Worse)*, ed. Joe Biel and Richard Kraft (Los Angeles: Siglio, 2015), 20. See also Jeremy Millar, ed., *Every Day Is a Good Day: The Visual Art of John Cage* (London: Hayward Publishing, and New York: Distributed Art Publishers, 2010).
8. Douglas Crimp, "Getting the Warhol We Deserve," *Social Text* 59 (Summer 1999): 49–66.
9. Fishman, conversation with the author, January 23, 2019.
10. See, for example, Jonathan D. Katz, "Agnes Martin and the Sexuality of Abstraction," in *Agnes Martin*, ed. Lynne Cooke, Karen Kelly, and Barbara Schröder (New York: Dia Art Foundation, and New Haven, CT: Yale University Press, 2011), 177–78.
11. Fishman, conversation with the author, September 14, 2017. See also Schaffner "Getting Small," and Melissa E. Feldman, *Louise Fishman* (New York: Robert Miller Gallery, 1993).
12. These leporellos, along with *Book I* (1992), marked Fishman's return to her work after a fire devastated her upstate New York studio in 1990. Her journals and sketchbooks from the time are still singed.
13. Fishman, conversation with the author, January 23, 2019.
14. More than seventy-five videos from the series *On Art and Artists* are catalogued from 1974 to 1988 on VDB's website, http://www.vdb.org/artists/blumenthalhorsfield. Other interviewees in the series included Chantal Akerman, Laurie Anderson, Louise Bourgeois, Sol LeWitt, Agnes Martin, Joan Mitchell, and Martha Rosler. Blumenthal and Horsfield founded Video Data Bank in 1976 and eventually combined their series with other video resources on contemporary artists; for a full inventory of the project, see Kate Horsfield and Lucas Hilderbrand, eds., *Feedback: The Video Data Bank Catalog of Video Art and Artist Interviews* (Philadelphia: Temple University Press, 2006).
15. Kate Horsfield, "Lyn Blumenthal: A Brief Work History," *Lyn Blumenthal: Force of Vision* (Los Angeles: LACE Los Angeles Contemporary Exhibitions, 1989), 4.
16. All are reproduced in Posner, *Louise Fishman*.
17. Fishman, conversation with the author, January 23, 2019.
18. For more on Fishman's family history, see especially *Generations: Louise Fishman, Gertrude Fisher-Fishman and Razel Kapustin* (Philadelphia: Woodmere Art Museum, 2012).
19. *It's Good to Have Limits* (1977) stretches to the paper's edges. This work was published in the *Heresies* journal issue on lesbian art and artists that Fishman coedited that same year. See *Heresies: A Feminist Publication on Art and Politics* 3 (1977).
20. Susan Frecon, "Traveling in Louise Fishman Terrain," *Turps Banana* 17 (January 2017): 45.

10

Untitled, 1975

Oil on paper
31⅛ × 22⅞ inches

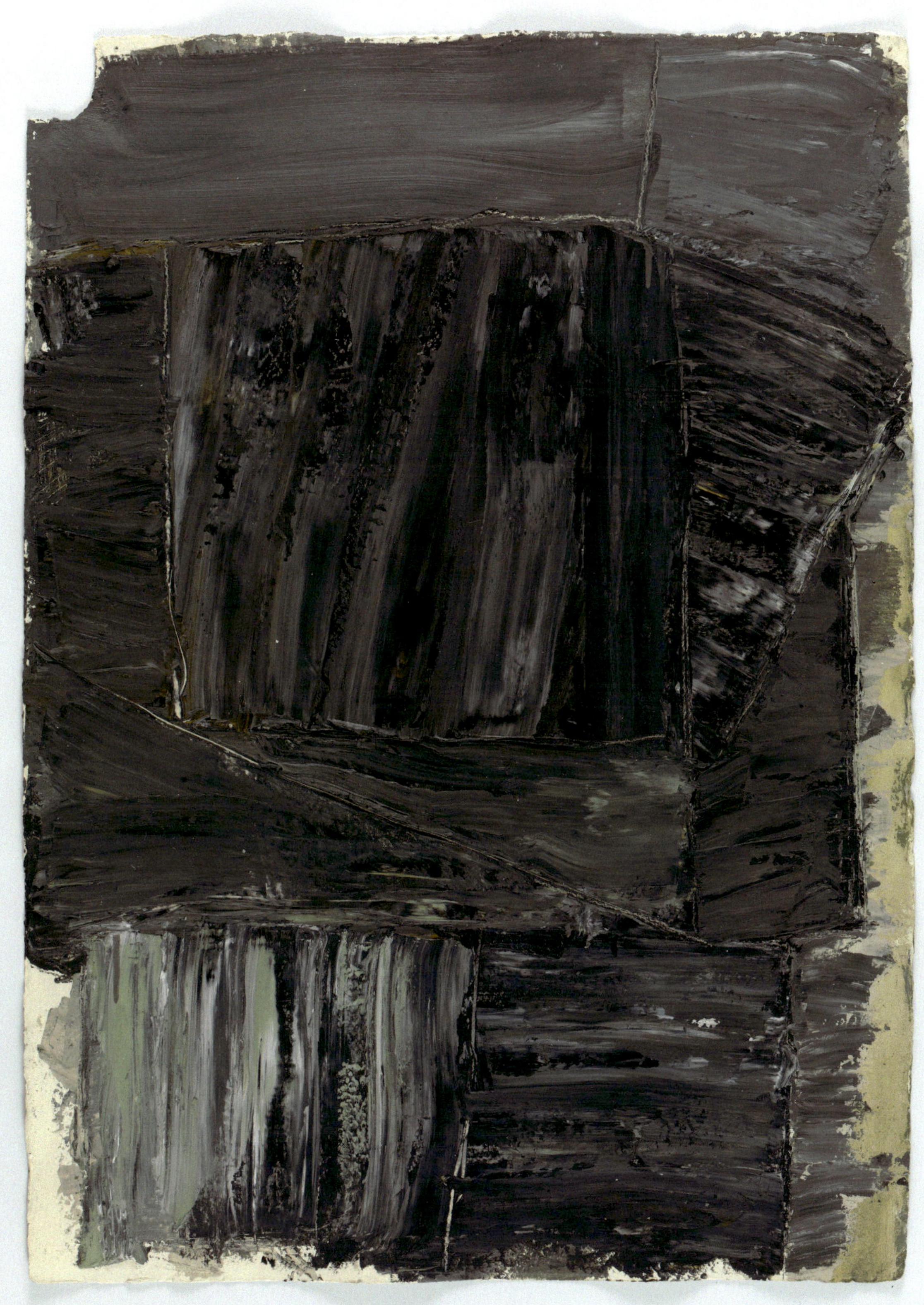

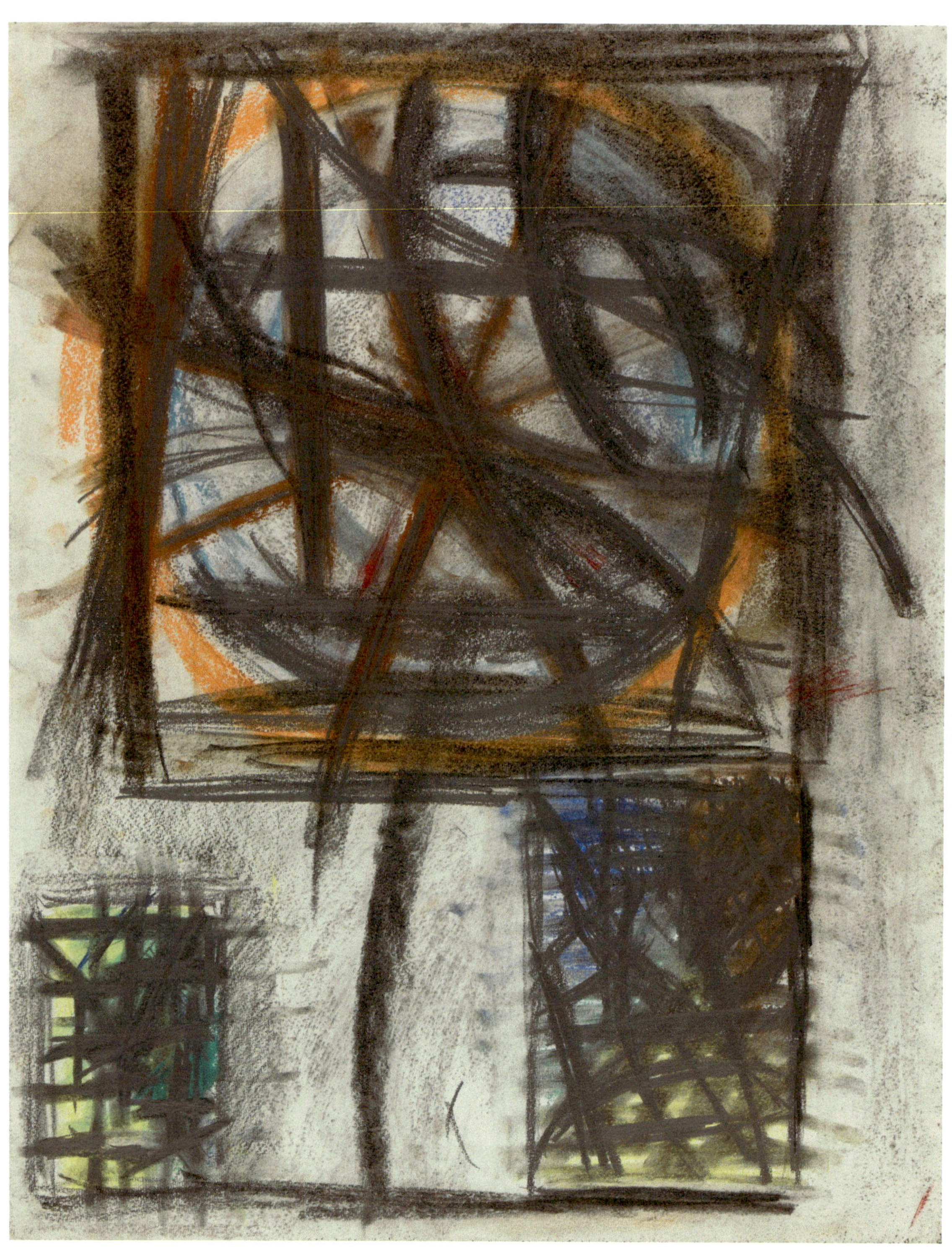

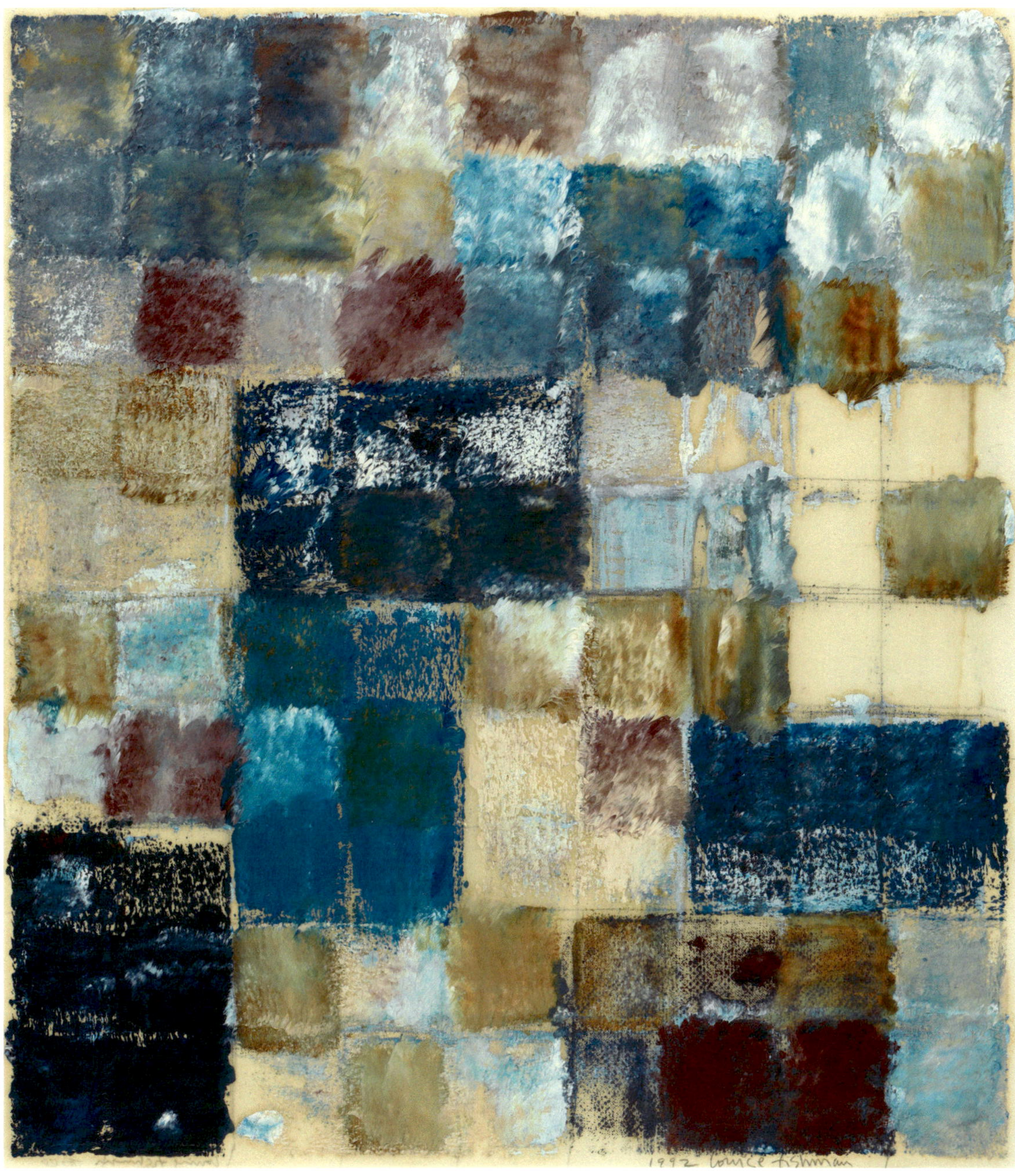

11

Untitled, 1985

Graphite, charcoal, and pastel on paper
23¾ × 19 inches

12

Untitled, 1992

Charcoal and oil on tracing paper
20½ × 18½ inches

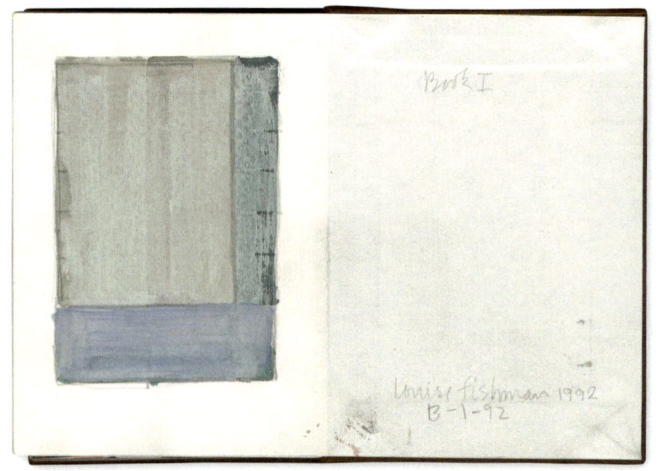

1

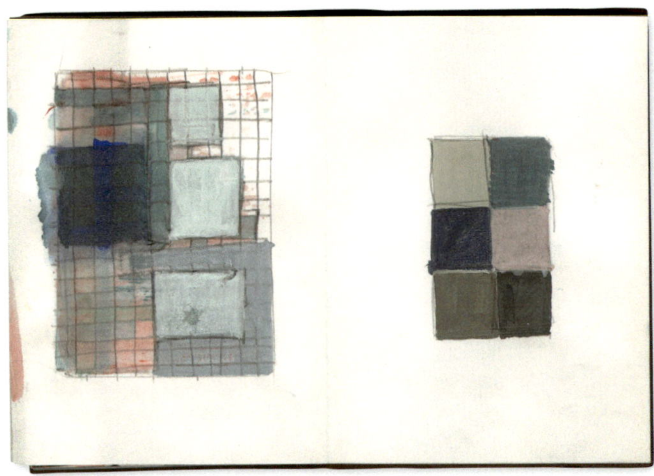

2

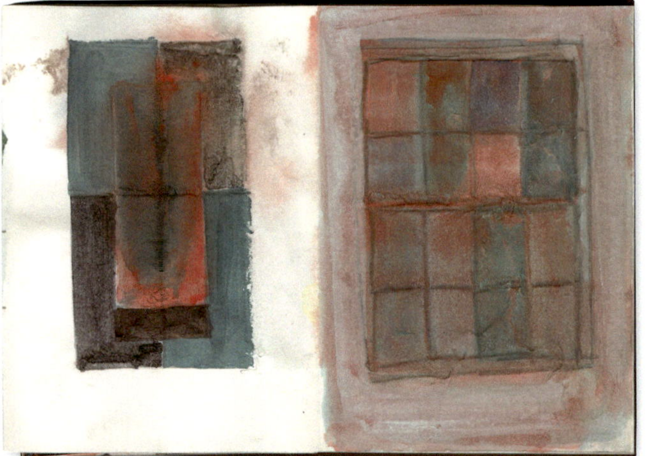

3

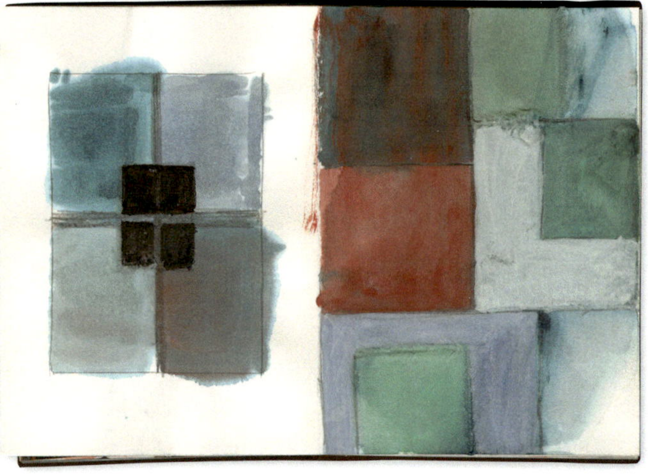

4

13

Book I, 1992

Gouache and graphite on paper; Japanese leporello binding
4⅞ × 3⅝ × 1¼ inches (closed)

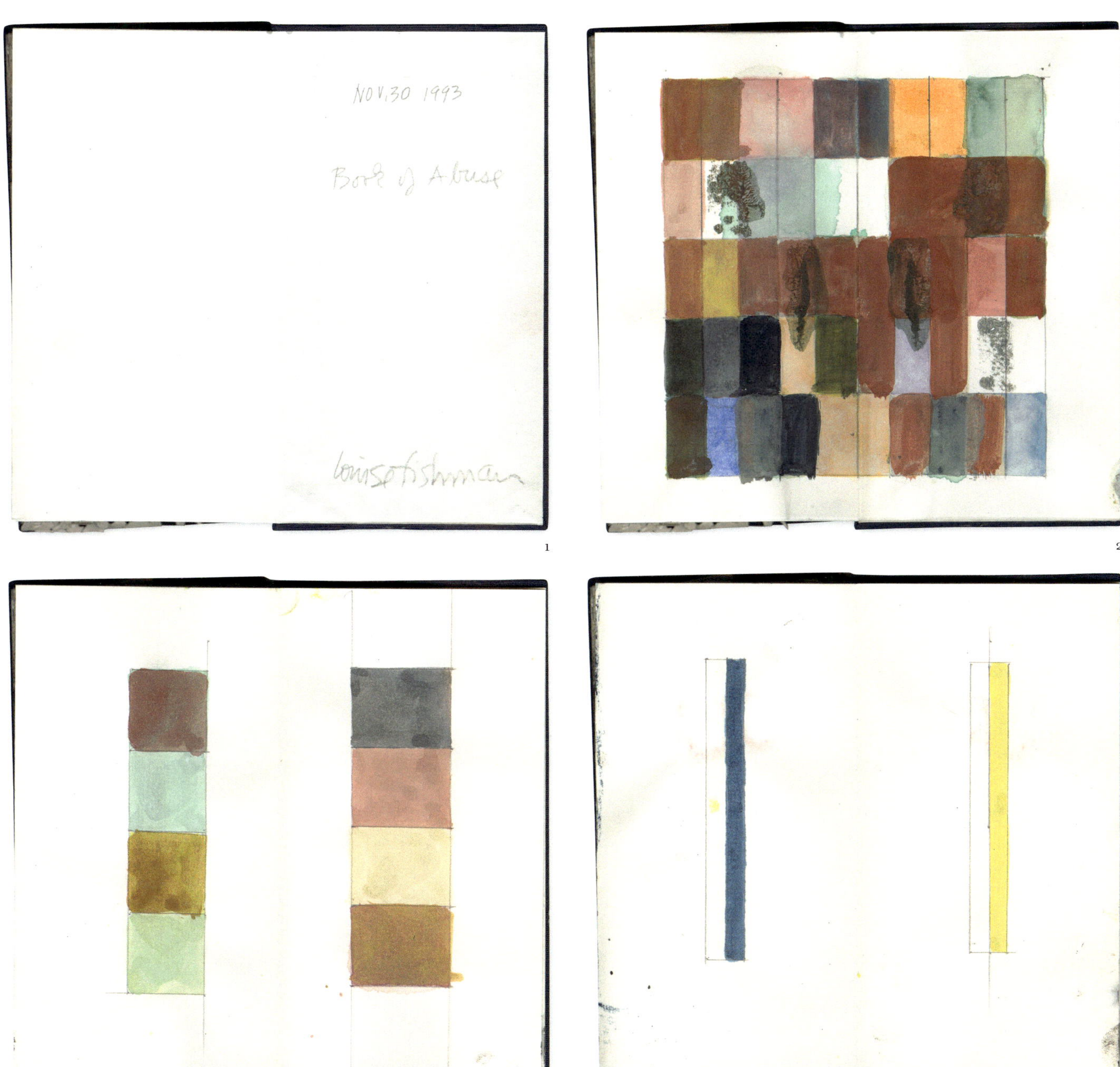

3 4

14

Book of Abuse, 1993–94

Acrylic, oil, oil stick, graphite, staples, and wire with aluminum and paper collage on paper; Japanese leporello binding
6⅜ × 3⅝ × 1⅝ inches (closed)

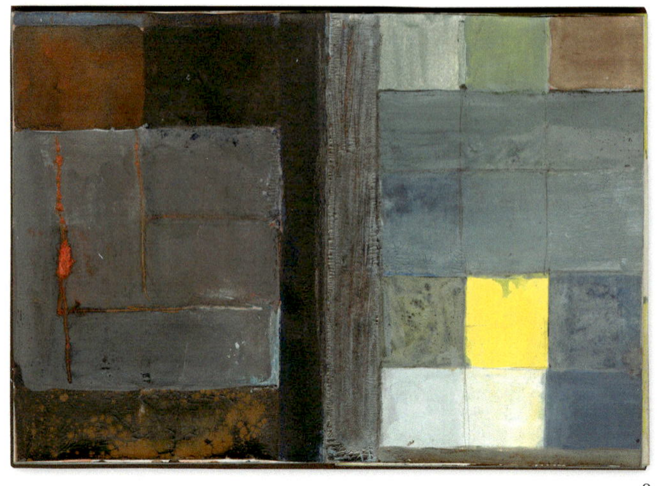

9

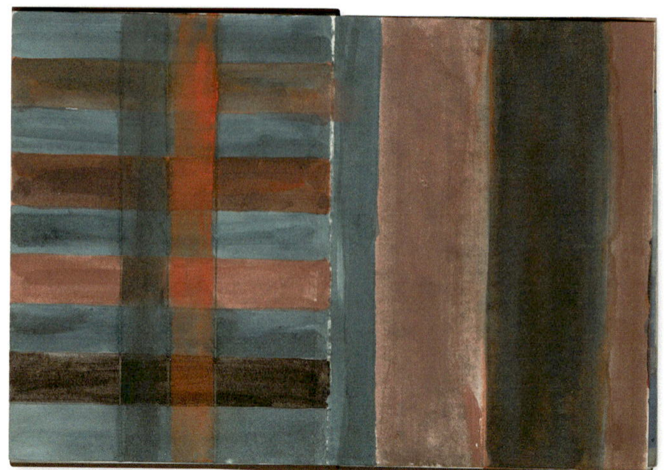

10

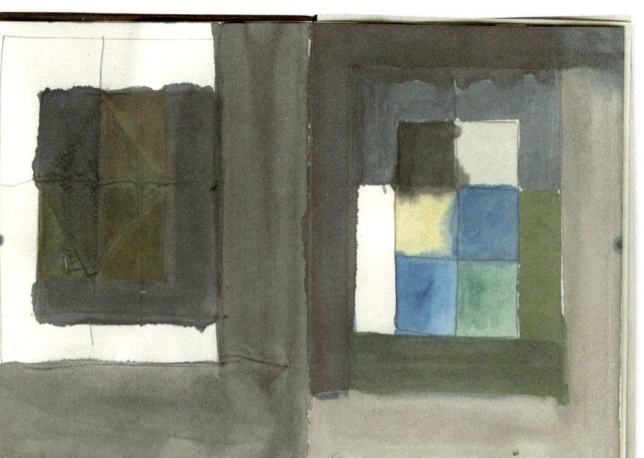

11

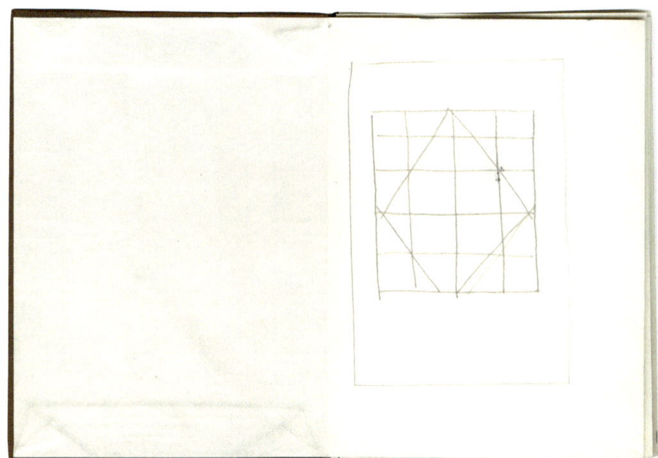

12

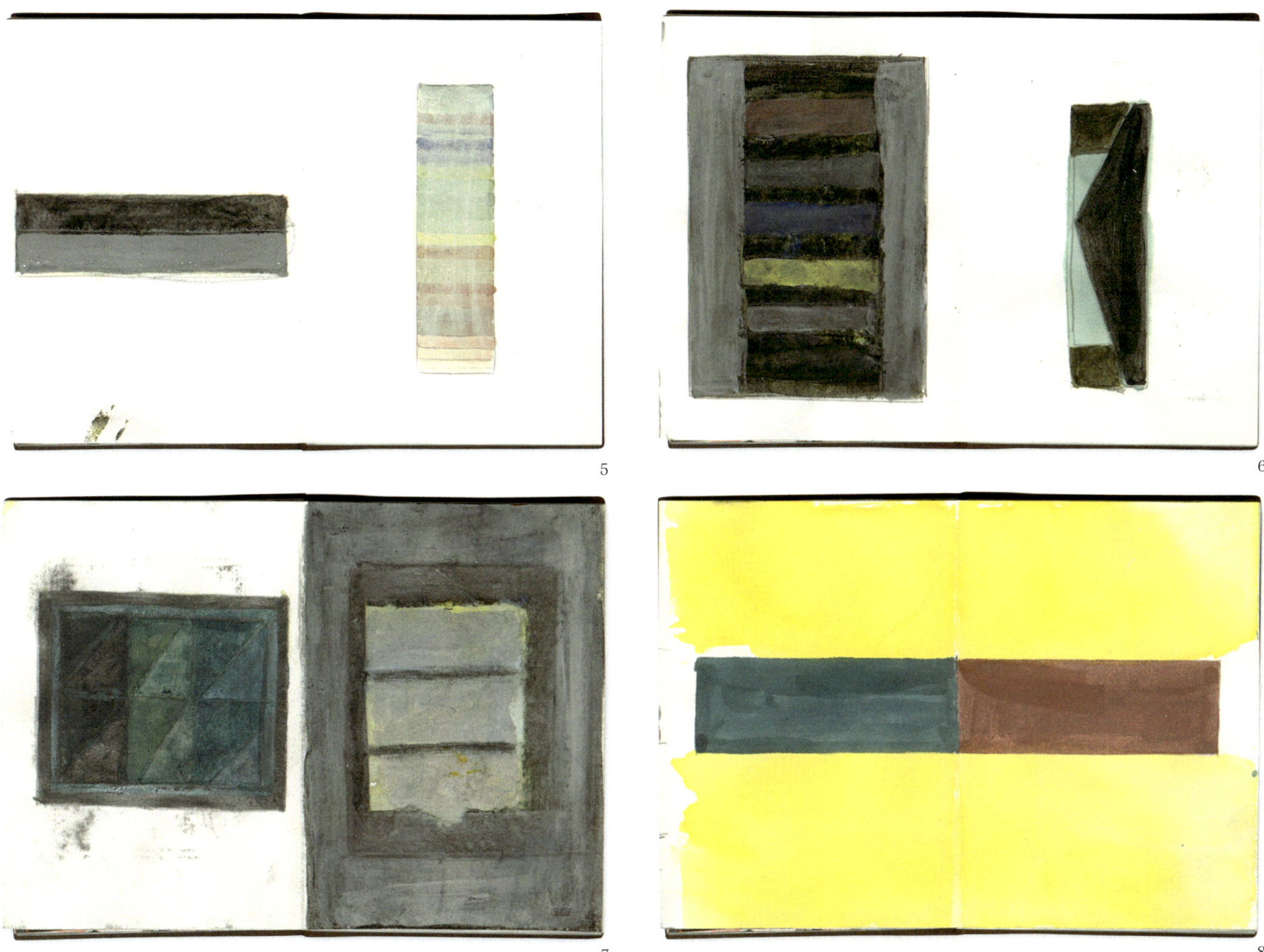

5

6

7

8

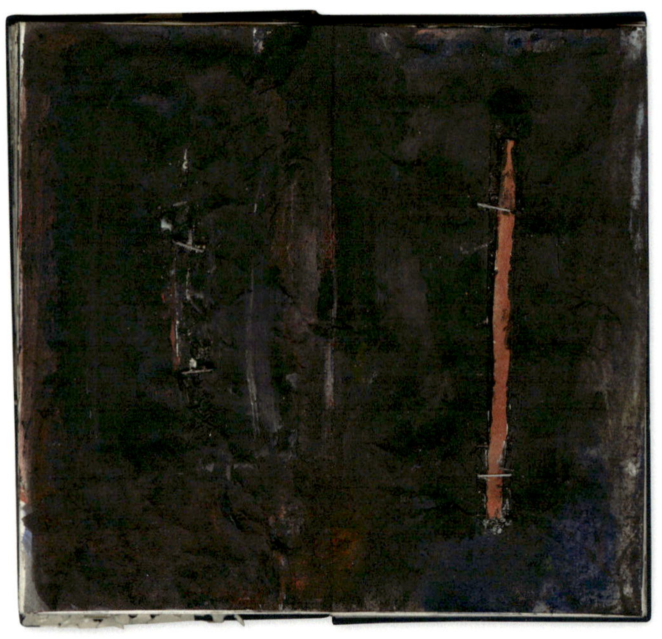

5

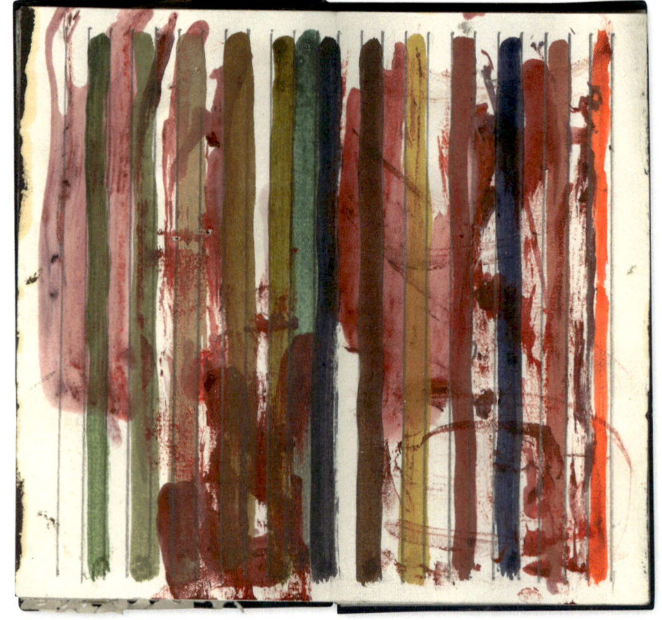

6

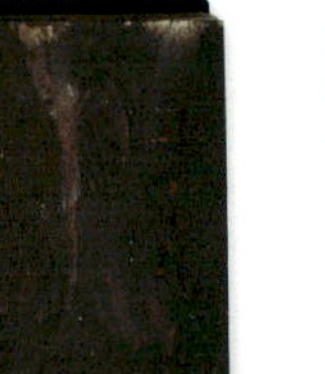

7

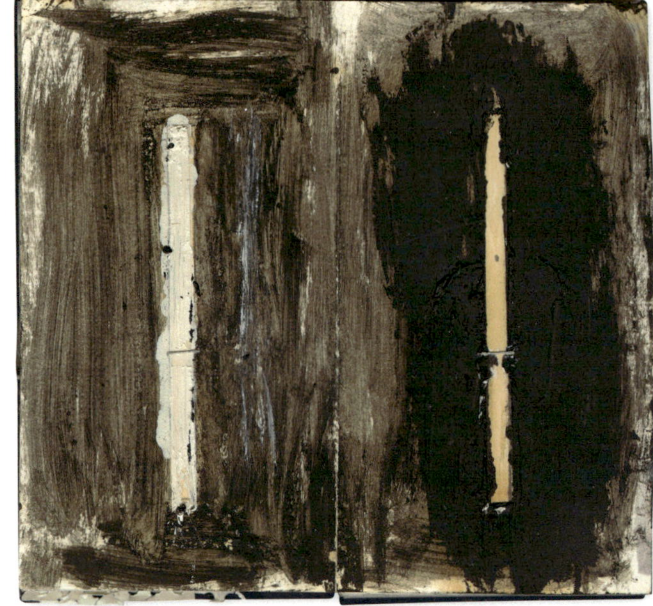

8

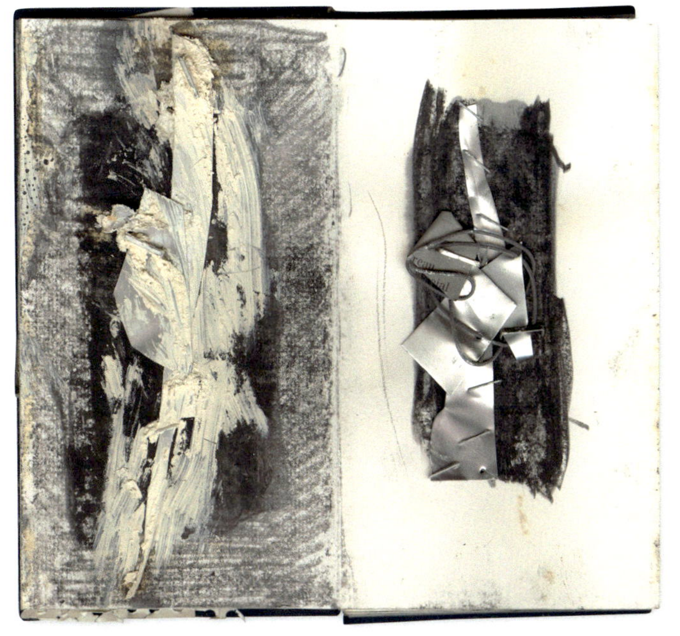

9

10

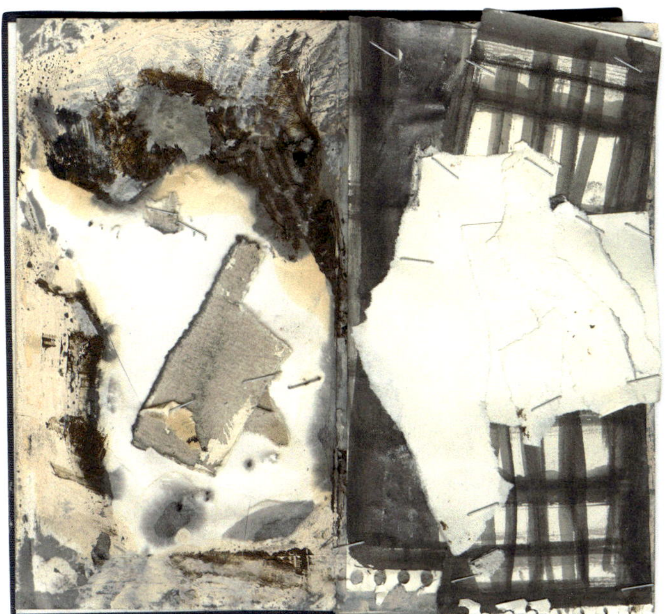

11

12

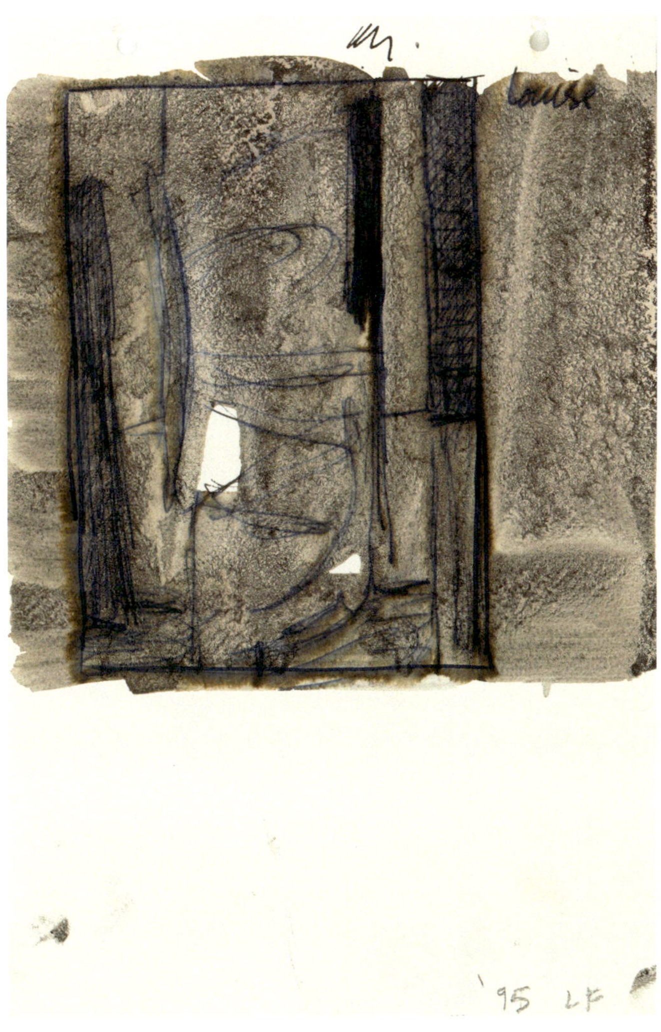

15
Untitled, 1990
Oil on paper
31 × 22¾ inches

16
Untitled, 1995
Watercolor and ink on paper
9⅜ × 6⅜ inches

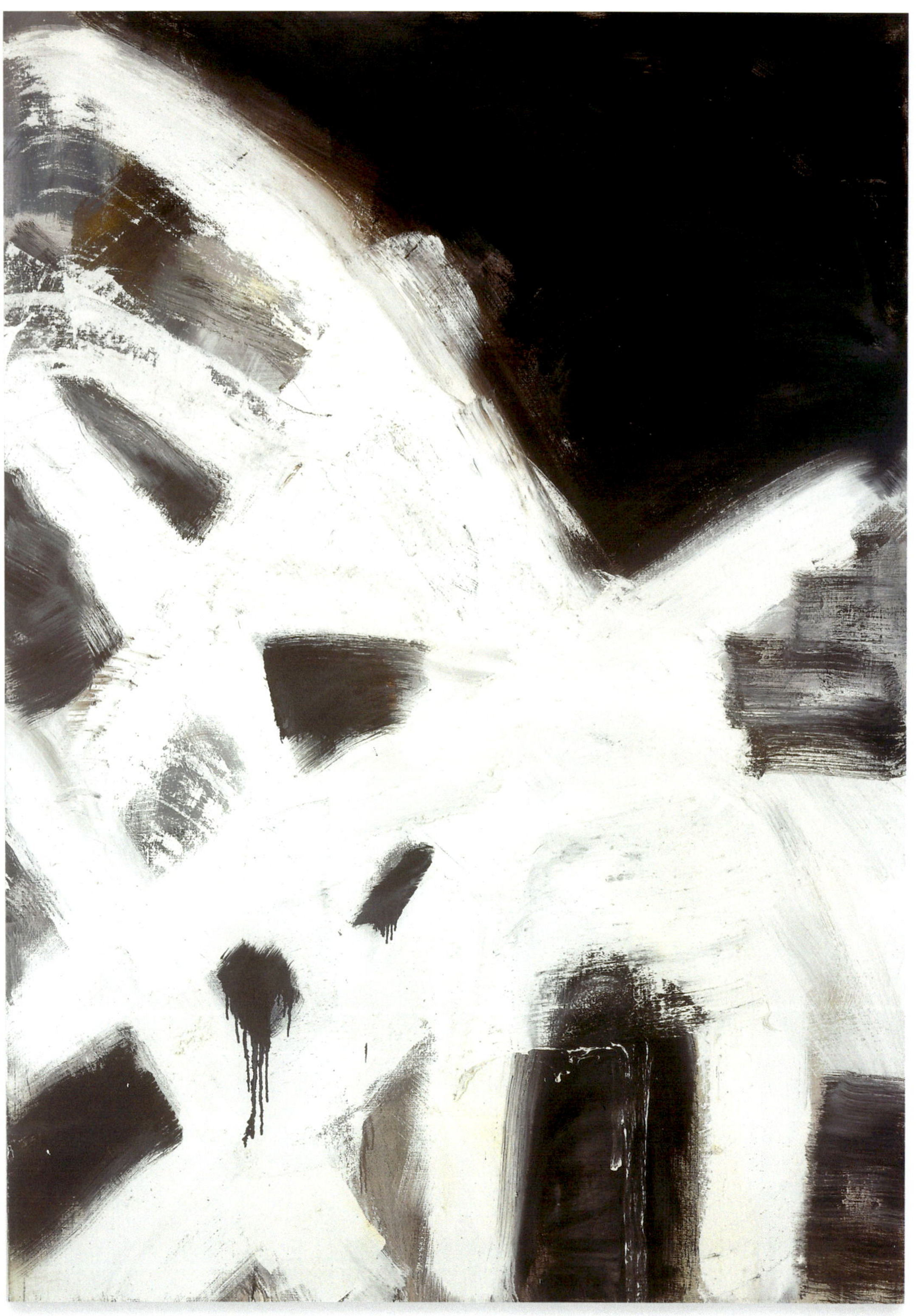

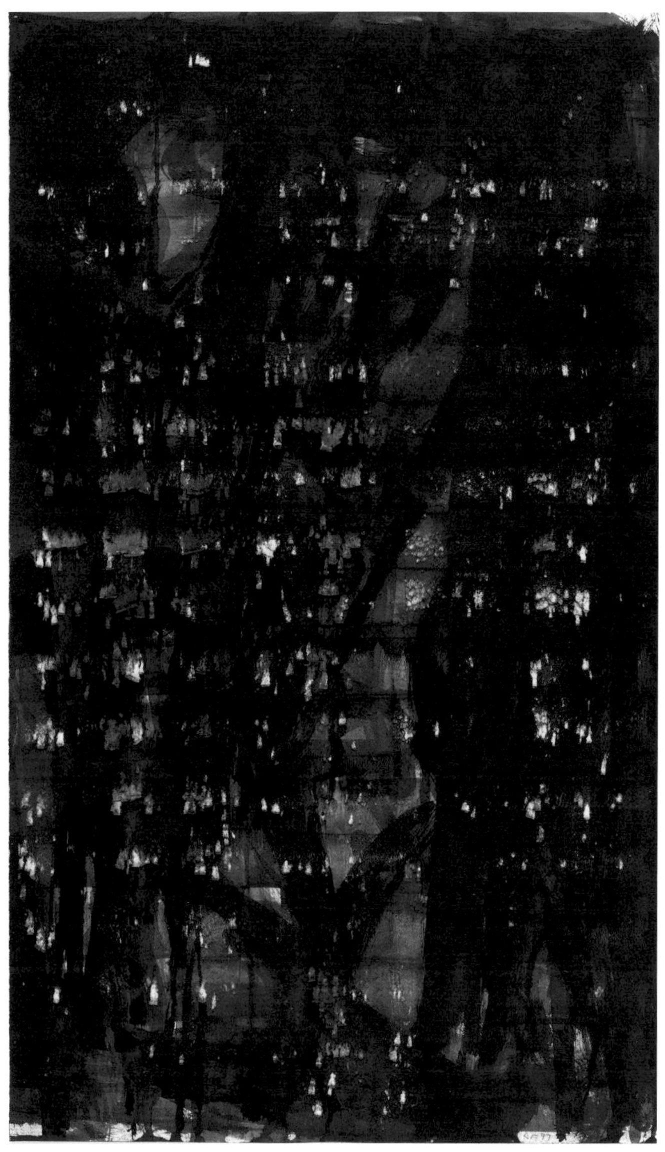

17

Blonde Ambition, 1995

Oil on linen
90 × 65 inches
Krannert Art Museum, Museum Purchase through the John N. Chester Fund and the Richard M. and Rosann Gelvin Noel Fund, 2019-1-1

18

Untitled, 1997

Oil and ink on paper
30 × 18 inches (framed)

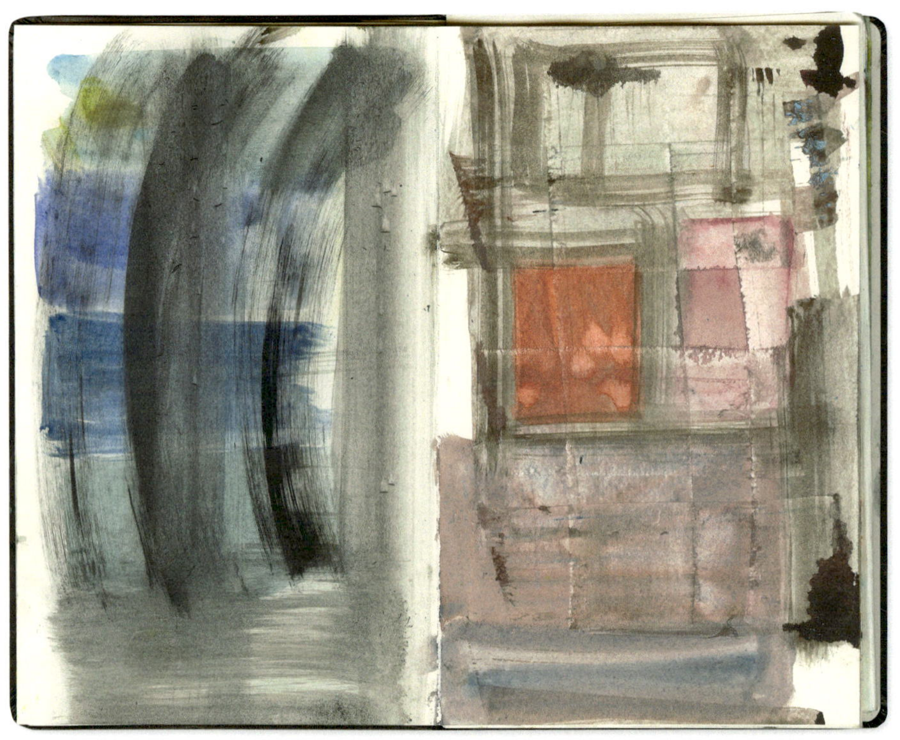

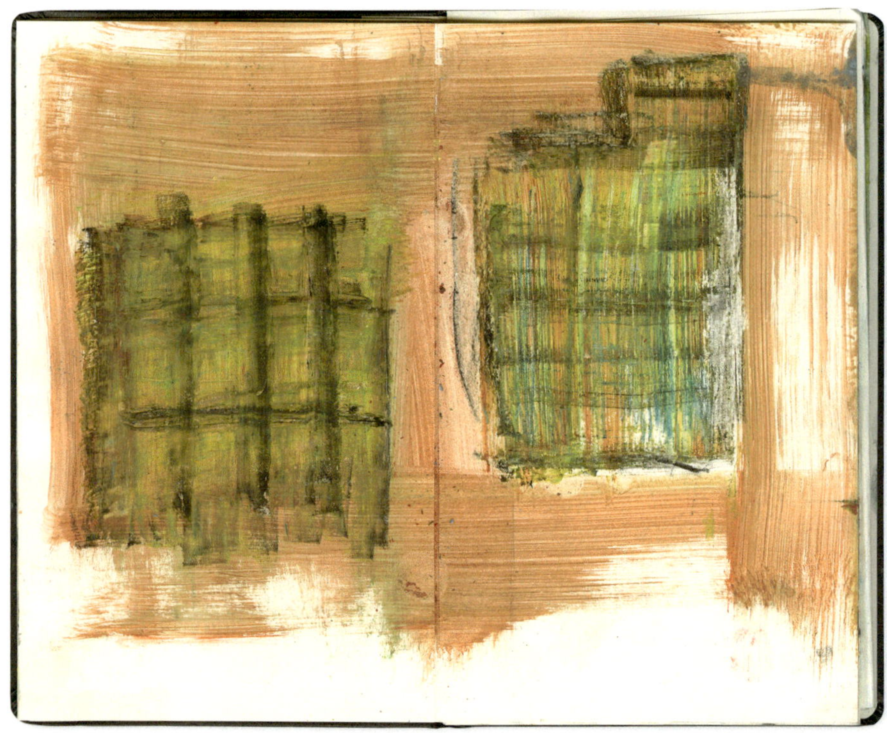

19

From **Vaporetto Leporello No. 1**, 2016

Watercolor and tempera on paper; leporello binding
8¼ × 5 × ¾ inches (closed)

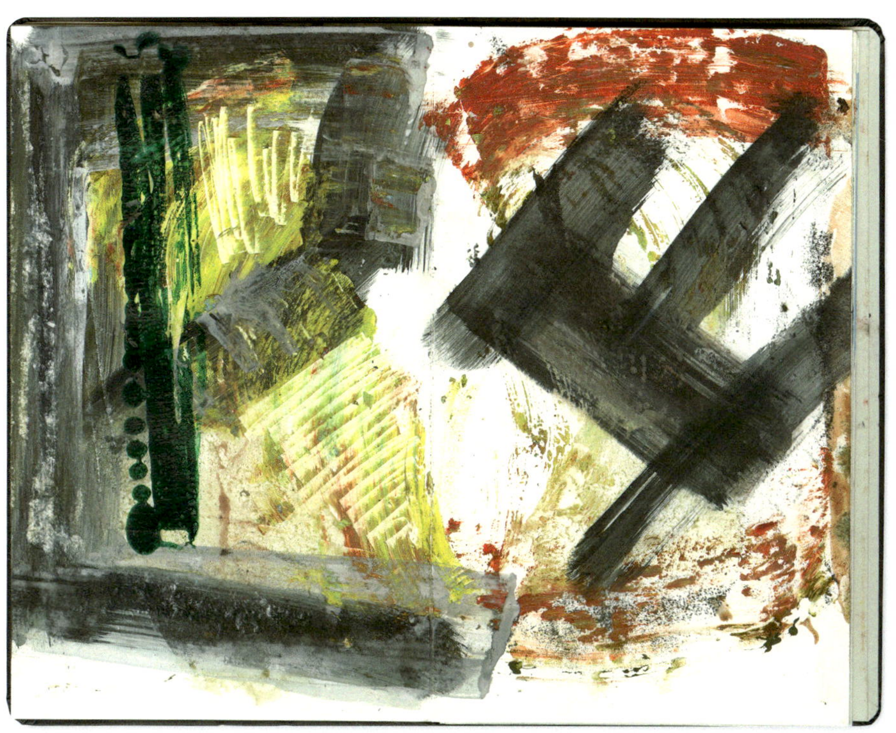

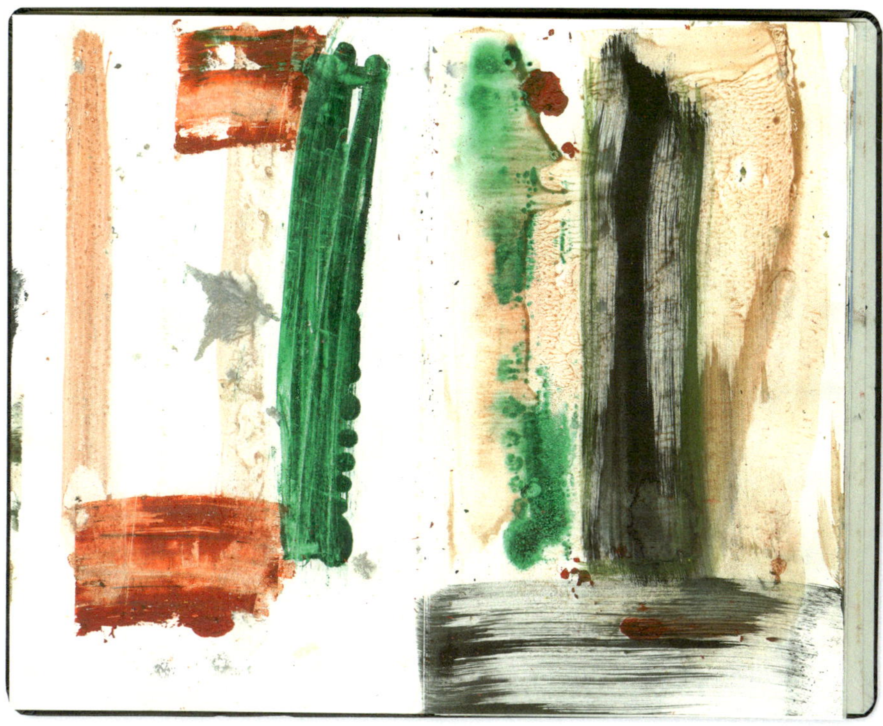

From **Vaporetto Leporello No. 3**, 2016

Watercolor and tempera on paper; leporello binding
8¼ × 5 × ¾ inches (closed)

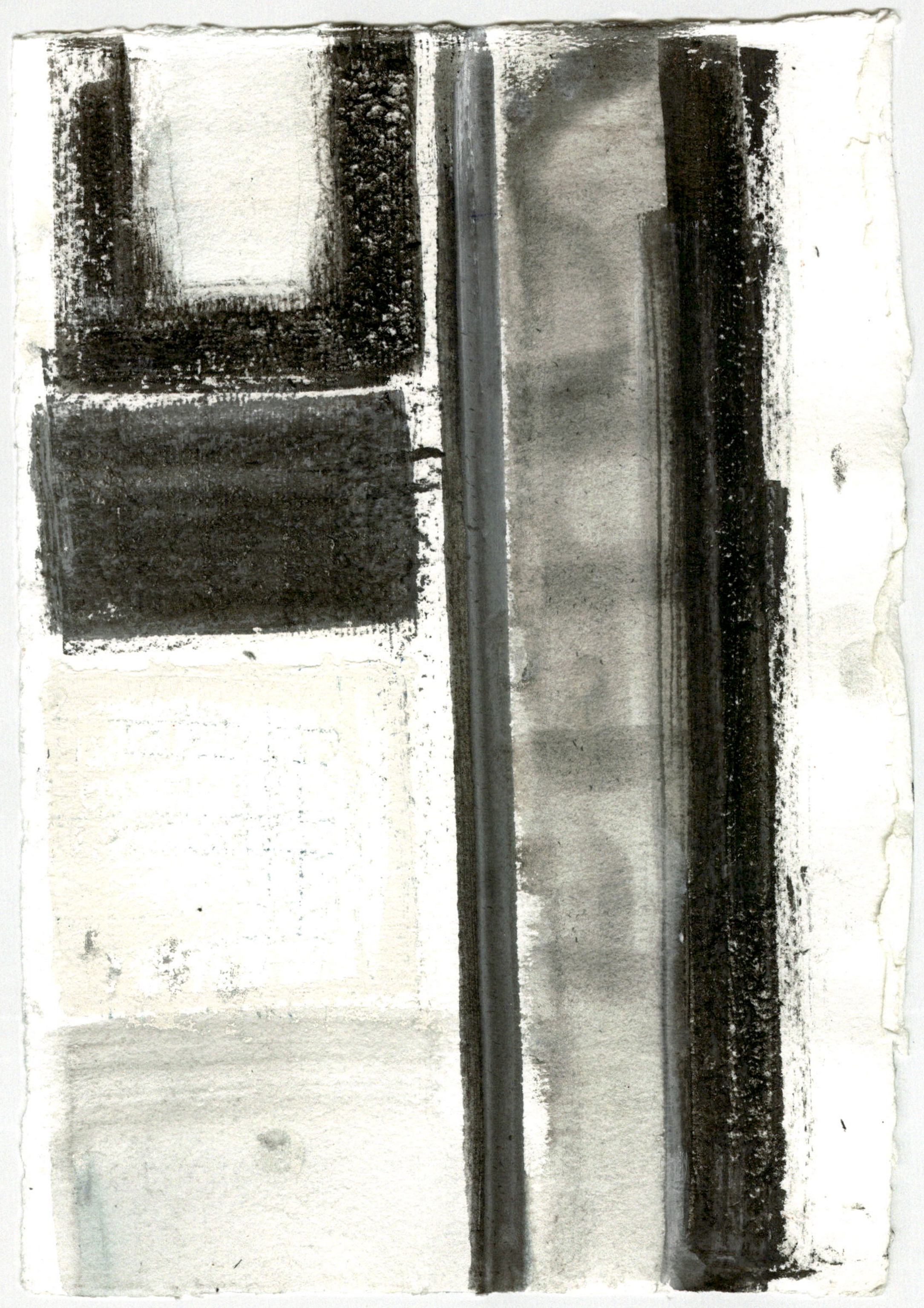

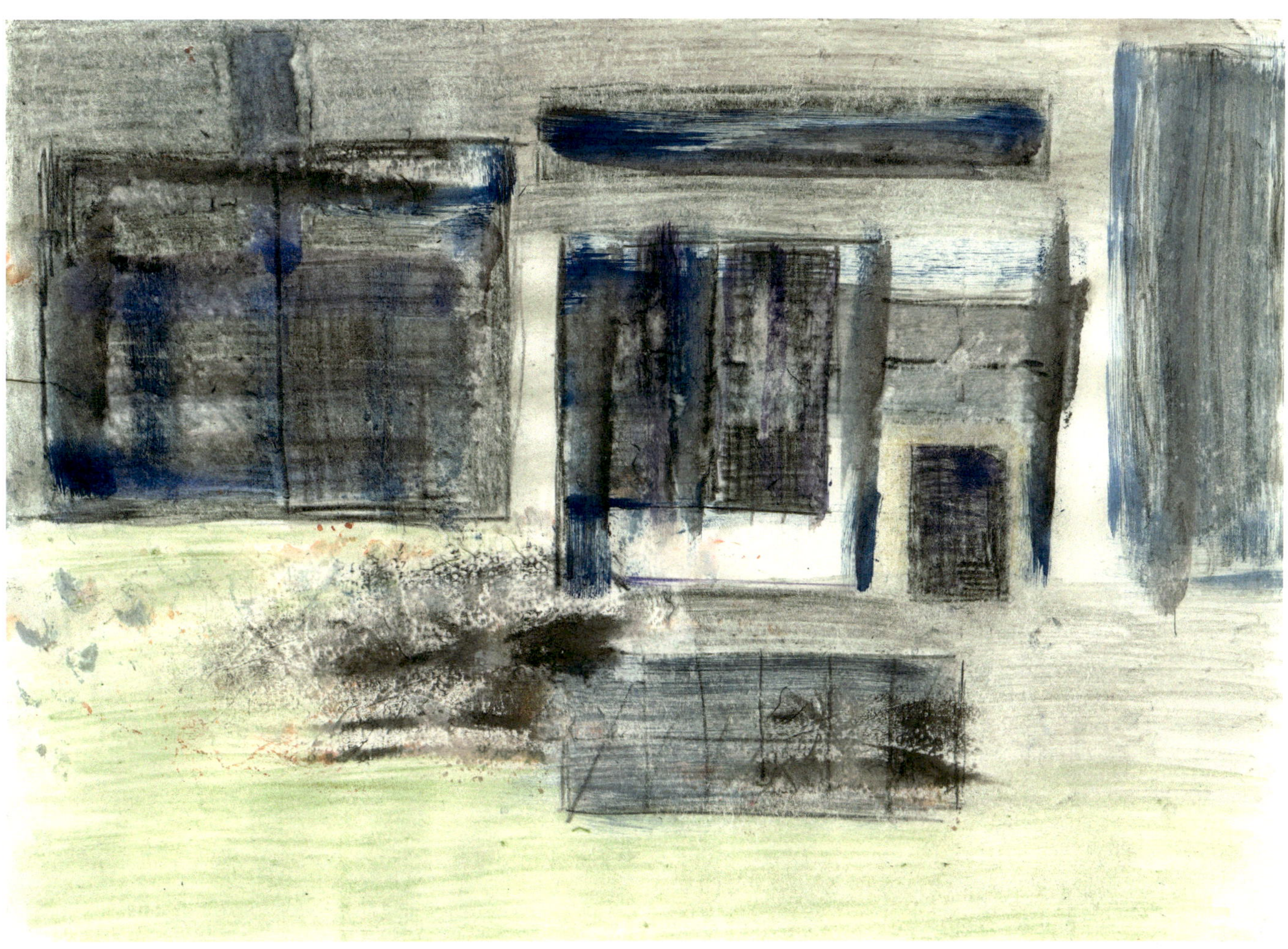

21

Untitled, 2016

Watercolor on paper
15½ × 11¼ inches

22

Untitled, 2016

Watercolor on paper
12⅝ × 17⅝ inches

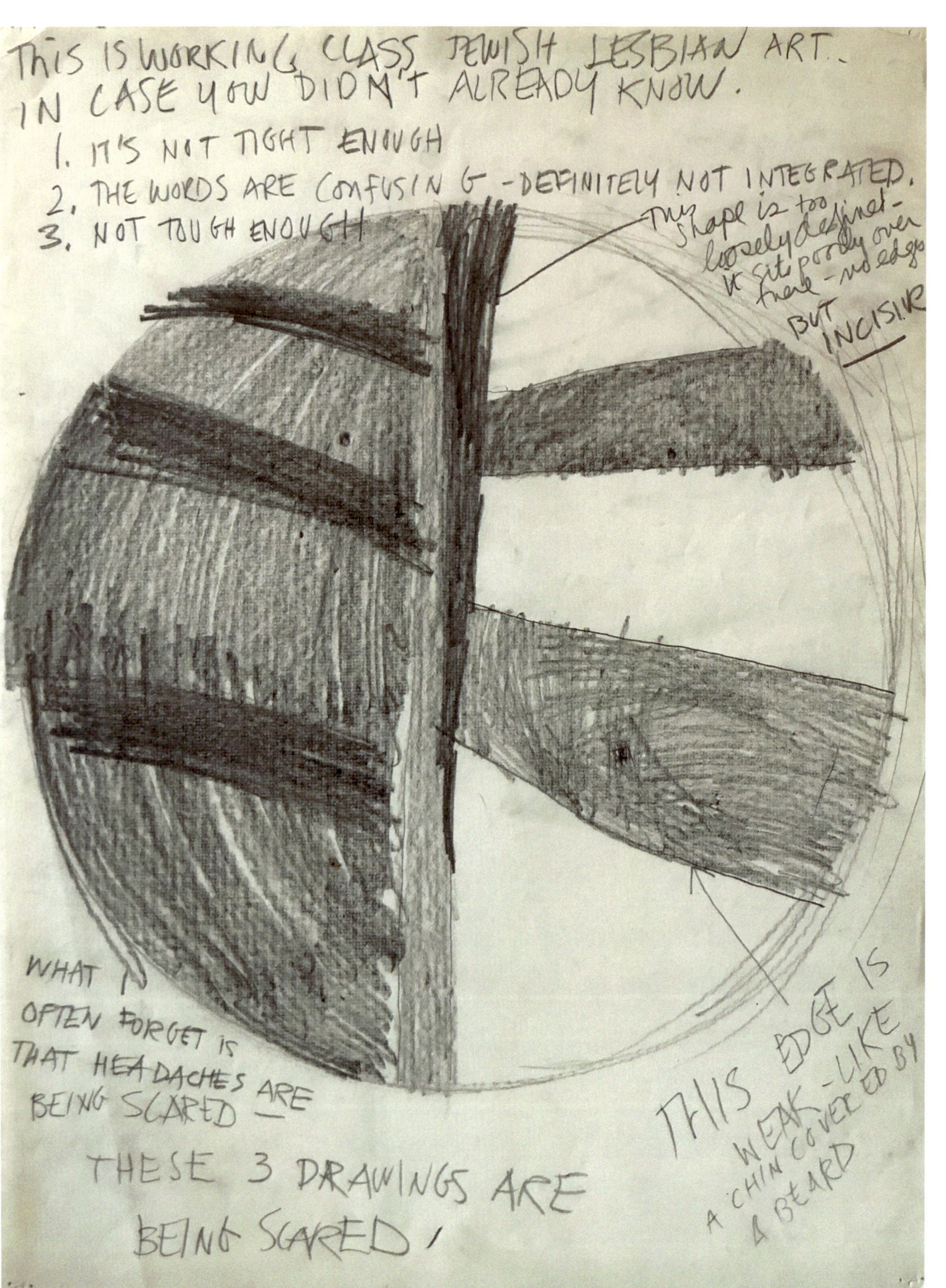
THIS IS WORKING CLASS JEWISH LESBIAN ART.
IN CASE YOU DIDN'T ALREADY KNOW.
1. IT'S NOT TIGHT ENOUGH
2. THE WORDS ARE CONFUSING - DEFINITELY NOT INTEGRATED.
3. NOT TOUGH ENOUGH
This shape is too loosely defined - it sits poorly over there - no edges
BUT INCISIVE
WHAT I OFTEN FORGET IS THAT HEADACHES ARE BEING SCARED
THESE 3 DRAWINGS ARE BEING SCARED!
THIS EDGE IS WEAK - LIKE A CHIN COVERED BY A BEARD

Queer Expressivity; or, the Art of How to Do It with Louise Fishman

Jill H. Casid

The charged form and sheer force of Louise Fishman's art is tough to disentangle from the relational forcefield of the claiming power of her exes. And yet, rather than extricate Fishman from that field, what happens if, instead, we take the risk of exploring what she does with the exes who claim her? We might start with the amorous declarations of those powerhouse book dedications to Fishman.

Never content to settle for the norm-conserving powers of mimesis or the plaintive notes of lyric address, Bertha Harris, in her 1993 introduction to the re-publication of her experimental novel *Lover* (1976), returns to the novel's dedicatory address to Fishman: "*Lover* is for Louise Fishman."[1] Recasting the "for" into an active "to," Harris flexes the volatile powers of art not merely to address or describe interdicted bodies, worlds, and loves, but also to materialize and affect them: "I wrote *Lover* to seduce Louise Fishman."[2] As we are given to understand, which is to say, to feel it, *Lover* was not just based on Louise but did Louise. For, as Harris concludes with the daring condensation of a two-word boast: "It worked."[3]

That the work of art might work is no small claim. With that stroke of wild condensation, we are made to reckon with what I would like to call a certain mad expressivity that we could also name *queer* in its pressing of the limits of what art can do when produced by those structurally barred from its genius ranks and consigned only to being done by it. We are made to face the not-at-all-trivial question of what such art can make us feel beyond the limits of a patriarchal and heterosexist real — such as tremble the here and now with the palpable sense of another world and other ways to come.

A certain mad expressivity professes no less with the dedication of anthropologist Esther Newton's *My Butch Career*, a memoir of what it takes to turn the gender and sexual outlawry of becoming, as she puts it, a "girl refusenik" into an academic vocation: "For LOUISE FISHMAN: my first great love."[4] As Newton recounts it, her "love for Louise" was an essential part of the "ferment" of the "lesbian world" cracking open in 1969 and 1970 into a world-quaking movement: "You could feel it on the streets, at GLF [the Gay Liberation Front], and in the bars."[5] From watching Trisha Brown and Steve Paxton perform to seeing Andy Warhol films and having tea with painter Elizabeth Murray, Fishman "opened the world of downtown art" to Newton. Through the mundane tremors of downtown art and lesbian worlds colliding and altering the world that arrogates to itself the status of real, Newton relays that she and Fishman talked "endlessly" about the question of feminist writing and art, which Newton re-articulates with a transposition that replaces the *ex* in expressionist with a variant of *in*: "Should it be realist, abstract impressionist [*sic*], protest, or could it be anything by a woman?"[6]

In or out? This is a relational spatio-temporal and political problem of form in formation and deformation at the center of the push-pull energetics of Fishman's working of the work of art. And yet, whether modified by the draw of the *in* or press of the *ex*, it is abstraction that has come to characterize Fishman's articulated refusal of the demand to play the role of native informant who represents

Fig. 2.1. No title (This is working class Jewish lesbian art. In case you didn't already know), 1973. Graphite on paper, 24 × 18 inches.

their unrebuffed marginality in recognizable terms. In a 2017 conversation in *Interview* magazine on the occasion of her first comprehensive museum survey (*Louise Fishman: A Retrospective* at the Neuberger Museum of Art in Purchase, New York), the then-77-year-old artist threw down the critical gauntlet while bringing into frictional relation the terms — queer, lesbian, woman, abstraction, and let us not forget "old" — that have come to define the uneasy critical frame for Fishman's work: "It has always been a problem for my career that I am one, queer, two, a woman, and three, doing plain old abstract paintings. There's not the subject matter that you see in other lesbian work — subject matter makes things more accessible and easy to write about. Abstract painting is not easy to write about."[7] Easy or not, the interview's title, "Louise Fishman's Abstract Activism," is its own demonstration of a major surge of investment in attending to the political work of what has come to be known as queer abstraction.[8] And yet, what if abstraction, with or without qualification, were not exactly the main problem at the heart of Fishman's experiments in what art can do when not dutifully staying in the lanes of representation and the prescribed givens that condition legibility?

Let's confront directly that other claiming ex: the ex of Ab-Ex, the ex that positions Fishman as if a queer, feminist inflection of a derivative inheritance — that is, as one reviewer puts it on the way to an ostensible defense: "Louise Fishman aptly describes herself as a 'third generation Abstract Expressionist.'"[9] In his 1946 *New Yorker* review on "Assorted Abstractions," critic Robert M. Coates asserted that Hans Hoffman "is certainly one of the most uncompromising representatives of what some people call the spatter-and-daub school of painting and I, more politely, have christened abstract Expressionism."[10] Coates's claim to the name was preceded by Alfred Barr's deployment of the phrase "Abstract Expressionism" to map the "Blue Rider Group of Munich Expressionists" (with particular emphasis on Wassily Kandinsky, Franz Marc, Lyonel Feininger, Paul Klee, and Hans Arp) in the catalogue to the 1936 Museum of Modern Art exhibition *Cubism and Abstract Art*. Despite the effort exerted to find a fitting name, for neither Barr nor Coates is the expression in and of Abstract Expressionism at issue. Indeed, it almost goes without articulation. With the exception, that is, of two moments in Barr's discussion of Kandinsky's method. In approaching the problem of the potential power of form to not just affect but also animate the spectator, Barr declaims: "Kandinsky's method was the logical expression of his theory."[11] This method for making the spectator vibrate may be apprehended, Barr specifies, in the way that Kandinsky's 1913 *Improvisation no. 30* (now in the collection of the Art Institute of Chicago) takes affecting form "as an expression of lyrical spontaneous excitement."[12] Expression, as an unproblematized delivery mechanism (the method carries the theory while the form conveys the excitement) and radically truncated mapping of sources (method comes from theory and form from excitement), would here seem to do the work of making manifest — with, it might seem, an accent on the *man*. And yet, in this circuit of excitement that excites, in which method is also a theory at work, the logistics of expression teeter toward an excess that troubles mapping them back to a man behind the canvas or paint. This excess leads onto the immanent potentials of an unruly expressivity with its own defiant energies that I will designate as *queer* for the way queer expressivity, as an affecting agency and aesthetic force of potential, works and works us.[13]

Queer expressivity troubles the policing of substance and its ostensible inheritance, the biopolitical regimes dedicated to controlling production and reproduction with binary-gendered, antisemitic, and antiblack racializing and heterosexist implications for the fates of bodies and worlds rendered disposable. It is perhaps not surprising, then, that in the 1930s and 40s, just as expressivity became a cornerstone of genetics as a way to describe a gene's materializing manifestation, the term was also introduced by Austrian Jewish refugee philologist and linguist Leo Spitzer's 1948 *Linguistics and Literary History: Essays in Stylistics*, which demonstrated what has come to be known as "expressive stylistics" in action. In Spitzer's anatomization of eighteenth-century polymath and art critic Denis Diderot's affecting mimicry of bodily movement or sensation, which Spitzer diagnoses as a kind of Enlightenment nervous system of style, expressive stylistics makes a point of its failure to "disentangle the manner of expression from the manner of thinking."[14] For it is not just the question of who or what does the expressing that haunts the enterprise. It is also that, as Spitzer attributes to Diderot, an expressivity in excess of the subject threatens to not just do but also undo the subject: "The self-destruction brought about by excessive expressivity was seen by Diderot as a danger to which any artistic nature is exposed."[15] What interests me here is not to further ascribe particular afflictions to something called "artistic nature," but to put pressure on the way expressive stylistics raises, however inadvertently, the creatively ontogenetic and autodestructive potentials of a subject-eroding and altering expressivity, an expressivity in excess.

It must be acknowledged that the danger in taking expressivity seriously is that any expressivity, when attributed to those from whom no one wants to hear, risks being marked as excessive. This is especially true when it is understood to come from those barred from the universal or general — that is, from those whose work is ever ascribed to the particular and, thus, to the marginalized minor without generalized public purview. Discounted as nothing but raw and even illegible noise, expressivity can, therefore, only be dismissed as the shamed outpourings of personal experience that does not know its place. The recent revival (in Zoe Leonard's strategically placed signage at the Whitney Museum of American Art and emblazoned across T-shirts by Maria Grazia Chiuri for Dior) of "Why Have There Been No Great Women Artists?" — the interrogative puncture that gives its title to Linda Nochlin's landmark 1971 essay — calls on us to confront the particular problem expressivity poses for those disqualified from the start from what constitutes the expressible capacity for greatness. As Nochlin puts it: "The problem lies not so much with some feminists' concept of what femininity is, but rather with their misconception — shared with the public at large — of what art is: with the naïve idea that art is the direct, personal expression of individual emotional experience, a translation of personal life into visual terms. Art is almost never that, great art never is."[16] Here, Nochlin clears the way for the possibility of "great art" by those structurally barred from it. But she does so by cleaving what art can and should do not just from excess expressivity but also from expression. Period. Expression is designated as abject, that is, as matter out of place, of which we somehow ought to be ashamed.

What is the cost of accepting the terms of this regulatory field dividing real or great art from expression? Must we accept this cleavage that positions expression as the humiliating evidence of ostensibly naïve investment in the direct transmission of emotional experience, as the necessarily *merely* personal? For we could argue that this abjection of expression is still caught within the problem (not at all exclusive to feminist thought and politics) of what is attributed to femininity. Rejecting expression as the communication of a maligned substance or essence associated with emotional experience does not merely relegate the temerity to assert their mattering to ostensibly merely personal life. Consigning expression to the zone of an abjected femininity denies the general condition of living matter: the potential to be reduced to abject nothingness that we all share. We might think here of Andrea Long Chu's rereading of Valerie Solanas's 1967 *SCUM Manifesto* and largely forgotten 1965 play *Up Your Ass* to make the provocative claim for the terrifying universal of self-negation, "Everyone is female, and everyone hates it."[17] Hated or loved or all of the above, expression is hard to excise, for what is abjected always lands somewhere.

Fishman's working of the work of art offers us a way to grapple with the potentials of excessive expressivity as a queer, feminist creative praxis that draws on and with what is in excess of the regulated subject, both the abjected aspects of what is consigned to the merely "personal" and "emotional" of experience and also the immanent of the as yet — including what we might yet become. And, in attending to Fishman's working of the work of art, we can revisit the question or problem of queer abstraction by focusing not on the how and why of its tactics of abstraction, but on what art can do when it is not representing. To do so is to unfold not the abstract in Abstract Expressionism but its embarrassed other side: the queer and problematic powers of expressivity — which Fishman's experiments with art as an affecting and altering force raise as a timely concern. I turn here to sketch out this art of how to do it with Fishman via an open-ended diagram of thirteen key aspects of Fishman's experiments in and with the powers of queer expressivity as an unruly force in excess of the individual that, nonetheless, refuses the abjection of the ostensibly merely personal as a condition for making art with an intensity that dares.

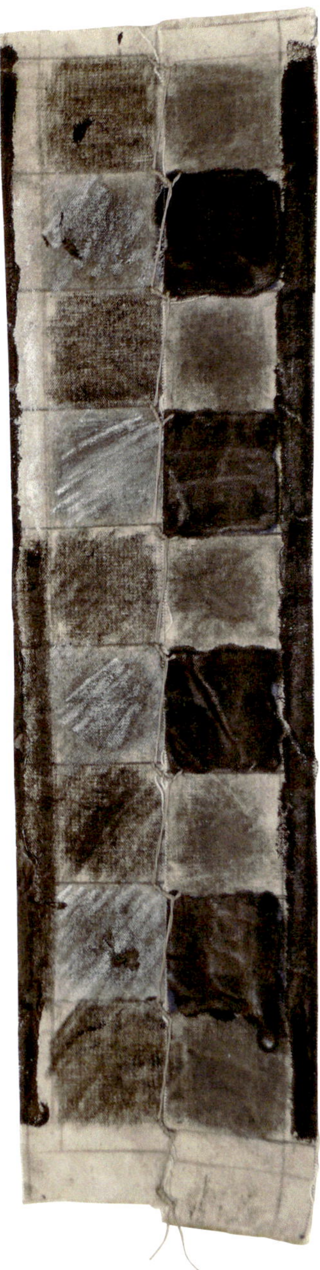

Fig. 2.2. *Untitled*, 1971. Acrylic, chalk, graphite, and thread on canvas, 19 × 5¼ inches.

1 *Queer expressivity risks working with the consigning names and identifications that claim the artist's life and work as a means to refuse their possessive confinement.* Fishman shows us how to work it, across a career of negotiating the insistence that the style and content match the assigned substance, by defying without disavowal. We could take as exemplary the taking apart of the emphatic all-caps assertion at the top of an untitled 1973 drawing, "THIS IS WORKING CLASS JEWISH LESBIAN ART. IN CASE YOU DIDN'T ALREADY KNOW" (fig. 2.1). Consider it a diagramming how-to with staying power in its energetic redrawing of the conventions not just for dividing (subjects, identities, bodies, worlds) but for setting the parts against one another. It draws with the pain and fear we might wish to deny ("WHAT I OFTEN FORGET IS THAT HEADACHES ARE BEING SCARED—THESE 3 DRAWINGS ARE BEING SCARED!") as a potential resource for the resilient working of ascribed weakness.

2 *Queer expressivity risks working with an athletic aesthetics that refuses binary gender consignment, employing tactics for extending the sense of the action of making to make physical process palpable through the work's working as dynamic, still-active material presence.* As Fishman demonstrates in working with an athletic aesthetics also often called "gestural abstraction," the extension of the vital sense of the action of making is not a matter of ableist investment in winning prowess. Nor is it to secure qualification for competition on the turf of an Abstract Expressionism already ceded to binarized gender on the kinaesthetic training grounds of the basketball courts or baseball diamonds to which the dynamized grids across Fishman's work (fig. 2.2) are so often analogized.[18] It is, rather, to make us feel how the vitality ascribed to virility was never the exclusive property of one form of what is attributed to genetic expression. Or, to put this another way, we could think of the risks of Fishman's working of queer expressivity as the making sensible of Monique Wittig's line that "lesbians are not women" by way of Jill Johnston's incitement that "it's not easy to see."[19]

3 *Queer expressivity risks working with relations to previous work that commits to lifelong training kept in frictional tension with a practice of undoing mastery.* How to do it with Fishman? It's a muscular practice of the ex and the in. Looking, doing, and undoing form the basis for a queer expressivity that risks excess out of the rhythms of a certain "integrity" of practice that has to be stretched, tested to produce its tensile strength. As Fishman demonstrates with "How I Do It: Cautionary Advice from a Lesbian Painter," which appeared in the 1977 special issue of *Heresies* dedicated to "Lesbian Art and Artists," it's not just a matter of "take what you want and leave the dreck" but relational judgment forged through a practice of looking that refuses identitarian purity: "Don't

stop looking at El Greco because he's not Jewish, or Chardin because he's not an abstract painter or Matisse because he's not a lesbian. By all means look at Agnes Martin and Georgia O'Keefe and Eva Hesse. But don't forget Cézanne, Manet and Giotto."[20] And yet it's also about disciplined meditative clearing practices that expel to make space that is also allied with a practice of a certain humility, which ranges in its exercise from the early cut-ups to a persistent refusal, across the work, of a signature look or formula.

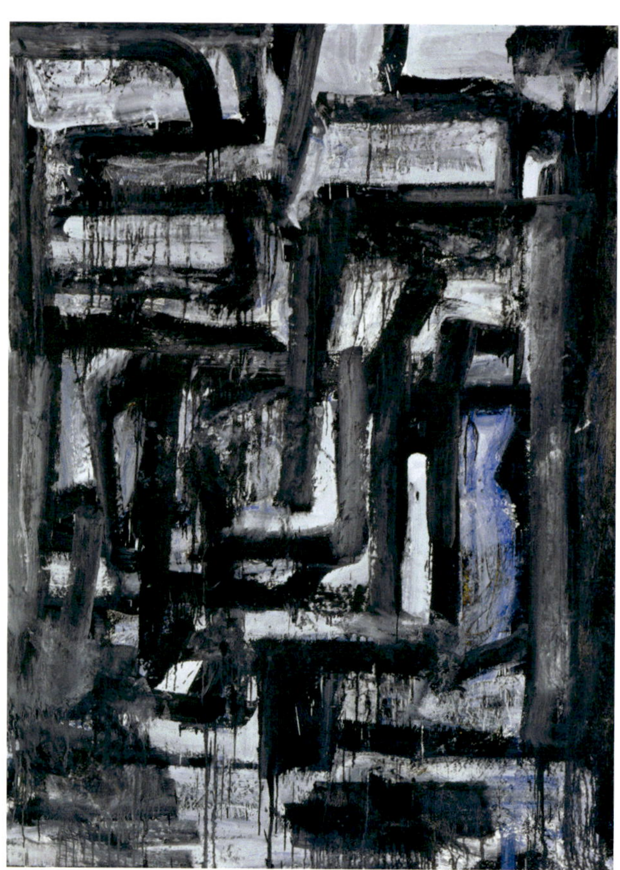

Fig. 2.3. *The Art of Losing*, 2003. Oil on linen, 80 × 60 inches.

4 *Queer expressivity risks its tensile and ductile powers by committing to a practice of painting that, in moving across materials and techniques not necessarily proper to painting, risks not being.* As Fishman demonstrates across a career of paint on paper that persists in unhinging painting from its canvas and wood supports while also continuing to explore what it does with fabric, the undoing of mastery as a queer-feminist praxis is not merely a formative stage of feminist consciousness raising that excises the patriarchal and heterosexist lurking inside with mat knife, stapler, and even needle in hand. It is a lifelong gambit hinged on making loss not content or subject but an aesthetic practice of resilient self-erosion. It is *The Art of Losing* (fig. 2.3), as Fishman puts it, titling a 2003 oil-on-linen painting with black-and-blue gray slashes and drips after Elizabeth Bishop's exclamatory ("*Write* it!") instructions for doing things with being undone.[21]

5 *Queer expressivity risks the further intensification of the knots of not-being by refusing the priorities of developmental order as well as those of size and scale.* That the drawings are not preparatory works on the way to the real thing. That the use of acrylic and oil on paper is not merely a matter of the economic contingencies of a particular life moment without a studio, though it is also a matter of recognizing and working with precarity. That the exploration of not just the extremity of the tiny but the big or just bigger than miniature refuses to give in to the dictates of malignant growth and unhooks the force and intensities of what affects from the presumption that the great equates to the large. These are the lessons across the exhibition *A Question of Emphasis* in exploring how to work with tying, tightening, and loosening into the knots of not-being we don't choose as a way to be with and do an art of losing — as a practice of undoing mastery that, in the process, intensifies its powers to affect (figs. 2.4 and 2.5).

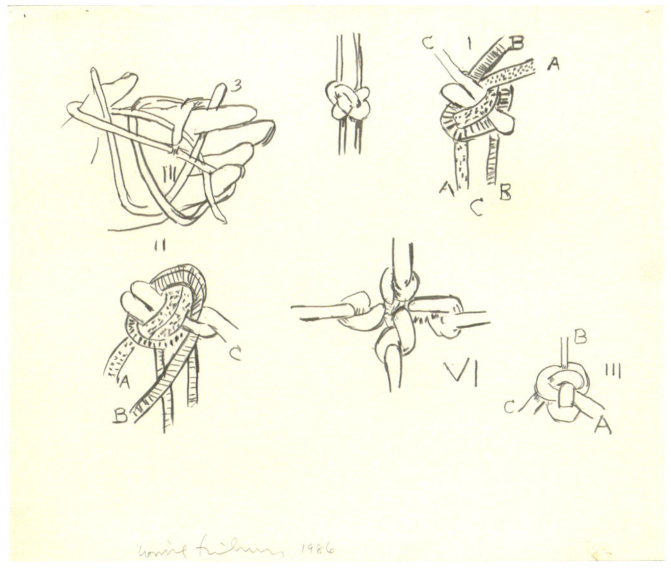

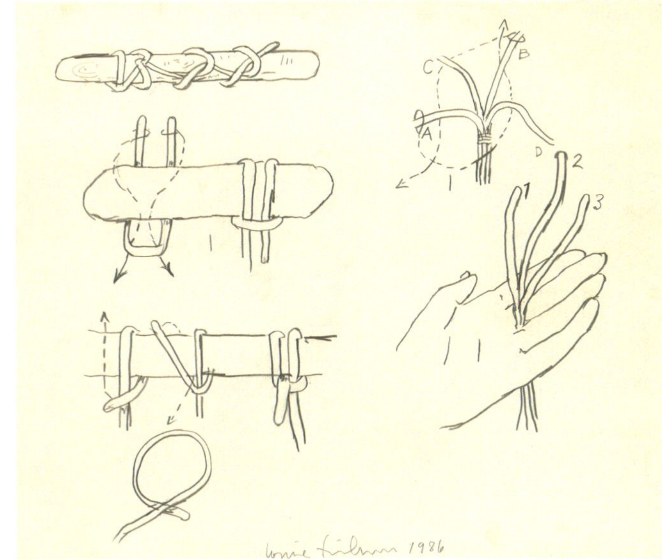

Fig. 2.4. No title (Knots), 1986. Graphite on paper, 13⅞ × 17 inches.

Fig. 2.5. No title (Knots), 1986. Graphite on paper, 13¾ × 16¾ inches.

6 *Queer expressivity risks working with the potentially self-eroding exposure to and relational dependencies on the vagaries of judgment.* Consider a group of circles from 1974 drawn out of "leftover colors" with pencil markings of precarious address ("THINKING ABOUT SOUTINE AT THE BARNES," "TO PLEASE JENNY AND JEFF," "THINKING ABOUT THE AUDIENCE"; see fig. 1.7) that expose these exercises to and yet work with relational dependencies on the anticipated and actual ways in which the working of the work of art may also, and even necessarily, work in the mode of the express in that other verb sense of sending by special delivery in the hope of the "letter" always reaching its destination. That they may not exactly reach their intended addressee is also critical to their felt intensification of the power of deflationary exposure as conduit. An "afterword" penciled in Fishman's characteristic capitals, speaking to what art can do with what it can't do, puts it this way: "RUSH TO GET ESTHER [Newton] TO SEE CIRCLE DRAWINGS. KNOWING ON THE WAY IT WOULD BE BETTER TO LOOK AT THEM FOR A WHILE MYSELF—BUT TOO INVOLVED ALREADY WITH HER LOOKING AT THEM. BUT ESTHER IS SLEEPING." And snap. With that doubled stroke of a drawn-out sense of rebuff that intensifies the many ways we miss one another, it's hard not to be called to attention to what may be left after it's ostensibly over.

7 *Queer expressivity risks intensifying the potentially self-eroding vulnerability of working with not just the ostensibly merely personal of direct address but also the matter of generation and inheritance.* Here we could

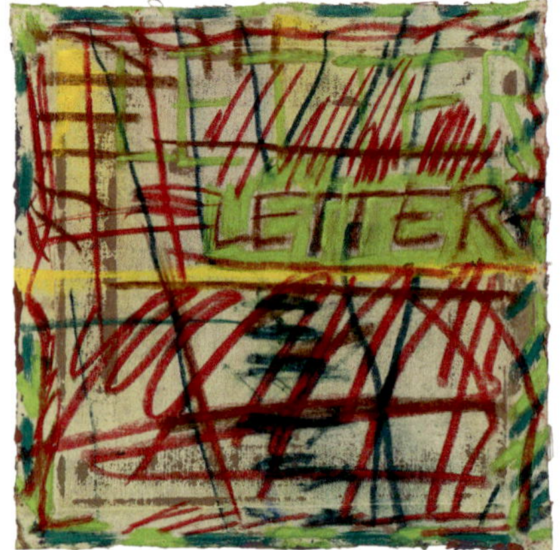

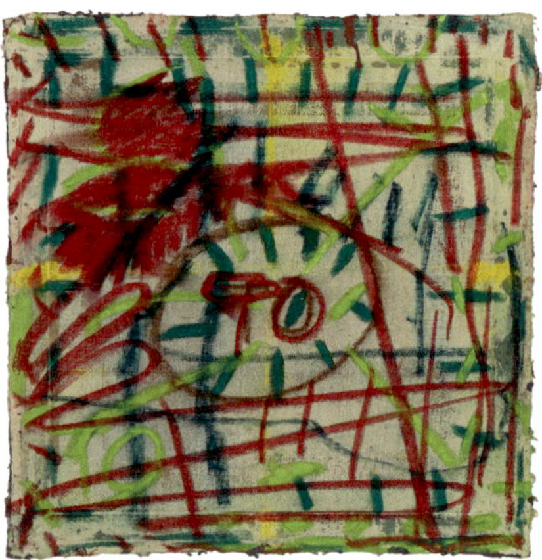

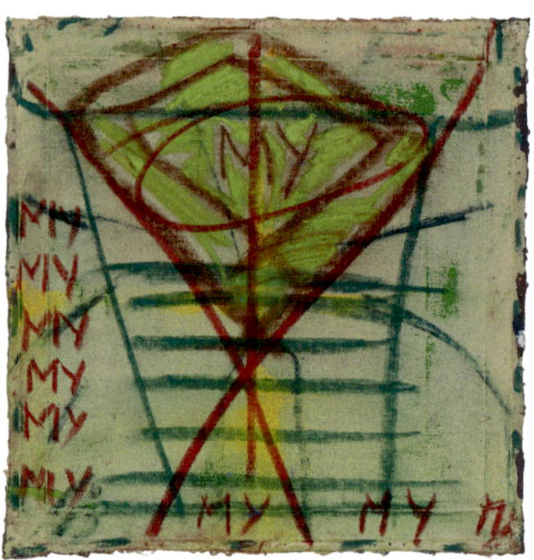

Fig. 2.6. *Letter to My Mother about Painting*, 1972–73. Oil on canvas, 13¾ × 14 inches each, two sided.

take as exemplary the audacious experiment in direct address of *Letter to My Mother about Painting* scrawled in oil across six double-sided panels from 1972–73 (fig. 2.6) that risks our taking it only as at once the acting out and the working through of Fishman's particular charged relation to the matter of her mother, Gertrude Fisher-Fishman, for whose 2011 catalogue of artworks Fishman provided the framing text.[22] Such a story of legacies, inheritances, and expectations regarding being or becoming an artist like and/or not like one's mother may be one that Fishman confesses in acknowledging: "I struggled for years to make sure that my mother didn't think I was going to be an artist."[23] But this would be to miss the way that the risk of working with the ostensibly merely personal of direct address puts the express in excessive expressivity in another way. That is, such queer expressivity makes the personal of volatile and charged ambivalence a vehicle for a general address that goes not just back, to forge the not-at-all-given bonds of generations by testing them, but also toward the future that gathers wild force in the summons of its errancy, which is crucial to its potential to draw in an expansive and expanding riot of a crowd of dyke, queer, and trans kin beyond its ostensible moment.[24]

8 *Queer expressivity risks working with ostensibly negative affects and the sharing out of the potentially unshareable as a summoning force.* That summoning force of amplifying anger blasts most vehemently across *Angry Louise*, *Angry Bertha*, *Angry Esther*, *Angry Jill*, *Angry Rita Mae* — just five of thirty "Angries" (most from 1973, plates 23–27) painted across the paper of insufficient infrastructures. That making of an "army of lovers" out of what undoes us may be positioned historically as Fishman's route back to painting. But that force also resists containment in its convoking intensity, which does the trans-temporal work of sharing out the potentially unshareable to make a

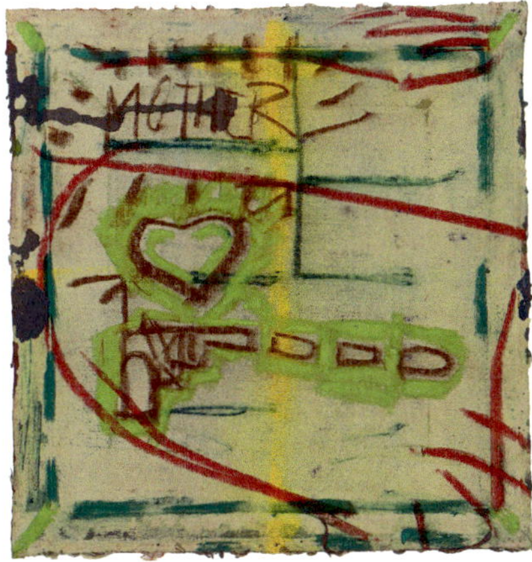

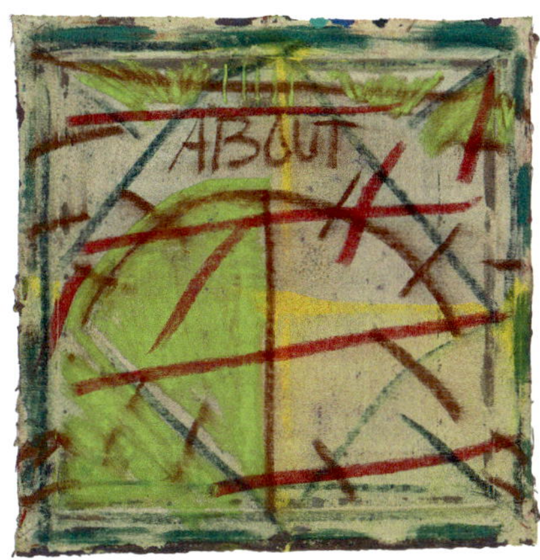

trans-feminist commons across time and space not out of shared substance but out of the bonds of rage as medium.[25]

9 *Queer expressivity risks working with the self-eroding force of the destructively unbidden to do things with being undone.* Doing things with the self-eroding blows of loss after loss after loss takes on an intensified charge with the studio fire that, as Fishman describes it, destroyed what she had gathered as her life and brought chronic fatigue syndrome in its wake. And yet Fishman's turn in the early 1990s to the fanning pleats of Japanese leporello books also comes in the wake of working with the exes that claim Fishman in other ways, from the ex of exile to that of extermination and the visit to Auschwitz — from which a rock, as Fishman recounts it, was one of the few objects to survive the fire. But which Holocaust, which sense of the insensible of *burnt whole*? And it is here where the impersonal, person-exterminating forces that produce denuded, bared life meet what takes hold of us at the level of the personal and at the scale of the handheld that *Book of Abuse* (1993–94, plate 14) shows us — with its wounding work — how to do things with what devastates.[26]

10 *Queer expressivity risks a material erotics of art not as content but as an unruly aesthetic affect that refuses specularizing legibility while risking working with the abjected of not just the "dirty" but a certain wash of what might be dismissed as the romantic or even sentimental.* That queer expressivity, in risking a material erotics of art, might be a problem — and not just for critics — is haunted by Susan Sontag's famous challenge: "In place of a hermeneutics we need an erotics of art."[27] If such an erotics is neither visible form nor expressed content, then it might seem that we are reduced to hallucinatory projection, a version of auto-theory in the confessional mode, or following

the directional vectors of the dedication. But consider what Fishman does in working into and through the folds of *Down and Dirty (A Book for Bertha Harris)* (1994, plate 29) to put the unexcised matter of relation to wilding use beyond merely a tit for tat or "Lover" does Bertha. *Down and Dirty* does a different version of the vice versa in exciting the page to incite and inciting the surface to excite.

11 *Queer expressivity risks working with the potential of the work of art to work, a vital version of a kind of animacy attributed to the naive that, at best, goes by the inadequate name of the spiritual.* Here we move from the pleats of the matter of the fold-in and fold-out books to the paintings Fishman activates with the dirt laden with charred remains that she collected from the disposal site at the Auschwitz II-Birkenau death camp, which Fishman reminds us to call the "Pond of Living Ashes," as well as to paintings such as *Golem* (1981, fig. 2.7) that force us to confront the active, vital potential of presumptively dead matter not merely as subject or even process of making (as in the way the form and facture of Fishman's painting resembles that of fabricating a figure out of earth and activating it by encircling incantations).[28] To put this another way, what is also at stake in the question of the working of the work of art is no less than the potential that life rendered disposable as life reduced to dead matter might yet act to contest the logics of a necropolitical ex without terminus.

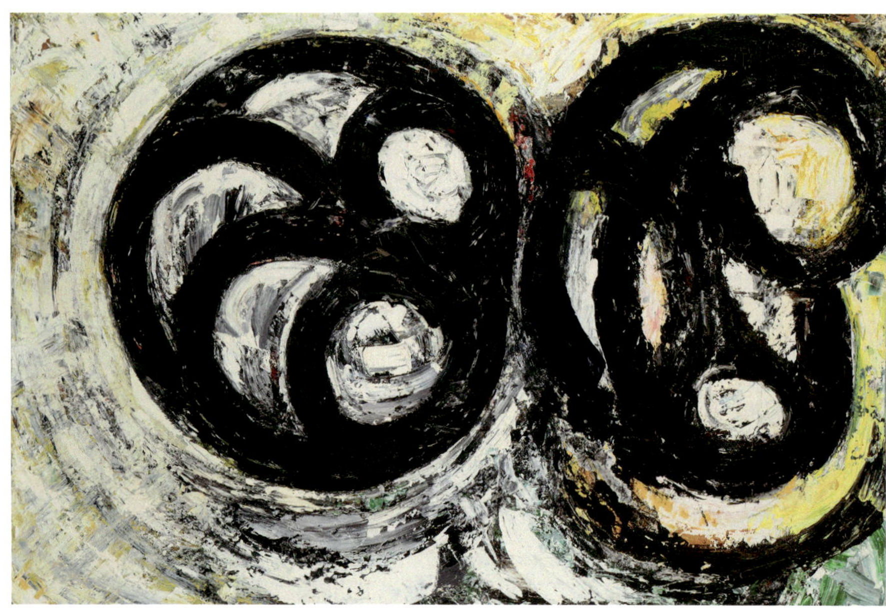

Fig. 2.7. *Golem*, 1981. Oil on linen, 32 × 48 inches. The Jewish Museum, New York, Gift of Francine and Samuel Klagsbrun, 1991-56.

12 *Queer expressivity risks the openness of the fan in the sense of both devoted enthusiasm and the accordion pleats that unfold.* Fanning back, let us return to those concertina-fold books that go by the name of Leporello, the servant in Mozart's opera *Don Giovanni* whose revelation of the libertine's liaisons unfolds a seemingly endless list of exes. Here we meet that inseparable other side of the vitalities of matter at stake in the working of the working of art so often dismissed as the spiritual, and this is the radical joy that goes by the no-less-inadequate name of seduction.

13 *Queer expressivity risks not belonging to the moment of its making, which is also to risk an openness to the as yet.* Fishman has avowed a relation not just to expression but also to Expressionism: "I've always thought of myself as an Expressionist painter. I associate it with a certain kind of passion and a certain kind of marking. A kind of immediacy."[29] But this is not to bury the lede at the end. It is, rather, to refuse the relegation of Fishman's work to Abstract Expressionist style with a queer-feminist content or another turn on the question posed by Helaine Posner, "What's left for an artist to express after the triumph of Abstract Expressionism?"[30] And this is not just because Fishman's exploration of the embarrassed potentials of potentially excessive expressivity troubles temporal progression with both an intensified relation to a past that is not over and an unforeclosed futurity. Rather, to revisit the beginning, Fishman's working of the risks of queer expressivity hazards not the confidence of "it worked" but an aesthetics of seduction without assurances that, nonetheless, moves with a mad sense of the immanence of other possible ways of being and doing — an as yet with the palpable immediacy of an urgent here and now.

Notes

1. Bertha Harris, "Introduction," in *Lover*, with a foreword by Karla Jay and new introduction by Bertha Harris (1976; New York: NYU Press, 1993), viii.
2. Harris, "Introduction," lxviii.
3. Harris, lxviii.
4. Esther Newton, *My Butch Career: A Memoir* (Durham: Duke University Press, 2018), v.
5. Newton, *My Butch Career*, 146.
6. Newton, 146.
7. William J. Simmons, "Louise Fishman's Abstract Activism," *Interview*, May 2, 2016. Not just a queer feminist defense but a robust re-theorization of abstraction in praxis had, by this time, already been mounted. See Barbara Hammer, "The Politics of Abstraction," in *Queer Looks: Perspectives on Lesbian and Gay Film and Video*, ed. Martha Gever, John Greyson, and Pratibha Parmar (New York: Routledge, 1993), 70–75; Linda Besemer, "Abstraction: Politics and Possibilities," *X-TRA* 7, no. 3 (2005): 14–23; Amy Sillman, "Ab-Ex and Disco Balls: In Defense of Abstract Expressionism II," *Artforum* 49, no. 10 (Summer 2011): 321–25; and Harmony Hammond, "A Manifesto (Personal) of Monochrome (Sort of)," reprinted in *Harmony Hammond: Becoming/Unbecoming Monochrome*, Tirza True Latimer (Denver: Redline Art Space, 2014), 4.
8. I am particularly indebted here to ongoing conversation with Lex Morgan Lancaster and their articulation of queer abstraction as not a style or look but, rather, a set of tactics for dragging away from the normative constraints on the domain of appearance. See particularly their dissertation, "Dragging Away: Queer Abstraction in Contemporary Art," University of Wisconsin-Madison, 2017; their articles "The Wipe: Sadie Benning's Queer Abstraction," *Discourse* 39, no. 1 (Winter 2017): 92–116, and "Feeling the Grid: Lorna Simpson's Concrete Abstraction," *ASAP/Journal* 2, no. 1 (2017); and their review of Jared Ledesma's exhibition "Queer Abstraction," *ASAP*, July 16, 2019, http://asapjournal.com/queer-abstraction-lex-morgan-lancaster/. For a speculative overview that places particular emphasis on the question of resistance to surveillance and an embrace of the impurity of abstraction, see David J. Getsy, "Ten Queer Theses on Abstraction," in *Queer Abstraction*, ed. Jared Ledesma (Des Moines: Des Moines Art Center, 2019), 65–75. That abstraction might rather be understood best as an impure tendency and, thus, even figuration by other means, see Charles Bernstein, "Disfiguring Abstraction," *Critical Inquiry* 39, no. 3 (Spring 2013): 488.
9. Daniel Kunitz, "Exhibition Note: On 'Louise Fishman: New Paintings,' at the Cheim & Read Gallery, New York," *The New Criterion* 38, no. 7 (November 2000), http://newcriterion.com/issues/2000/11/exhibition-note-2315.
10. Robert M. Coates, "The Art Galleries: Assorted Abstractions," *New Yorker*, March 30, 1946, 83.
11. Alfred Barr, *Cubism and Abstract Art* (New York: Museum of Modern Art, 1936), 66.
12. Barr, *Cubism and Abstract Art*, 66.
13. This essay's formulation of the concept of queer expressivity thinks with the foundational work on queer performativity by Eve Sedgwick and Judith Butler at the beginnings of what has come to be known as queer theory. See Eve Kosofsky Sedgwick, "Queer Performativity: Henry James's *The Art of the Novel*," *GLQ* 1, no. 1 (1993): 1–16; and Judith Butler, "Critically Queer," *GLQ* 1, no. 1 (1993): 17–32. It also extends my thinking on the "deformative" (a term used in both of these early essays yet never quite taken up) as the negative aspect and potential within the performative, which I developed in "Doing Things with Being Undone," *Journal of Visual Culture* 18, no. 1 (2019): 30–52, and "Queer Deformativity," *The Conditions of Being Art: Pat Hearn Gallery & American Fine Arts, Co. (1983–2004)*, ed. Jeannine Tang, Lia Gangitano, and Ann Butler (New York: Dancing Foxes Press, 2018), 213–37.
14. Leo Spitzer, *Linguistics and Literary History: Essays in Stylistics* (1948; Princeton, NJ: Princeton University Press, 2015), 168.
15. Spitzer, *Linguistics and Literary History*, 155.
16. Linda Nochlin, "Why Have There Been No Great Women Artists?," *ARTnews* 69, no. 1 (1971): 23–39, 67–71.
17. Andrea Long Chu, *Females* (New York: Verso, 2019), 11.
18. For the most recent narration of Fishman's athletic aesthetics and, in this case, through the device of live-action ballgame commentary, see Amy Sillman, "9 Innings: Notes of a Color Commentator," *Louise Fishman: 9 Works on Paper*, Karma Gallery website, April 28, 2020, http://karmakarma.org/viewingroom/louise-fishman-9-works-on-paper/.
19. Monique Wittig, "The Straight Mind" (1978), trans. Mary Jo Lakeland and Susan Ellis Wolf, in *Out There: Marginalization and Contemporary Cultures*, ed. Russell Ferguson, Martha Gever, Trinh T. Minh-ha, and Cornel West (New York: New Museum; and Cambridge: MIT Press, 1990),

57. Jill Johnston, “Cunningham in Connecticut” (1961), in *The Disintegration of a Critic*, ed. Fiona McGovern, Francis Sullivan, and Axel Wieder (Bergen: Bergen Kunsthall, and Berlin: Sternberg Press, 2019), 15.

20. Louise Fishman, “How I Do It: Cautionary Advice from a Lesbian Painter,” *Heresies* 1, no. 3 (Fall 1977): 74.

21. Elizabeth Bishop, “One Art,” in *Geography III* (New York: Farrar, Straus and Giroux, 1976), 41. Bishop’s poem begins, “The art of losing isn’t hard to master,” and concludes, “the art of losing’s not too hard to master/ though it may look like (*Write* it!) like disaster.”

22. Louise Fishman, untitled essay, in *Gertrude Fisher-Fishman: A Catalogue of Selected Work* (New York: Ink, Inc., 2011).

23. Ingrid Schaffner, “Getting Small with Louise Fishman,” in *Louise Fishman*, ed. Helaine Posner (Purchase, NY: Neuberger Museum of Art, and Philadelphia: Institute of Contemporary Art, 2016), 190.

24. Fishman’s *Letter to My Mother* was installed in the 2011 exhibition *Readykeulous: The Hurtful Healer: The Correspondence Issue*, organized by Ridykeulous (Nicole Eisenman and A.L. Steiner) at Invisible Exports, New York, with the wall text, “How’s My Painting: Call 1-800-EAT SHIT.” For a review and installation shot, see Rachel Wetzler, “Angry Art Letters on the Lower East Side,” *Hyperallergic*, February 3, 2011, http://hyperallergic.com/17693/angry-letters-exhibition/.

25. On the angry paintings, see especially Catherine Lord, “Their Memory is Playing Tricks on Her: Notes toward a Calligraphy of Rage,” in *WACK! Art and the Feminist Revolution*, ed. Cornelia Butler (Los Angeles: Museum of Contemporary Art, and Cambridge, MA: MIT Press, 2007), 440–57. For the call that “an army of lovers shall not fall,” see Rita Mae Brown, “Sappho’s Reply,” in *The Hand that Rocks the Cradle* (New York: New York University Press, 1971).

26. See particularly Carrie Moyer, “Zero at the Bone: Louise Fishman Speaks with Carrie Moyer,” *Art Journal* 71, no. 4 (Winter 2012): 36–53.

27. Susan Sontag, “Against Interpretation,” in *Against Interpretation, and Other Essays* (New York: Farrar, Straus & Giroux, 1966), 10.

28. Emily D. Bilski, “Louise Fishman’s Paint Golem,” in *GOLEM* (Bielefeld: Jewish Museum, and Berlin: Kerber Verlag, 2016).

29. Louise Fishman, quoted in Carter Ratcliff, Hayden Herrera, Sarah McFadden, and Joan Simon, “Expressionism Today: An Artists’ Symposium,” *Art in America* 70, no. 11 (December 1982): 66.

30. Helaine Posner, “Louise Fishman: The Energy in the Rectangle,” in Posner, *Louise Fishman*, 11.

23

Angry Marilyn, 1973

Acrylic on paper

26 × 40 inches (framed)

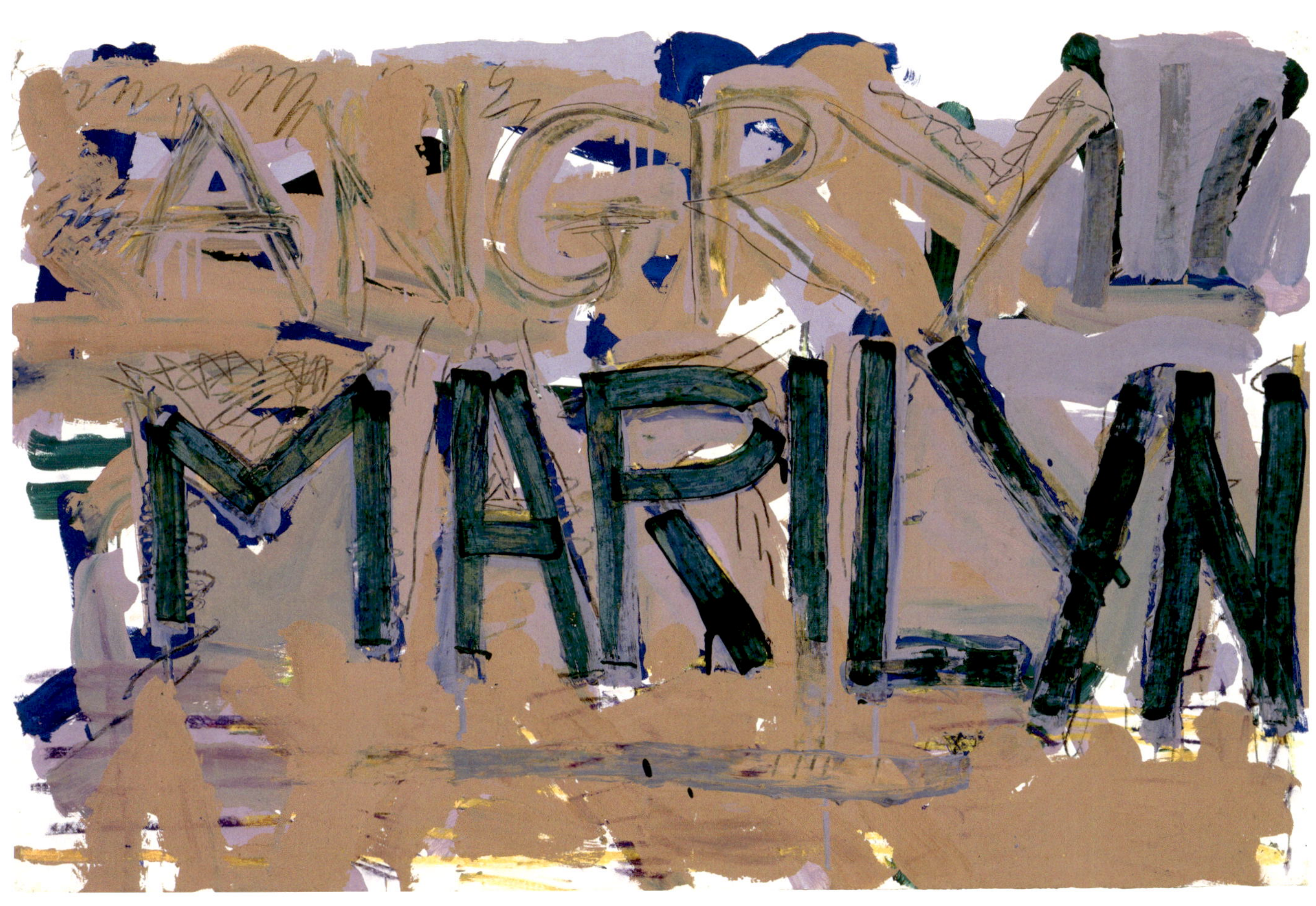

ANGRY
MARILYN

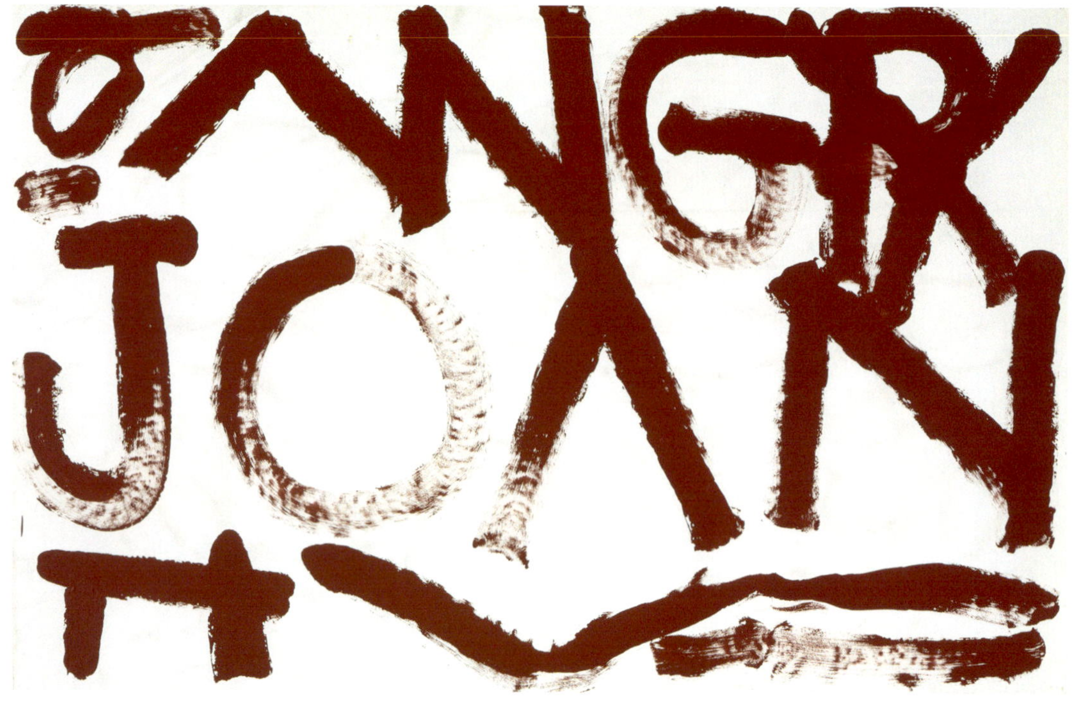

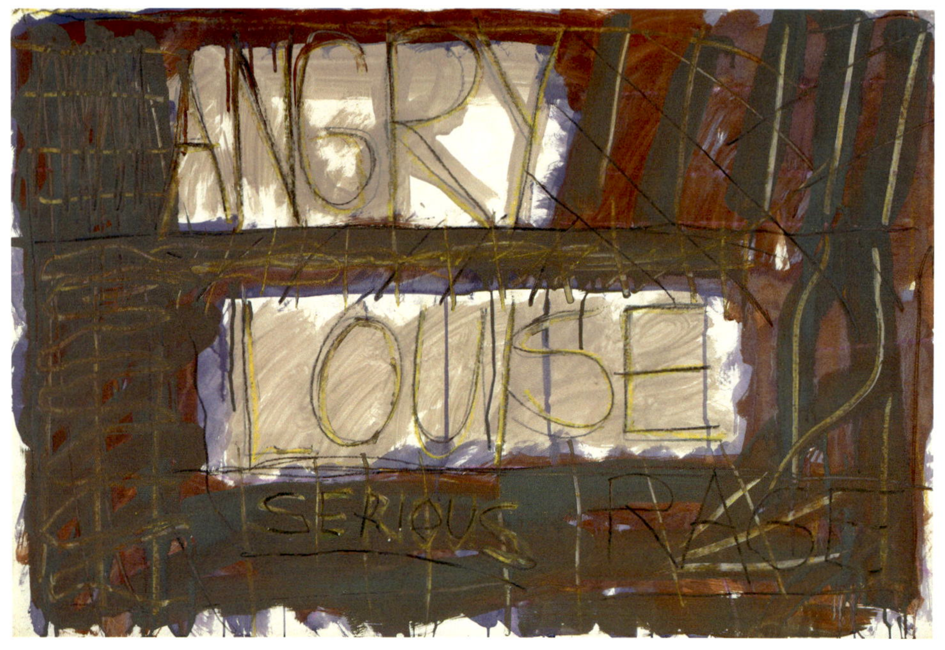

24

Angry Joan, 1973

Acrylic on paper
26 × 40 inches (framed)

25

Angry Louise, 1973

Acrylic on paper
26 × 40 inches (framed)

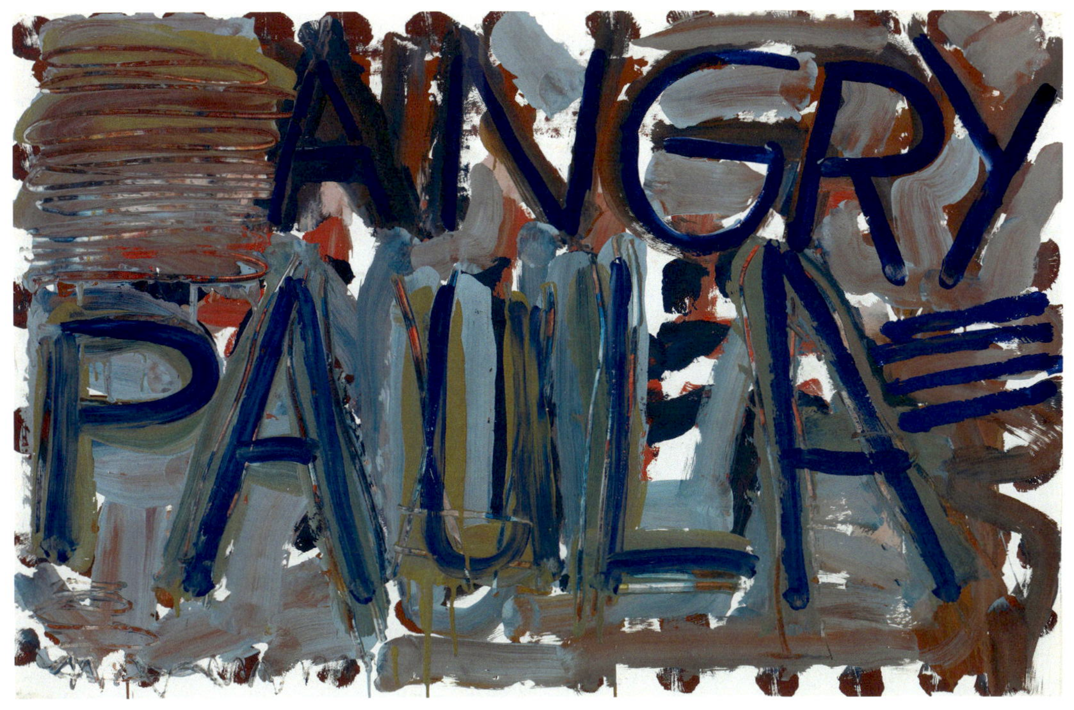

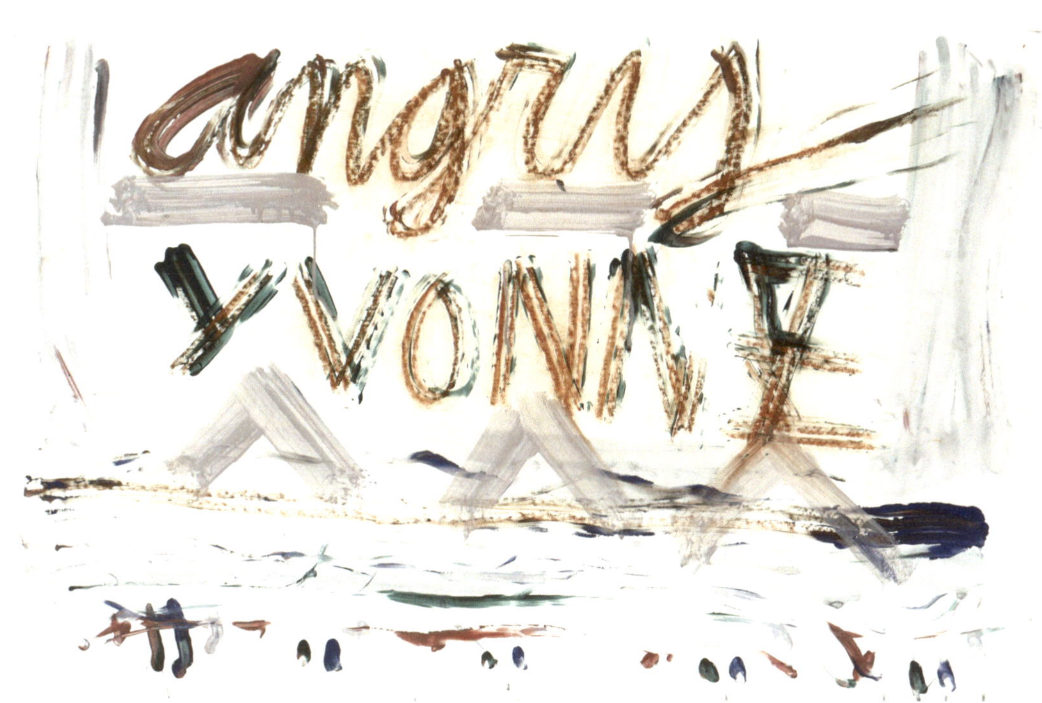

26

Angry Paula, 1973

Acrylic on paper
26 × 40 inches (framed)

27

Angry Yvonne, 1973

Acrylic on paper
26 × 40 inches (framed)

28

Untitled, 1992

Ink and acrylic on paper
52¾ × 42¼ inches

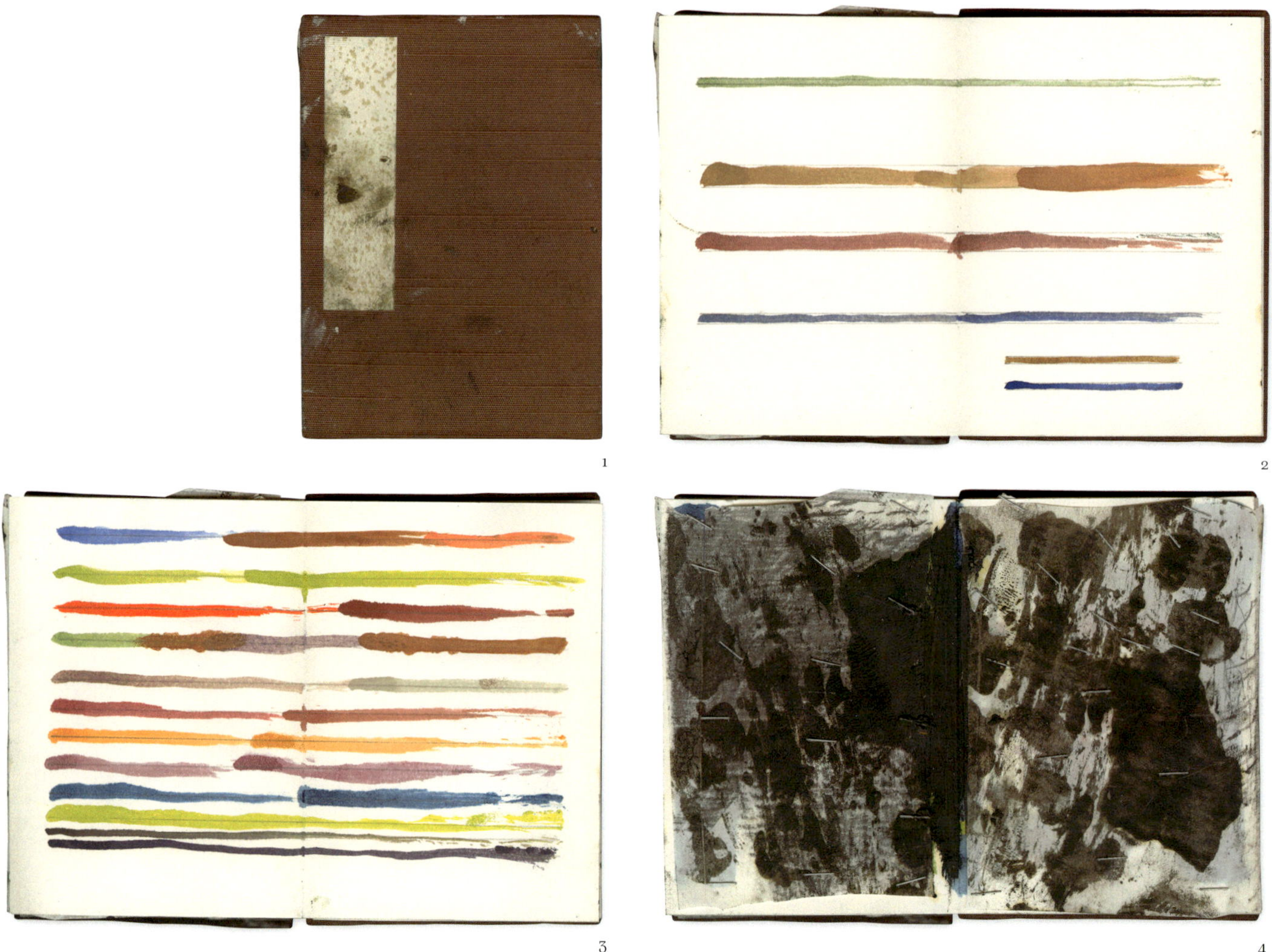

1 2 3 4

29

Down and Dirty (A Book for Bertha Harris), 1994

Oil, gouache, graphite, staples, and paper collage on paper; Japanese leporello binding
$4\frac{7}{8} \times 3\frac{5}{8} \times 2$ inches (closed)

1

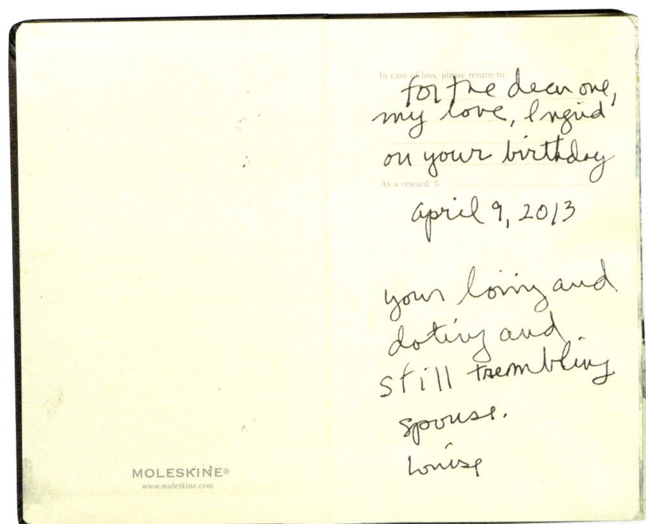
In case of loss, please return to:
for the dear one,
my love, Ingrid
on your birthday
As a reward: $
april 9, 2013
your loving and
doting and
still trembling
spouse.
Louise
MOLESKINE®
www.moleskine.com

2

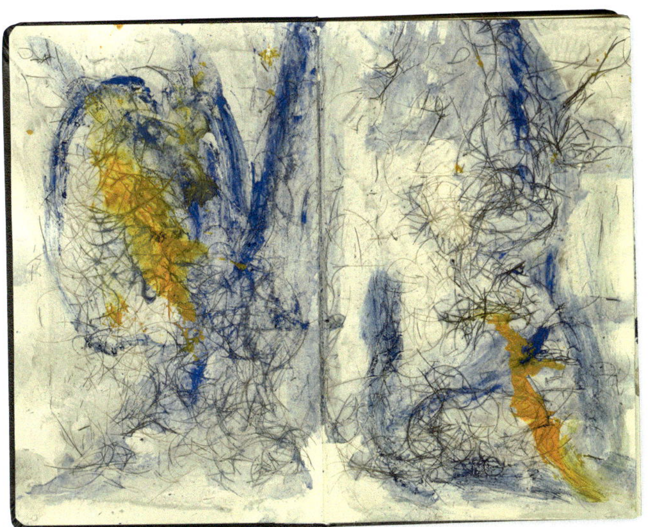

3

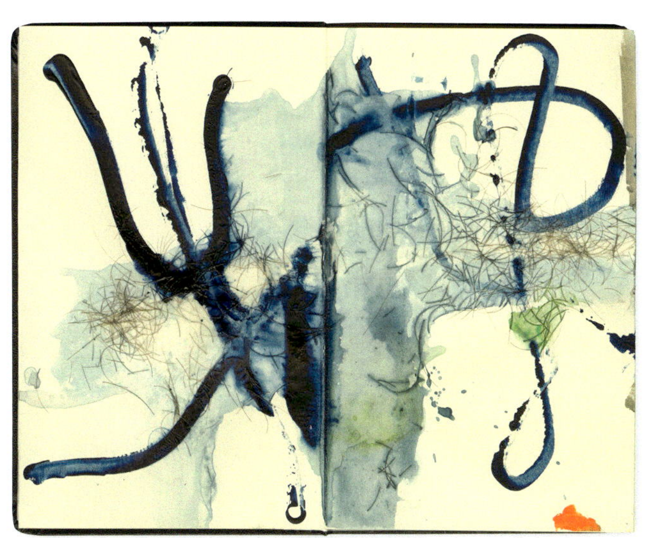

4

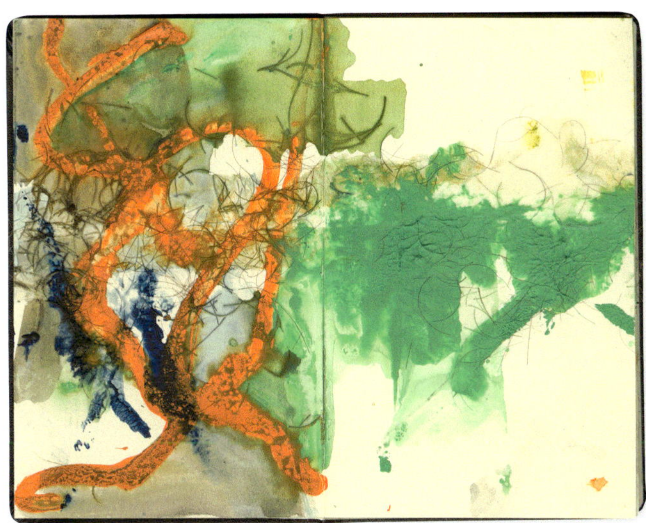

5

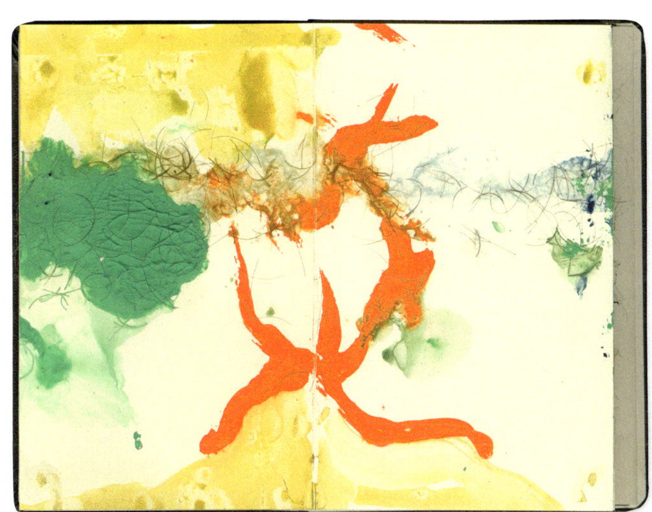

6

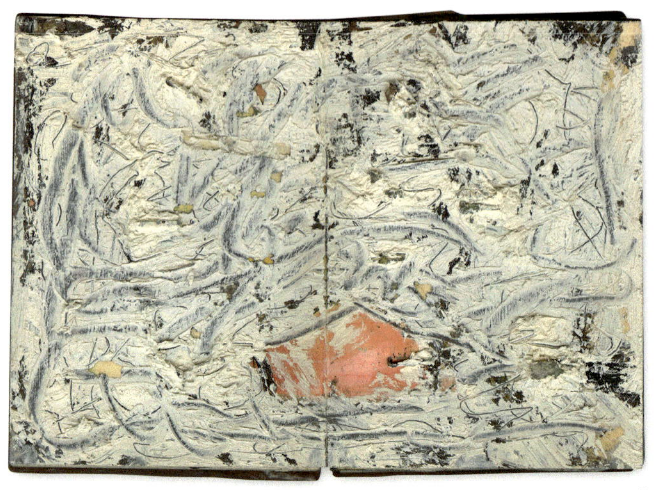

9

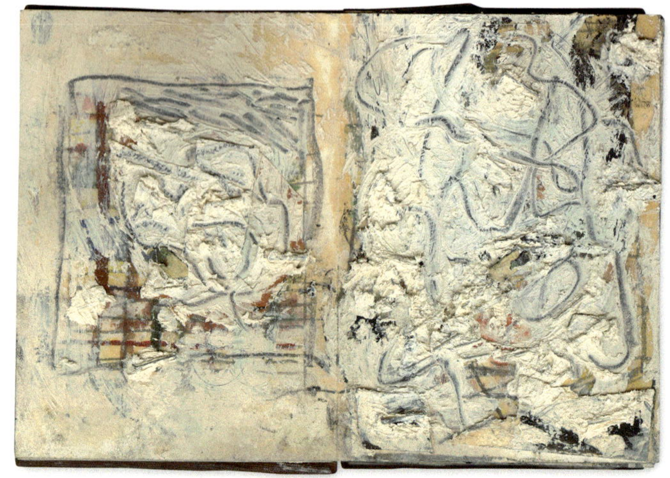

10

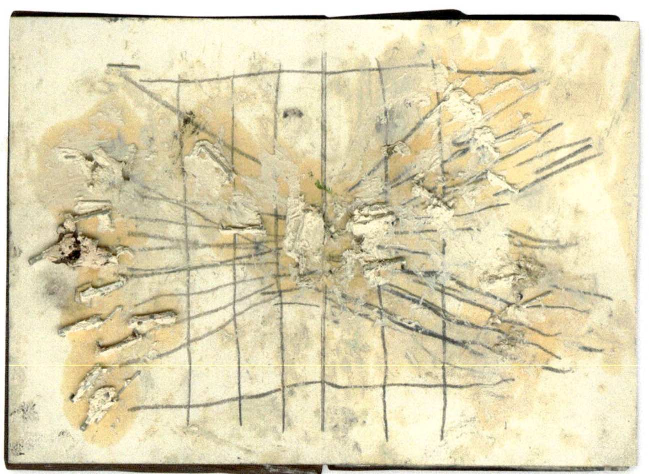

11

12

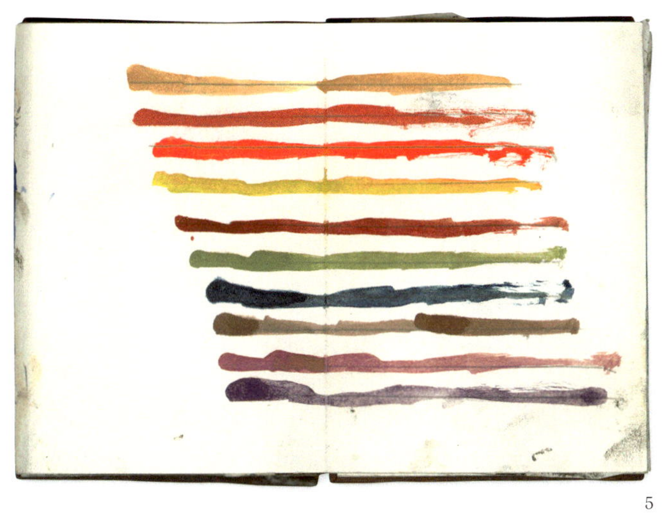

5

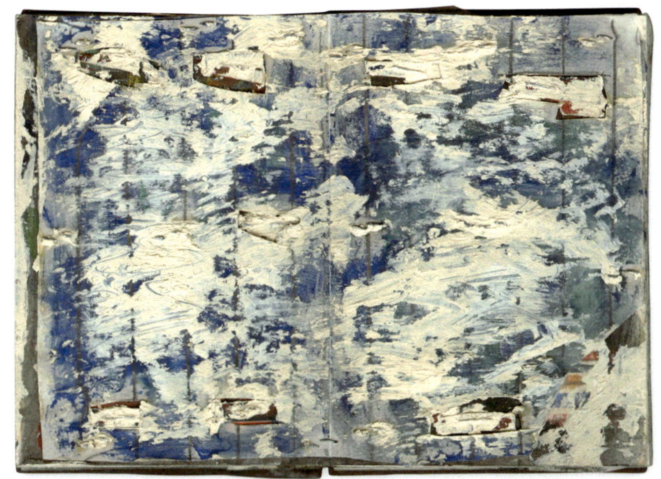

6

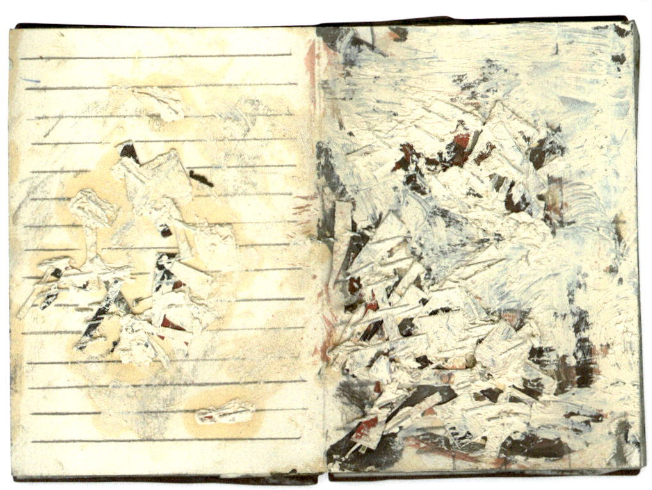

7

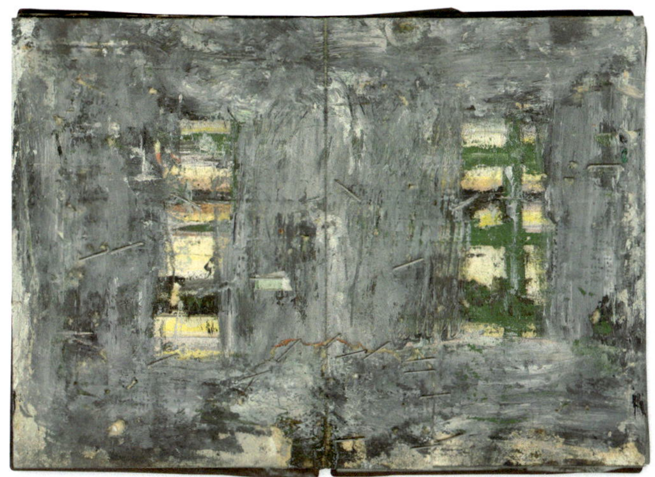

8

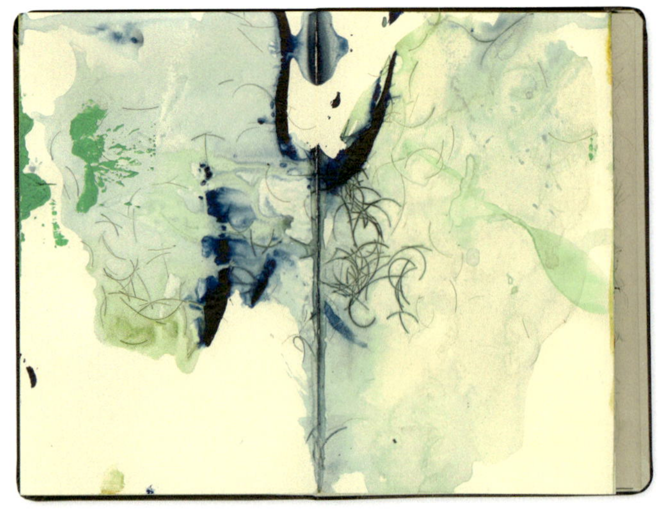

7

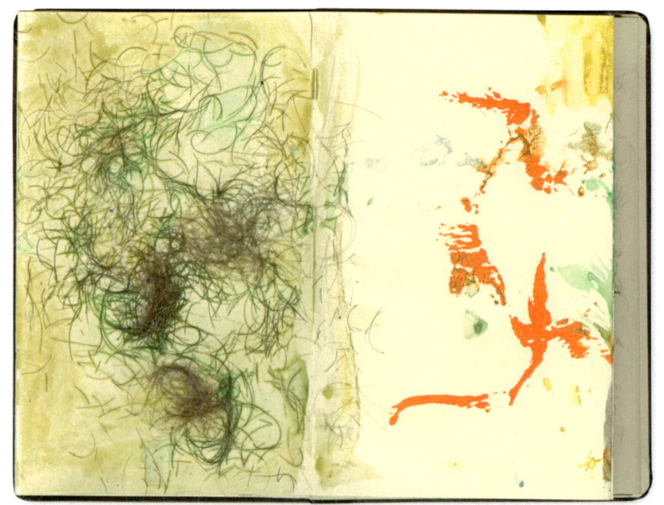

8

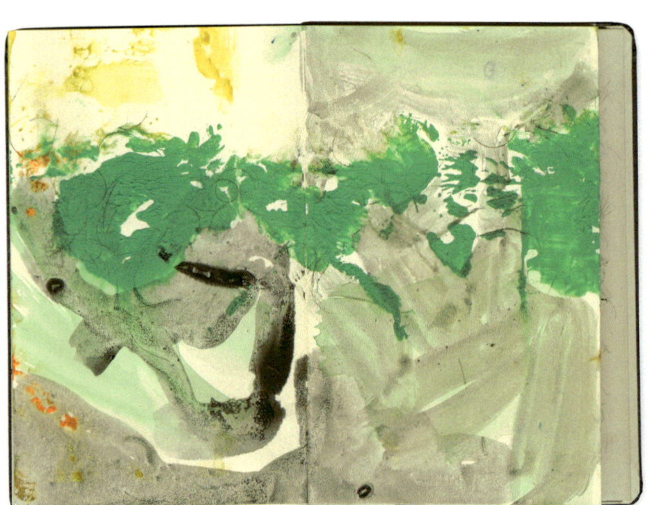

9

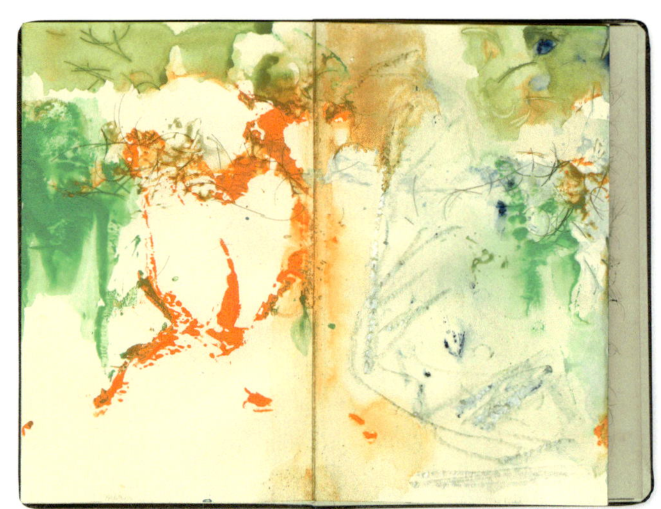

10

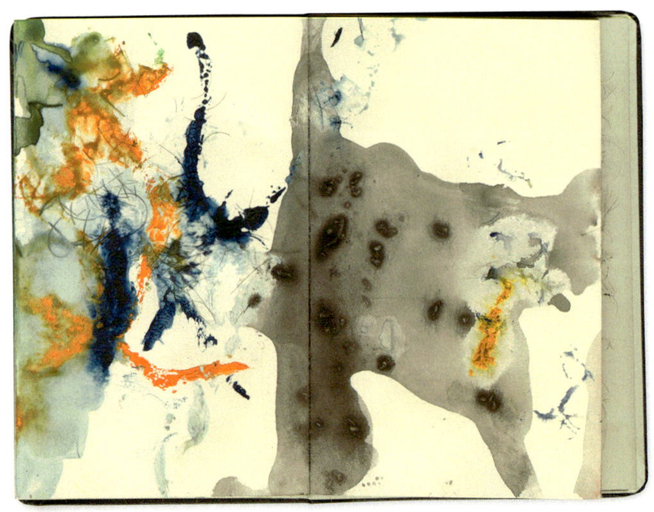

11

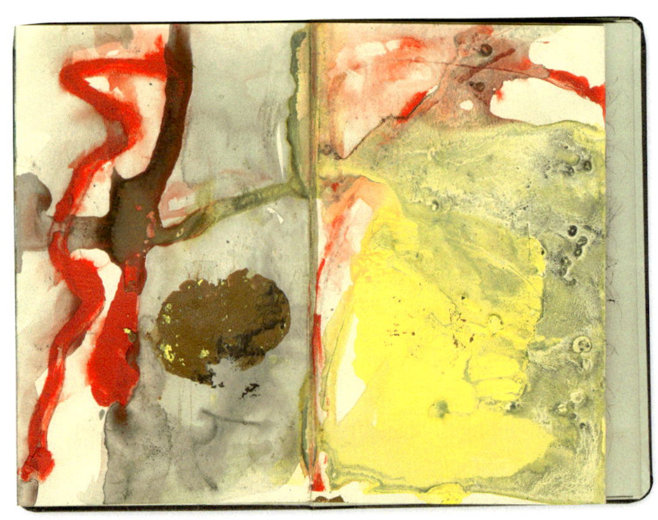

12

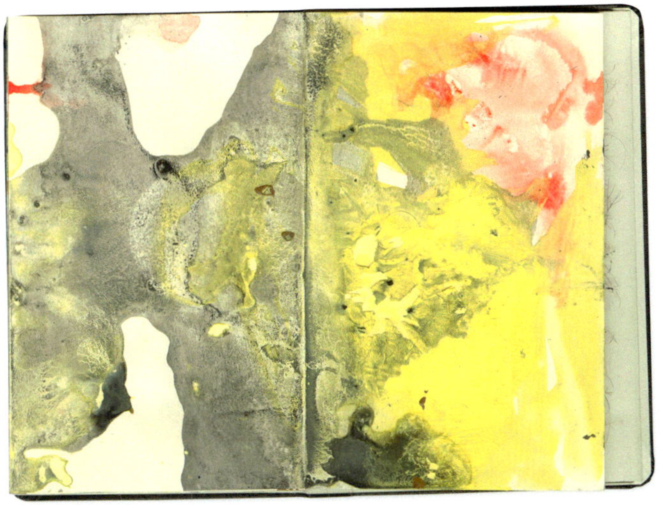

13

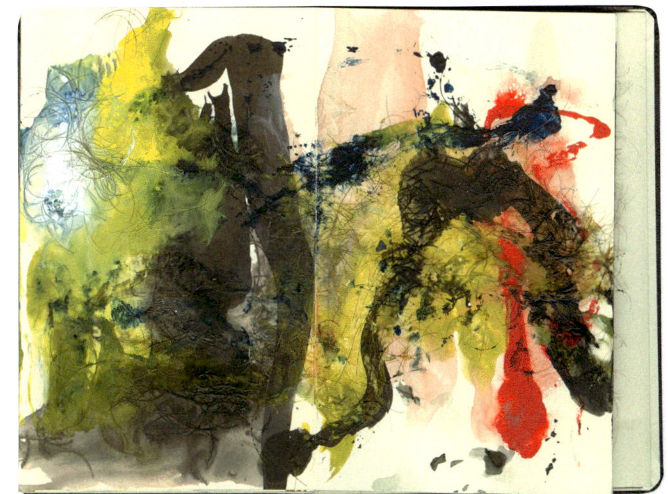

14

15

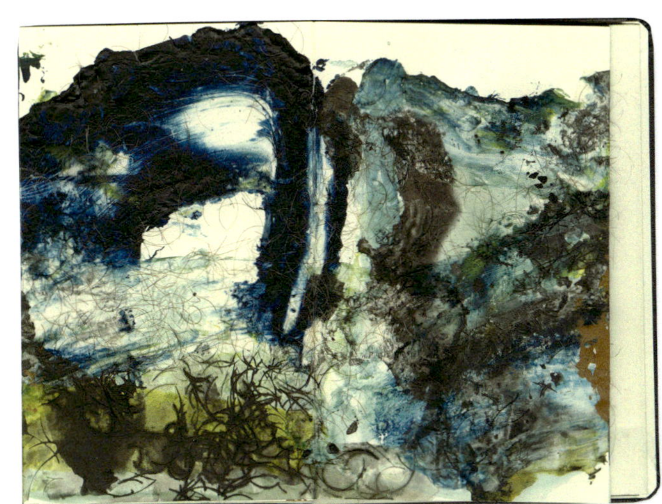

16

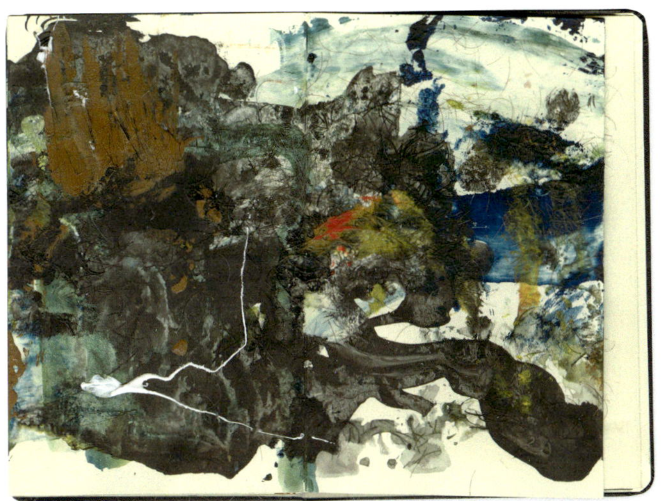

17

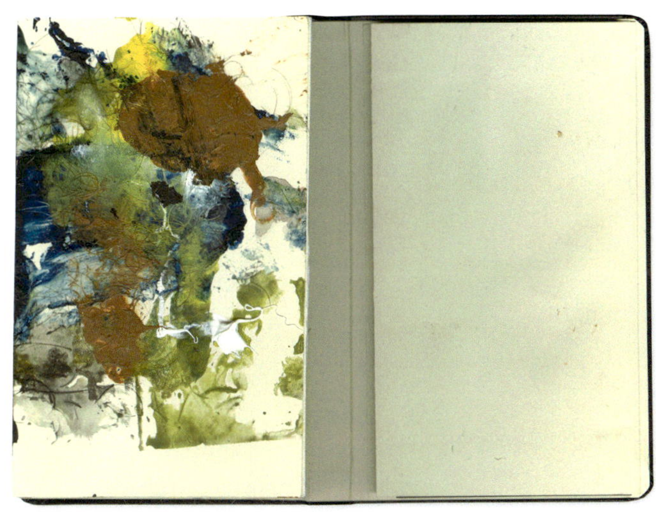

18

30 (PREVIOUS PLATE)

Ingrid, 2013

Watercolor and hair on paper; leporello binding
5½ × 3¾ × ¾ inches (closed)

31

Untitled, 2001

Oil on paper
30 × 22¼ inches

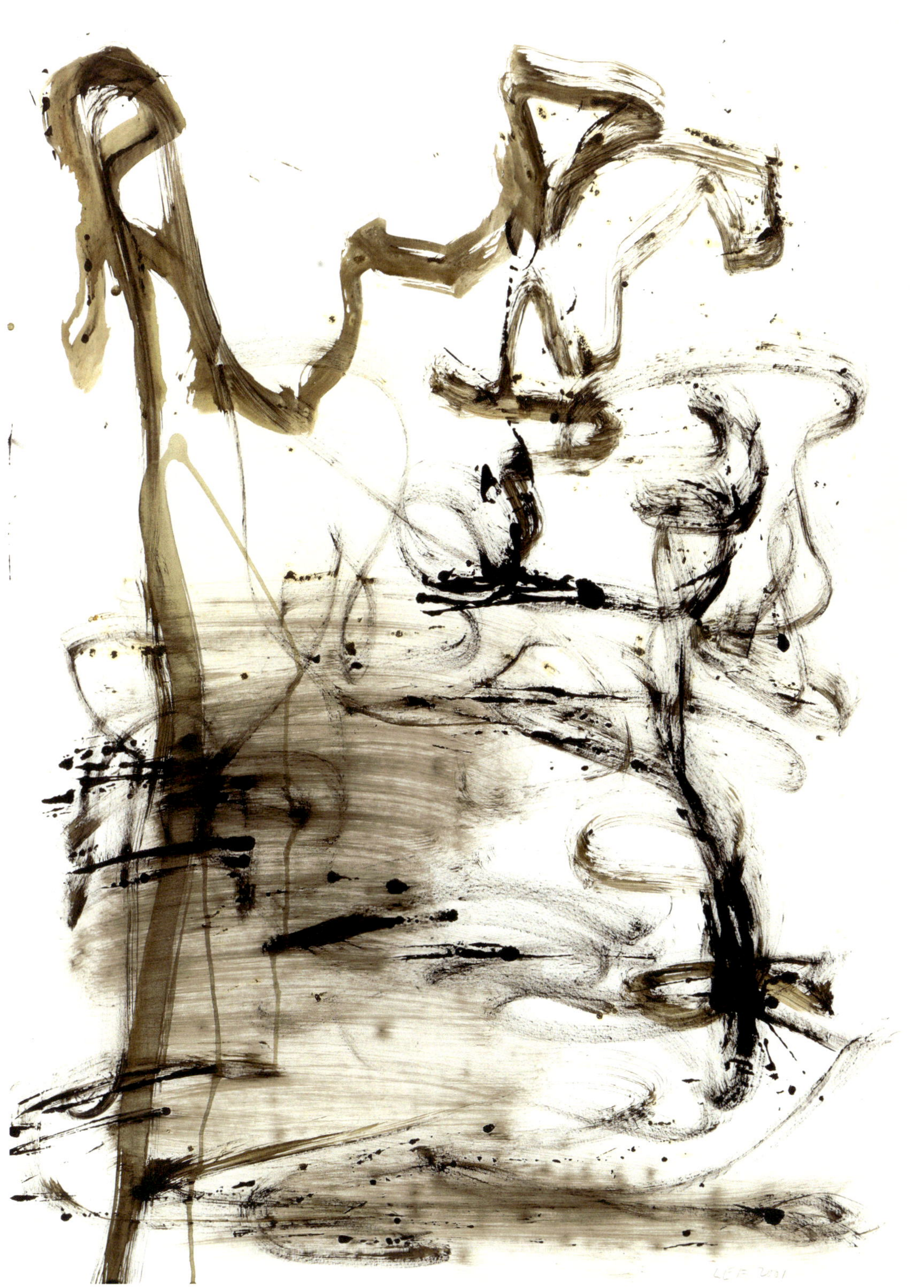

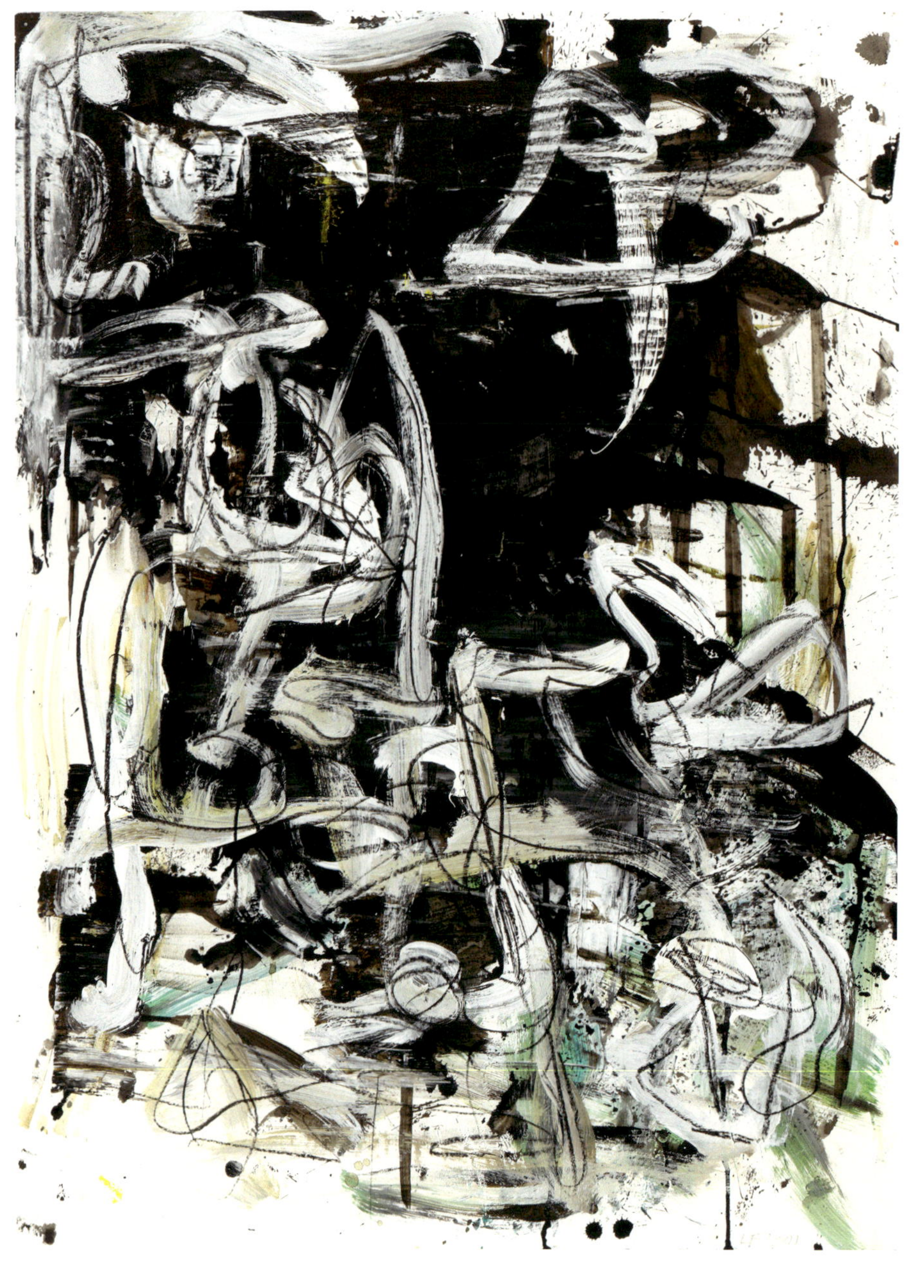

32

Untitled, 2001

Acrylic and charcoal on paper
30⅛ × 22¼ inches

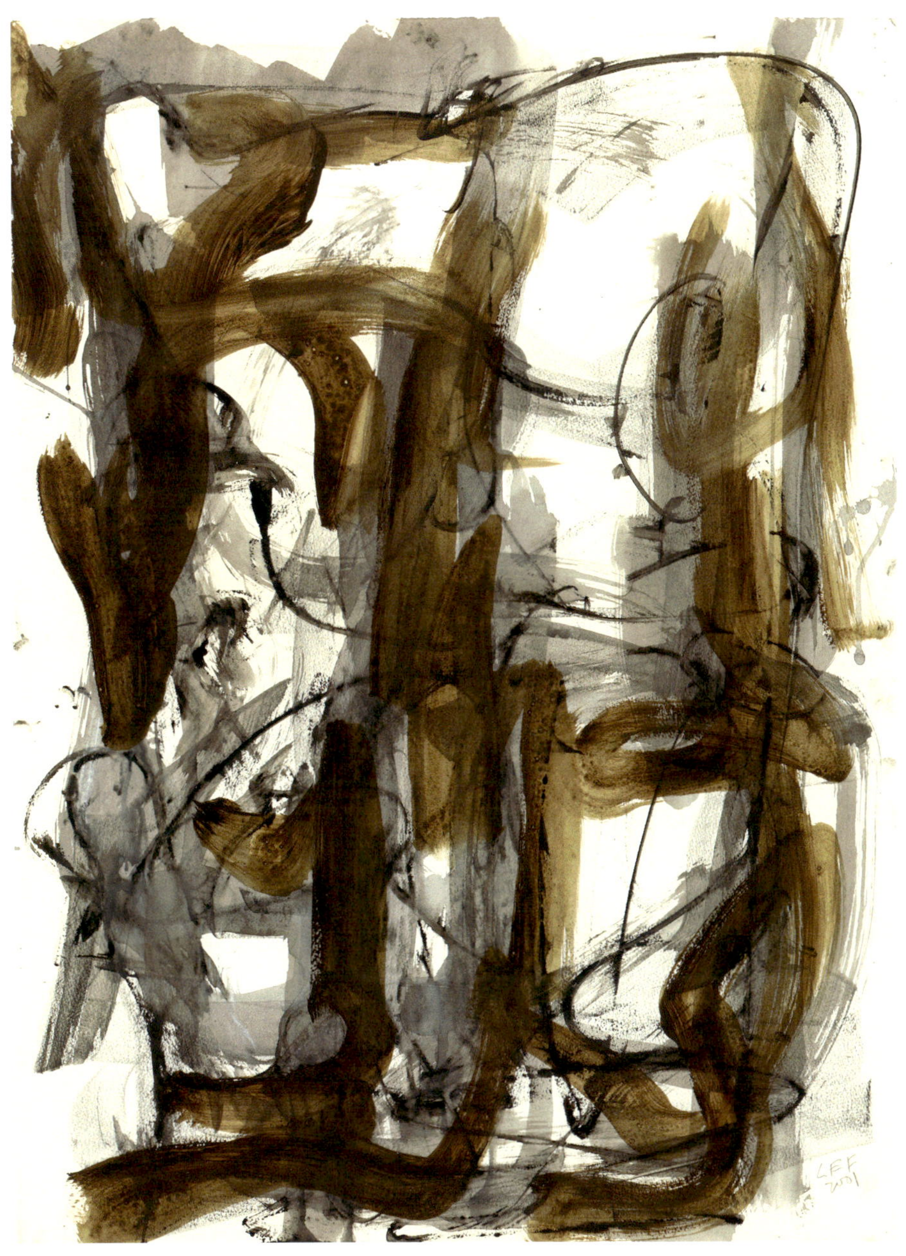

33

Untitled, 2001

Charcoal and gouache on paper

30⅞ × 22⅞ inches

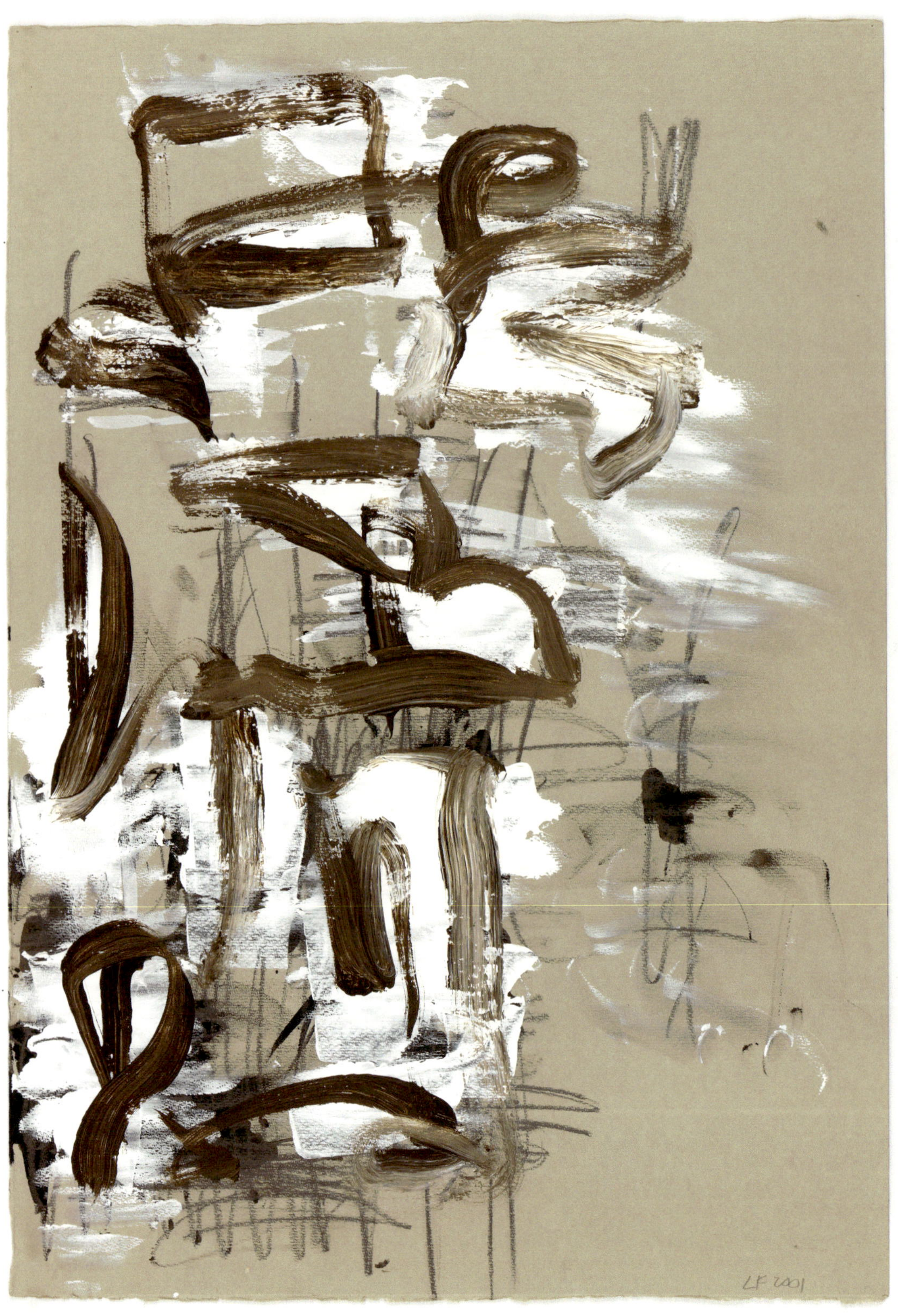
LF 2001

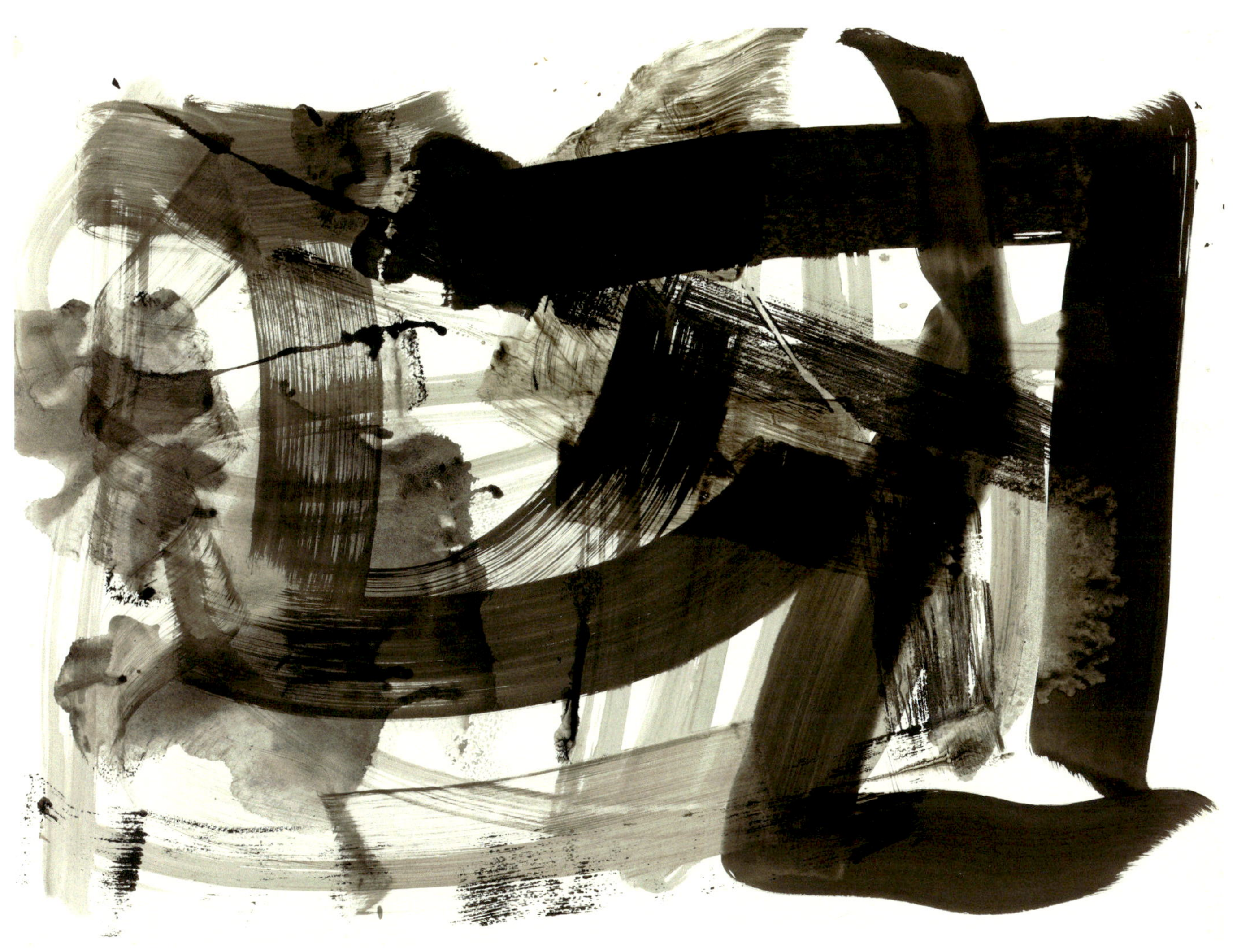

34
Untitled, 2001
Acrylic on paper
27⅝ × 19¾ inches

35
Untitled, 2004
Sumi ink on paper
22 × 30 inches

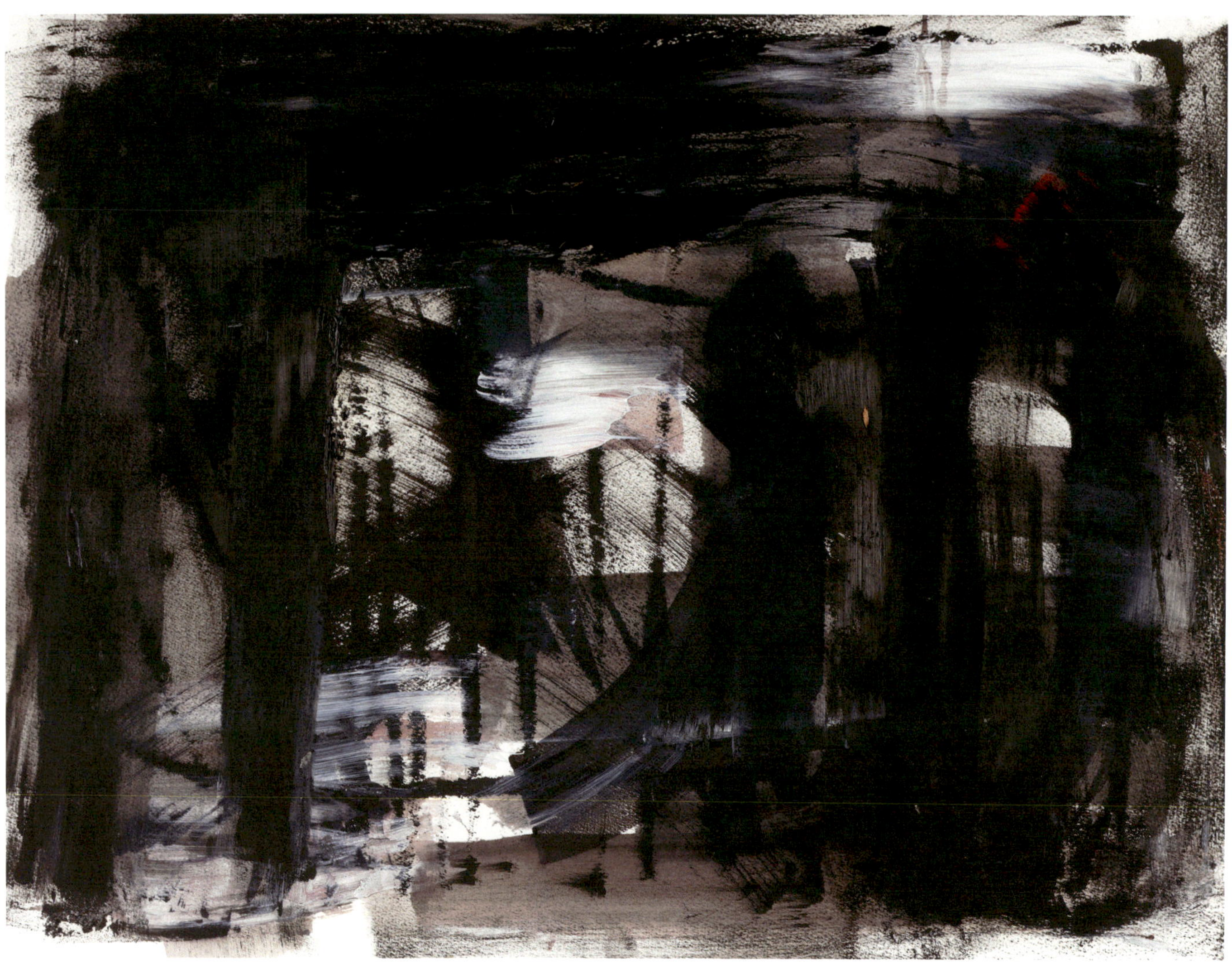

36

Untitled, 2016

Acrylic on paper
18 × 24 inches

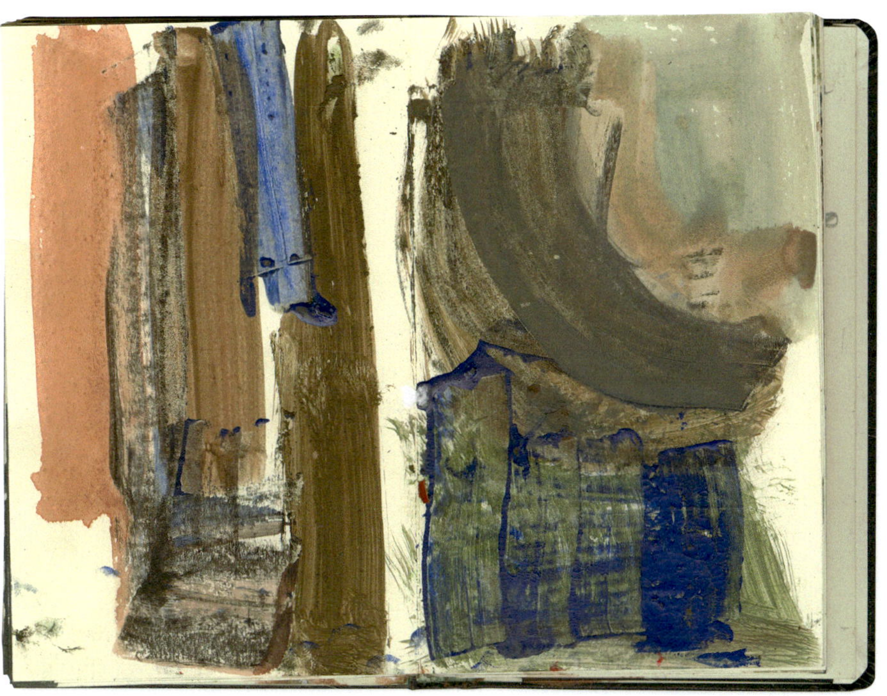

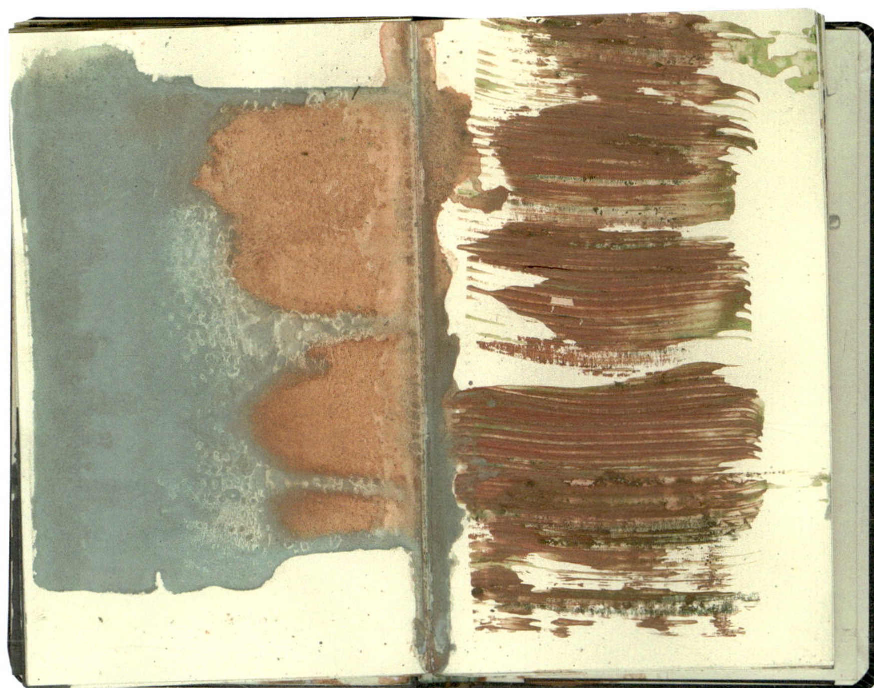

37

From **Vaporetto Leporello No. 5**, 2017

Watercolor and tempera on paper; leporello binding
5½ × 3½ × ¾ inches (closed)

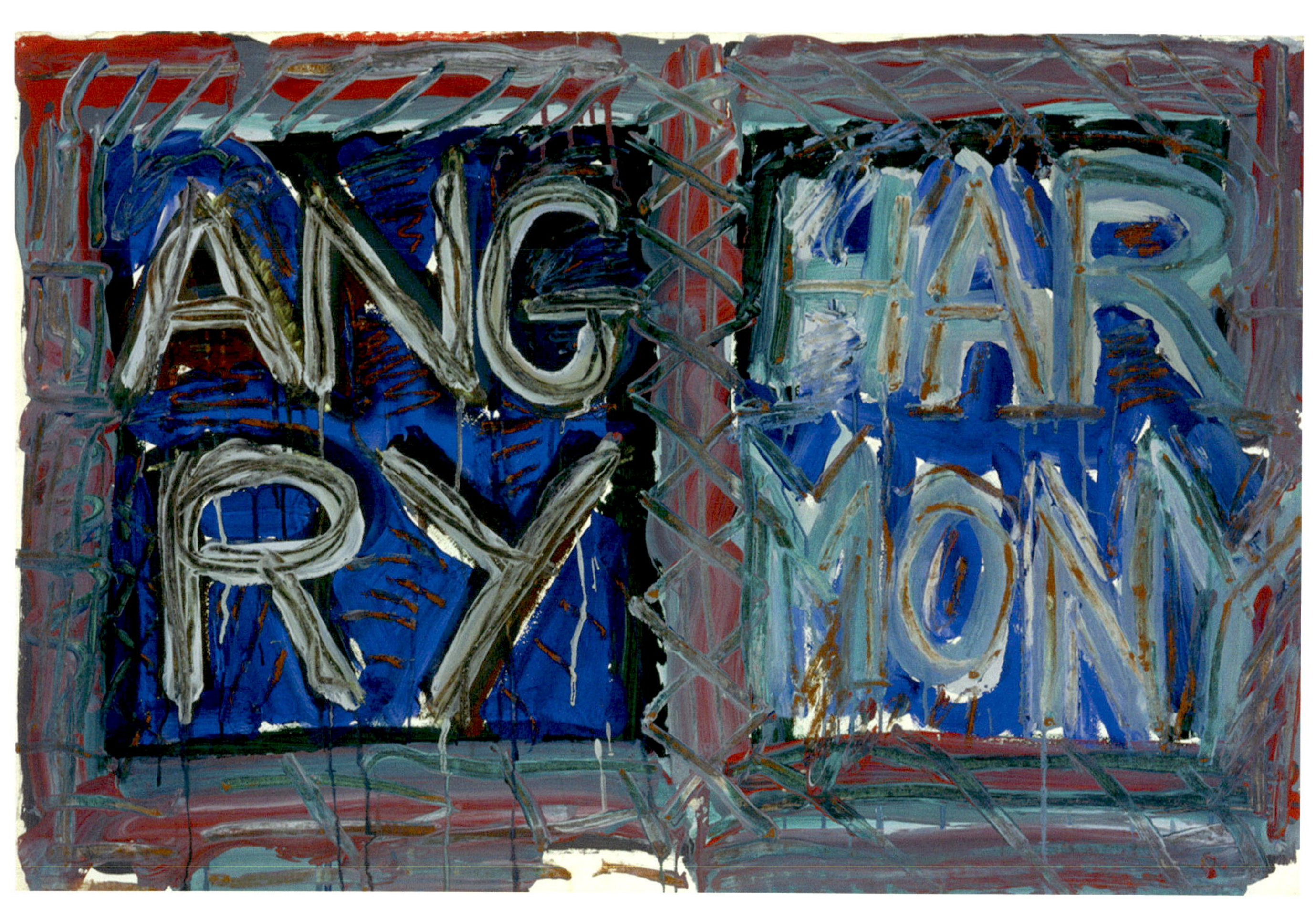
ANG
RY
HAR
MON

Abstracting Gender, Figuring Drag

Catherine Lord

I remember it in a corner, at the far left of the main studio wall, set apart from the grand abstractions hung in good light at the other end, the window end. (Though let it be said that the price of big-ticket items made by a woman wasn't then, and still isn't, as high as it should by rights have been.)

Gender is a drag. You can get that T-shirt online.

I first saw the painting almost twenty years ago. I had been invited to analyze something called "lesbian culture" for the catalogue *WACK! Art and the Feminist Revolution*, "lesbian culture" being apparently as credible a medium as painting or sculpture or video.[1] This opinion, at first, appalled me. Then it amused me. Then I rethought. To declare that lesbian culture is as solid an historical formation as painting could have its advantages in the art so-called world. Why not? I proposed to Connie Butler, curator of the *WACK!* show at the Museum of Contemporary Art, Los Angeles (now senior curator at the Hammer Museum in the same city), to write about Louise Fishman's "Angry Women" paintings. I hadn't met Louise at that point, and I hadn't actually seen any of the "Angry Women" in the flesh, but I gathered that she had made a lot of them. Such information permeates queer culture through the miracle of gossip — otherwise known as the viral transmission of subcultural craving.

I knew one of the "Angries" by reproduction: *Angry Harmony* (fig. 3.1). Even to say the title out loud yields paradox rather than the name of a particular woman — the artist Harmony Hammond — which explains why this instantiation of the series is so often seen in reproduction. If you're looking for a token floater in a project devoted to, say, the 1970s, or abstract women painters, *Angry Harmony* is an easy pick. It deftly combines a touch of irony with an implicit reproach to lesbians who are angry. But why wouldn't we be? Lesbian culture, indeed any minoritized culture, is inconceivable without anger. It wasn't and isn't only a matter of fucking, much less who or with what or when, but of intention, attention, motivation, need, the force of the will to change, and the farsightedness to glimpse utopia on the horizon.

There was, in fact, plenty to be pissed about in 1973 when Louise made the Angries: Joan Little, shock therapy, job discrimination, 59 cents on the dollar (or was it 69 cents?), way too few movies with lesbian anything, mullets, plaids, the absence of good vibrations, painful debates about porn, femme bashing, alcohol shame, depression shame, and custody battles. I hate progress narratives so much that it is hard to remember that things were not only worse but much worse and worse differently. Be that as it may, my job, self-assigned, was to write rage back into revolution. The Angries were a way to get there. Besides, I thought, if I wrote about those paintings for the *WACK!* catalogue, they would surely have to be included in the exhibition itself. Though they had not been on Butler's draft checklist, she agreed to include them and used a modest block of six or perhaps eight in Los Angeles. Then, because the network of women they created by the act of naming was specific to a site known as New York City, Butler decided to show the

Fig. 3.1. *Angry Harmony*, 1973. Acrylic, pastel, graphite, charcoal on paper, 26 × 40 inches.

entire preternatural, majestic, furious totality of the twenty-seven 1973 paintings at MoMA PS1 in 2008. Some of the women are celebrated, some are only coming to be known, some are unknown, forgotten even by Fishman, and untraceable. Among them are Fishman herself (plate 25), Rita Mae (Brown), Joan (Thorne, Snyder, and Mitchell) (plate 24), Jill (Johnston), Radclyffe Hall, Gertrude (Stein and Fishman, Louise's mother), Elizabeth (Weatherford and Bishop), Paula (Cooper, Webster, and Costanza) (plate 26), Bertha (Harris), Jane (O'Wyatt), Carol (Calhoun), Jenny (Snider), Sarah (Whitworth), Harmony (Hammond), Yvonne (Rainer) (plate 27), Phyllis (Birkby), Marilyn (Monroe) (plate 23), Djuna (Barnes), Razel (Kapustin), Nancy (Hoffman, Graves, Azara, Grossman, and Spero), Sue (Perlgut), Charlene (Sue Perlgut's lover, name lost from the lesbian memory bank), Ti-Grace (Atkinson), Patsy (Norvell), Jennifer (Bartlett and Wyland), Bianca (Lanza), and Esther (Newton).[2]

I digress.[3]

There I was in Louise's studio, shy, star struck, curious, an intruder with a paper-thin idea and not much to say about painting as a practice. There was Louise, lots of brushes, lots of tubes, Sammy the dog, tea, and something classical and fantastically sophisticated playing on a venerable sound system. Louise was kind. Maybe she thought I was cute. I found her hot. Louise and I have never spoken of these things. We have been disabled at times by our good manners.

Louise had found and put up a few of the Angries — big, brushy, calculated works made of neither pain nor paint but of a combination aimed precisely at that molecular level where rage sheltered in each of the women named. The names made gesture mean, and the names made the white space of the paper mean. The names were women Louise loved, whether or not she'd met them or touched them, whether or not they were alive. They were the women who made her world in 1973. Though I'm ten years younger than Louise, some of her Angries intersected with some of my Angries. These women had kept our heads above water, led us places, showed us when to flee and when to strike. Not all of our Angries were famous, but some of them were, and some of them might have been, had they been given a fair shake. They were a community, a network, a sisterhood, a tribe of siblings.

Over there on the left, near the storage racks, away from the window, was the small painting: *Portrait of Myself as a Man*, a vertical, seventeen by twenty-five inches, oil on canvas, 1983 (fig. 3.2). I didn't know what to say. Anything that came out of my mouth would have been blurt and clumsiness. I was smitten. Theft crossed my mind. I hadn't ever seen anything like it, and I did not understand how Louise came to make it when she did, back in the day. It was not Martha Wilson's *Posturing: Male Impersonator (Butch)* from 1973, or Ana Mendieta sticking a moustache on her face in 1972, or what Millie Wilson would do in 1989 in *Fauve Semblant: Peter (A Young English Girl)*. Catherine Opie was just beginning her moustaches. Peggy Shaw was not yet *A Menopausal Gentleman*. Besides, these other works were about transformation, about drag as a conscious practice, about the deliberate

Fig. 3.2. *Portrait of Myself as a Man*, 1983. Oil on canvas, 17 × 25 inches.

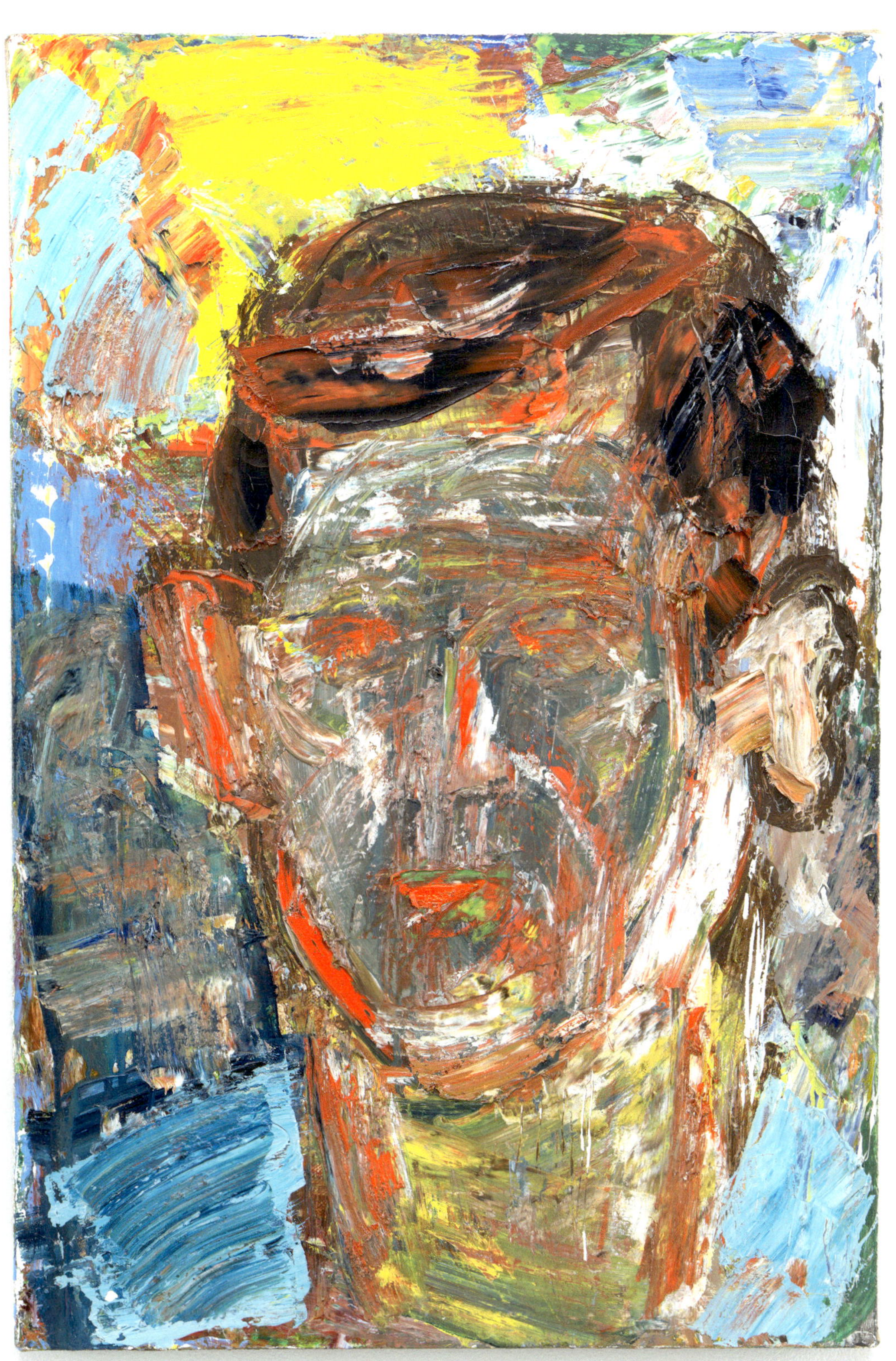

performance of butch, about the construction of masculinity as a costume for cis women, most of whom identified as lesbian.

Portrait of Myself as a Man was not about drag, or about lesbian or feminist or positive images or queer or any other sort of identity politics that were launched in the early 1980s. It was about paint and gender, paint and testosterone, paint and fiction, paint and performativity. This *Man* had no clue that gender was a copy without an original, a product of panicked heterosexuality, because Judith Butler was still in grad school and hadn't yet really been heard saying so. My *Man* was heading all the way to trans before Peggy Shaw was playing around with the idea. This *Man* was trans without benefit of high queer philosophizing and the sort of scholarly trans history produced by, for example, Sandy Stone or Leslie Feinberg or Maggie Nelson. This *Man* went trans in a skin of paint because a dyke with no particular interest in the antics of straight feminist artists, or in the trans community, combined the performance of her athletic, trained, muscular lesbian hand with oils.

Man and I met in person a few more times. When it wasn't up, over there by the storage racks, I'd ask Louise to take it out. She'd put it on the wall and watch me looking across the decades at her paint, or her man, or her gender, or her revolt. I'm reasonably sure that the gaze she aimed in my direction was butch, but I thought she wanted to see what I made of her painted man, her as man, her soul abstracted from her body to become a man, a man abstracted by paint from her dick, a man who had no need of dick.

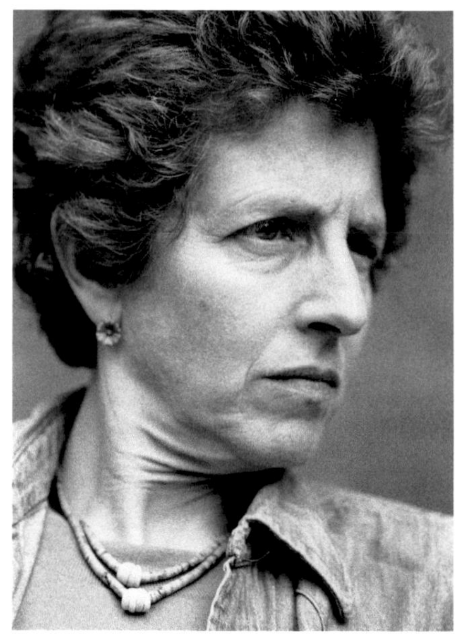

Fig. 3.3. Louise Fishman, 1982. Photo: Betsy Crowell. Courtesy the artist.

For all I know, Louise showed *Man* to lots of people, but I like to imagine that I was one of a select few. (Indeed, I gave it my own title: *My Little Guy*.) *Man* does, in fact, inhabit a more marginal, more liminal, and more tremulous space of precarity than most paintings can survive. For an exhibiting painter to put color on canvas is to assume the canvas has a public, a space for address, a space to call into being an audience. It's like writing a journal in the hope, or in the certainty, that your allegedly private ramblings will be read. Protests to the contrary, neither paper nor canvas is safely private. *Man* was shown once, in 2012, at the Woodmere Art Museum, an institution devoted to Philadelphia art and artists. The context was a show comprising work by Louise, by her mother, Gertrude Fisher-Fishman, and by her aunt, Razel Kapustin, all three of them card-carrying members of the sisterhood of the Angries. That, however, embeds *Man* in a family of women artists, and a family of women artists is not necessarily a queer family. *Man* has never been shown in New York, city or state. Until very recently, it would have been career suicide to show it. It was 1983. Dykes weren't especially interested in being mistaken for men because tendentious stereotypes about lesbians were literally too shitty to bother to step in.

In short, *Portrait of Myself as a Man* has spent almost forty years in the closet. It never entered the maelstrom of New York arguments about feminism, modernism, postmodernism, gender, intersectionality, race, sex, and so forth. It didn't advance the conversation on any of these topics. That tree never fell in the forest.

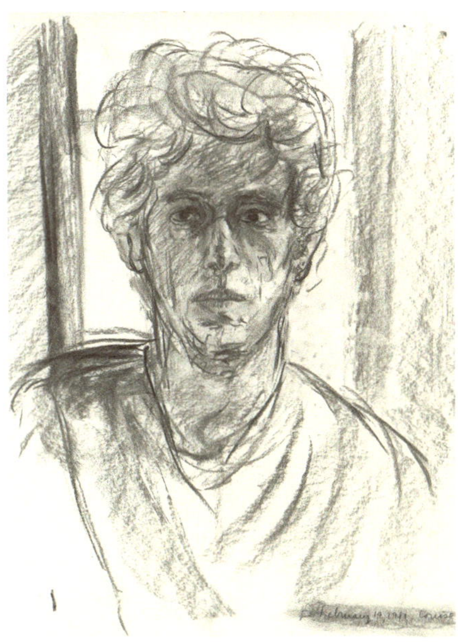

Fig. 3.4. No title (Self-portrait), 1981. Graphite on paper, 16¼ × 13 inches.

That stone sank with nary a ripple. *Man* was painted so long ago, in fact, that it may well be irrelevant to the current explosion of possibilities held by all things trans. *Man* didn't influence anything but its maker and a few friends. And if *Man* hasn't existed because it wasn't public, in what way can it now be public? I'm not going to position *Man*'s invisibility as a titillating act of self-censorship. Safer to say that Louise has been an enormously productive painter, and after she painted herself into *Man*, she went on to thousands of other things. Auschwitz, for example, and the atmospheric turbulence of Venice.[4] It's more generous, I think, and more productive, to think of *Man* as a liberatory gesture choreographed in a private space. An insistence on privacy can, of course, be identical to The Closet, but in this case it's a way of using the tools of abstract painting to articulate the artifice of gender, and then moving on to more immediate concerns. Not only do queers also have a right to privacy, but ever since her first gay march up Fifth Avenue, with not so many other brave souls, back in 1970, Louise has been generously and publicly out of The Closet.

Louise thinks hard about her titles, but none of the key terms here — portrait, man, or myself — help much. What could possibly be meant by portrait? Louise Fishman of the 1970s and early 1980s was certifiably a slender, frizzy-haired little baby butch jock (figs. 3.3 and 3.4), not a wholesome kind of Archie-and-Veronica comb-over with a thick neck. So, what self? Which self? What or who is being portrayed? Why man? Man, minus the italics, isn't a private construct. Man is a social presence, an ideological keystone, a performance for those cultures that make the gender binary the first in a series of (almost) inescapable choices.

Man wasn't made by looking at a photograph or in a mirror. In an eyes-wide-shut sort of process, it was a painting Louise made after looking across Eighteenth Street from her former studio window to one of those vanished light industries where guys made chains. Dabbing at canvas in her studio, thinking about figuration, haunted by the celebrated labor that Vincent van Gogh's boots represent and of which they are made, she looked at real men (at least so far as she could tell), doing real work, in real shifts. They arrived at 7:00 a.m. and left at 3:30 p.m. Their breaks were limited. That they worked on a regulated schedule, used different muscles, had different responsibilities, mixes Louise's queasy guilt about her class privilege into her impasto and scumbling, into the calculated drips and deliberate scrapes. Desire leaps gender and class. Louise as *Man* is a solid, stolid, rooted guy's guy, a guy who does more honest work than fine art painting. Think about that blue collar, light blue on indigo, sitting on the surface of an archaeology of recantation. This *Man* is neither a they nor a trans nor a nonbinary. This *Man* is a flagrant declaration of trespass in the land of cis masculinity.

Man is a palette upon which a painter tested the routes to a different embodiment of a different gender (fig. 3.5). It would have been easier to paint a naked dude with an impressive dick, but Louise isn't one for the easy route. Her gender is made of face, her face is made of paint, and the whole impossible project makes the

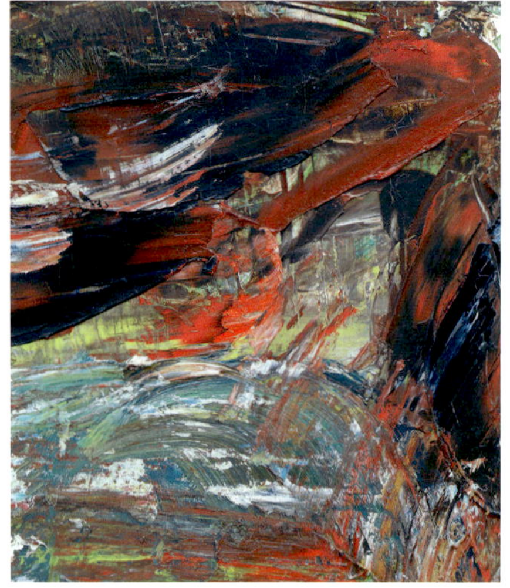

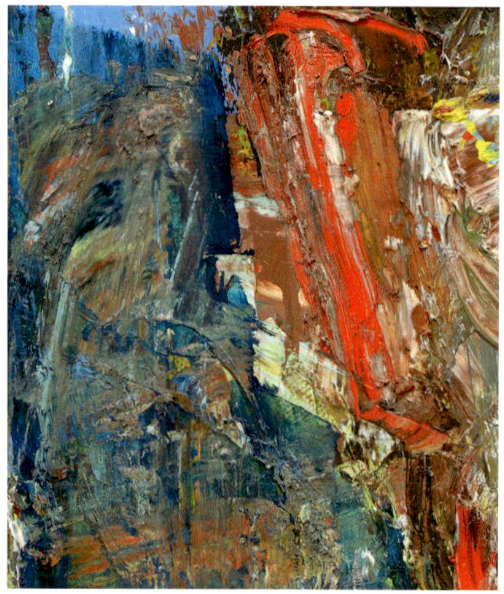

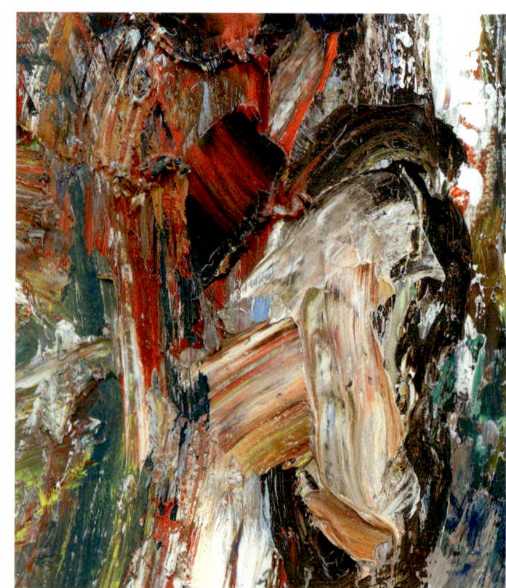

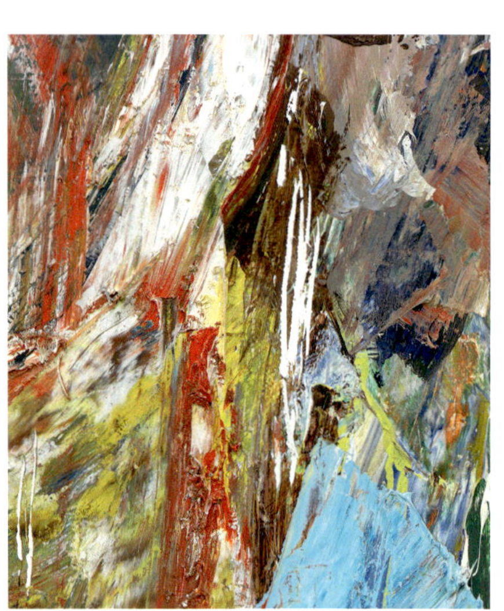

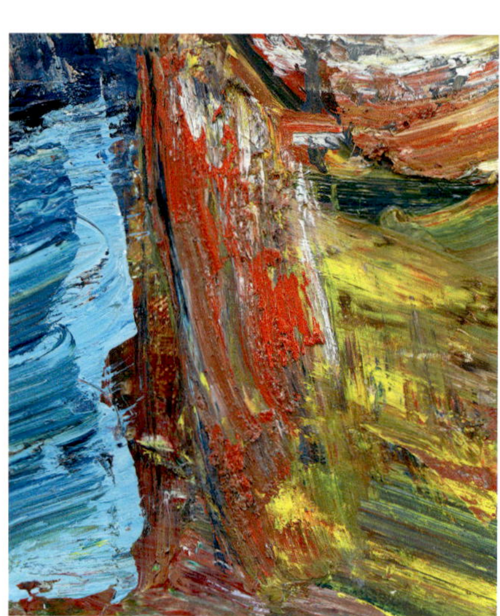

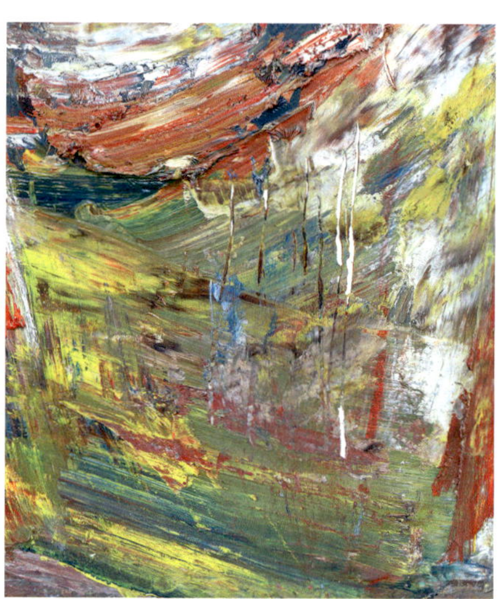

Fig. 3.5. *Portrait of Myself as a Man*, 1983 (details, fig. 3.2). Oil on canvas, 17 × 25 inches.

painting a surface upon which to think and to rethink, to speculate and to renounce. Tight, stabbing gestures, almost manic, cover a material inflected with a public future but that in this case serves as a ledger of failure, revision, reworking, and reinvention. The entire canvas is covered with daubs of color left over from the scraping away of possibilities. The ears don't come from the same universe. The edges of the painting make a face by outlining a head with smears of color that didn't work on the face, or that happened to be a surplus from somewhere else, maybe from one of those abstractions elsewhere in the studio. Skin has melted. Skeleton and musculature shine through. Flesh is bruised. The darkness of the hair is like nothing so much as dried blood. In that oval supported by a thick column of neck there has been so much scraping and repainting that it's as if layers of masks, or a small parade of men, or a series of auditions for possibilities for male, have distorted proportion, torqued anatomical fact, warped the relation of face to neck, and foiled the relation of face to its skin.

Man, I think, even if it had been shown at various points in the emergence of something called "queer art," couldn't have been seen. *Man* is queer, as is Fishman, but *Man* had nothing to do with the development of either queer or trans culture. In fact, I'd argue that it's best in the long run that it hasn't been seen. *Man* has been an outsider for decades, and the only way to describe the feminism in its gesture of embodiment is to acknowledge that some political conversations are conducted via experiments in form, that paint is one way to consider the malleability of flesh. Queer paints over van Gogh as well as Chaim Soutine.

In relation to the kind of histories that trace through-lines and in the various narratives that artists float and flick into the world, *Man* is a glitch, an anomaly, the ghost in the machine. It's a one-off, a work that deploys abstraction to imagine another class and another gender — the other gender, back in the day. *Man* takes figuration as far as it can plausibly go into abstraction. The painting understands and creates gender with the tools of abstraction, and so doing it superimposes one kind of construct upon another. In other words, *Man* is a sketch that toggles between two worlds. At once aesthetically skilled and theoretically curious, it outlines what would become commonplaces of gender theory with the tools of another discipline. More than photographs of Louise (no matter how fascinated the photographer may have been by the sprawl of her rangy presence), more than the modest pencil self-portraits she made by looking in the mirror, *Man* develops Fishman's understanding of gender, and perhaps herself, by muddling the tools and the terms. *Portrait of Myself as a Man* is a fabrication compressed from different registers of outsider status — Fishman's separation from the manual labor of working-class men, her problematic lesbian status in her family, her dissatisfaction with the feminist writers who made up the consciousness-raising groups she attended, and her exclusion as a woman from a male art world.

Gender.

Like abstraction, they are a set of habits and skills.

Notes

This essay is a revised version of "Gender Is a Drag," a talk delivered on April 27, 2016, in conjunction with the exhibition *Louise Fishman: A Retrospective* at the Neuberger Museum, SUNY Purchase, New York.

1. Catherine Lord, "Their Memory Is Playing Tricks on Her: Notes Toward a Calligraphy of Rage," in *WACK! Art and the Feminist Revolution*, ed. Cornelia Butler (Los Angeles: Museum of Contemporary Art, and Cambridge, MA: MIT Press, 2007), 440–57.
2. Fishman later made more of the Angries — including one around 2006, for me, and one in 2016, for Hillary Clinton.
3. I have always wanted to write this sentence. To allow that one has digressed is a code signaling that if the reader's attention has flagged, the problem is the reader. As women were, back in the day, the main audience for the novel, the convention alleges that their boredom was their own fault. Even though the author, usually male and usually paid by the word, had padded his own narrative, women, as a sex, were incapable of paying attention. Blame someone else for not getting to the fucking point, please.
4. In the 1980s, Louise made *Remembrance and Renewal*, a substantial series of paintings reflecting on a visit to Eastern Europe. In 2011, she began traveling to Venice as artist in residence with the Emily Harvey Foundation.

38

Untitled, 1980

Charcoal on paper
25¼ × 19 inches

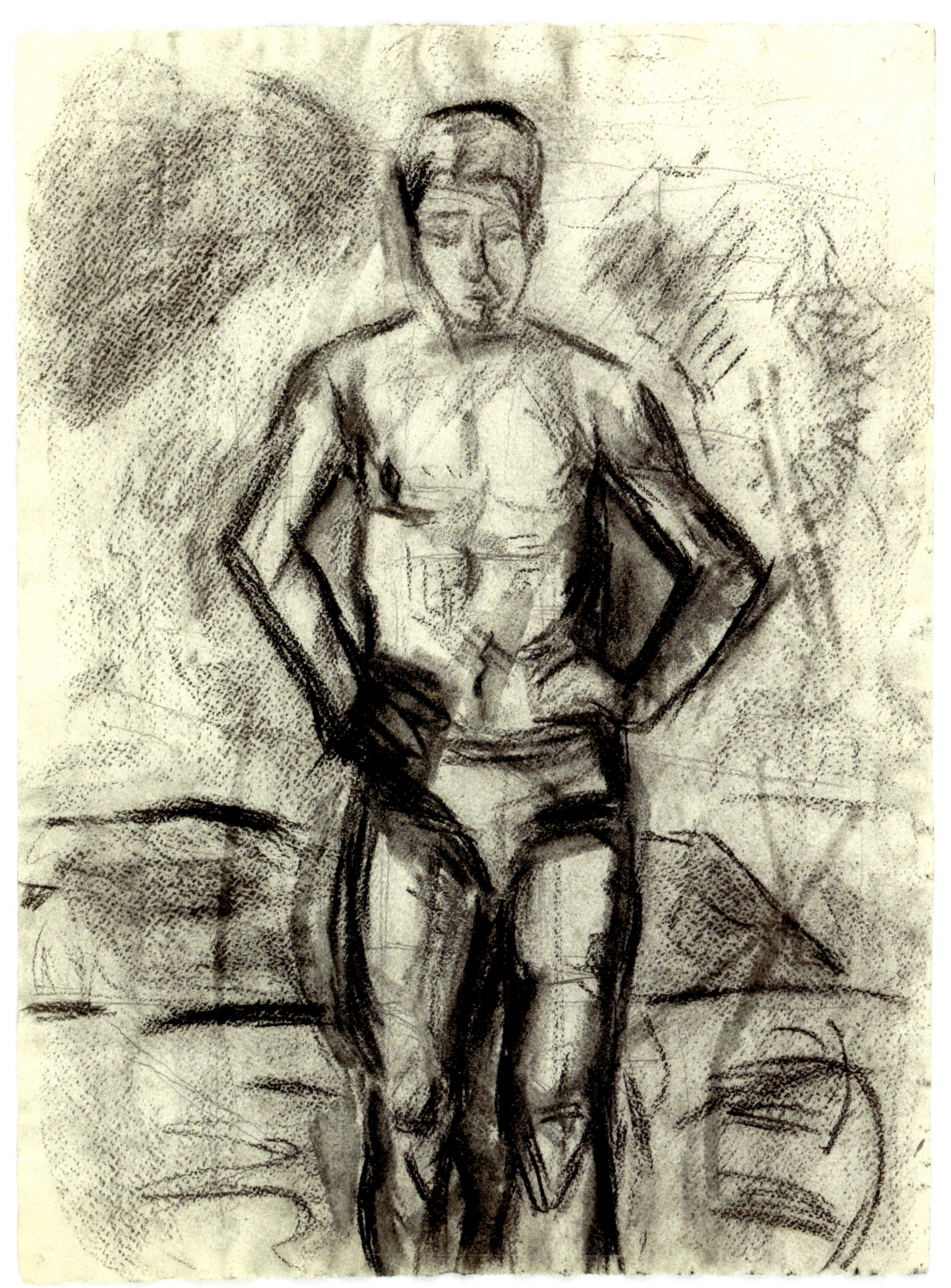

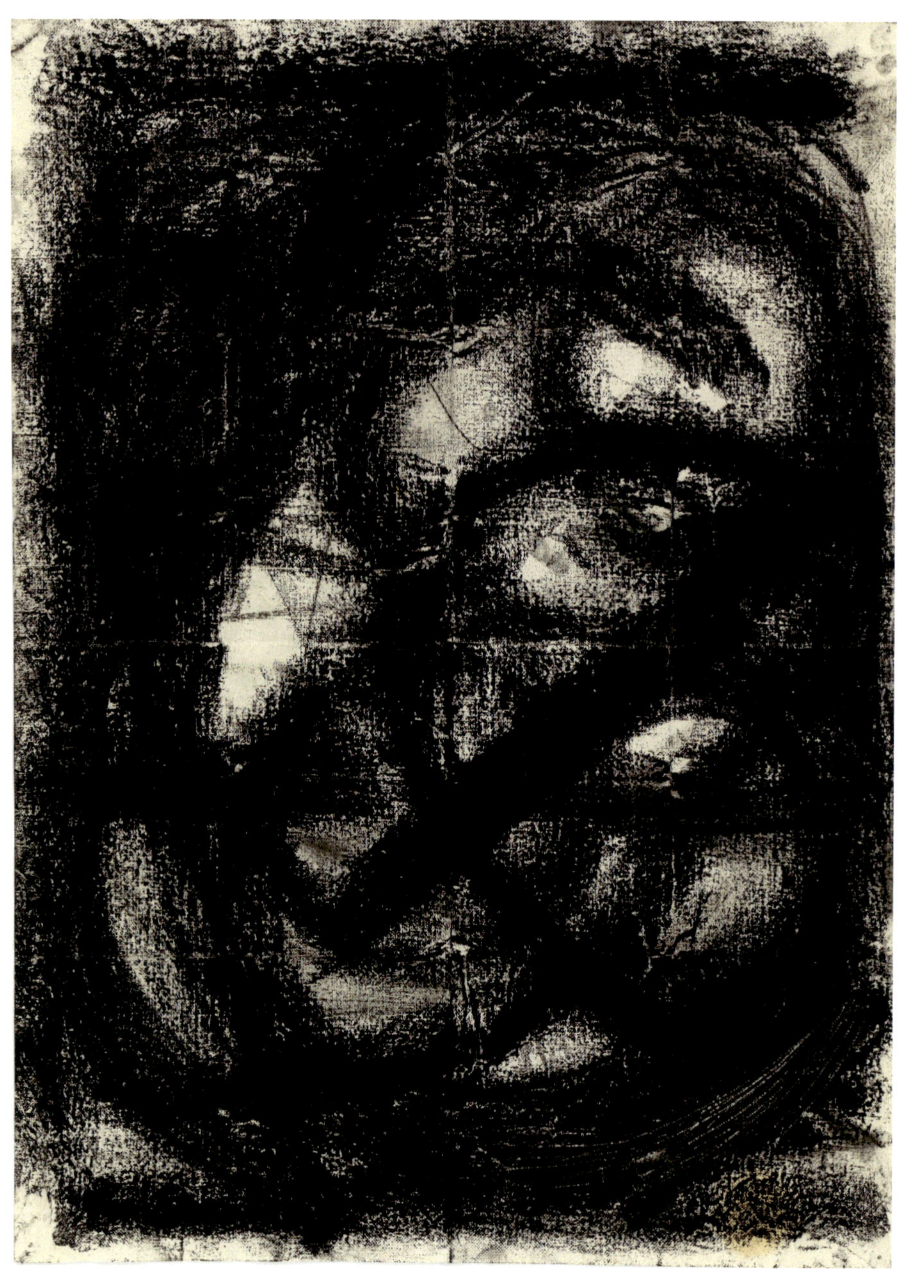

39

Untitled, 1982

Charcoal on paper
30 × 22 inches

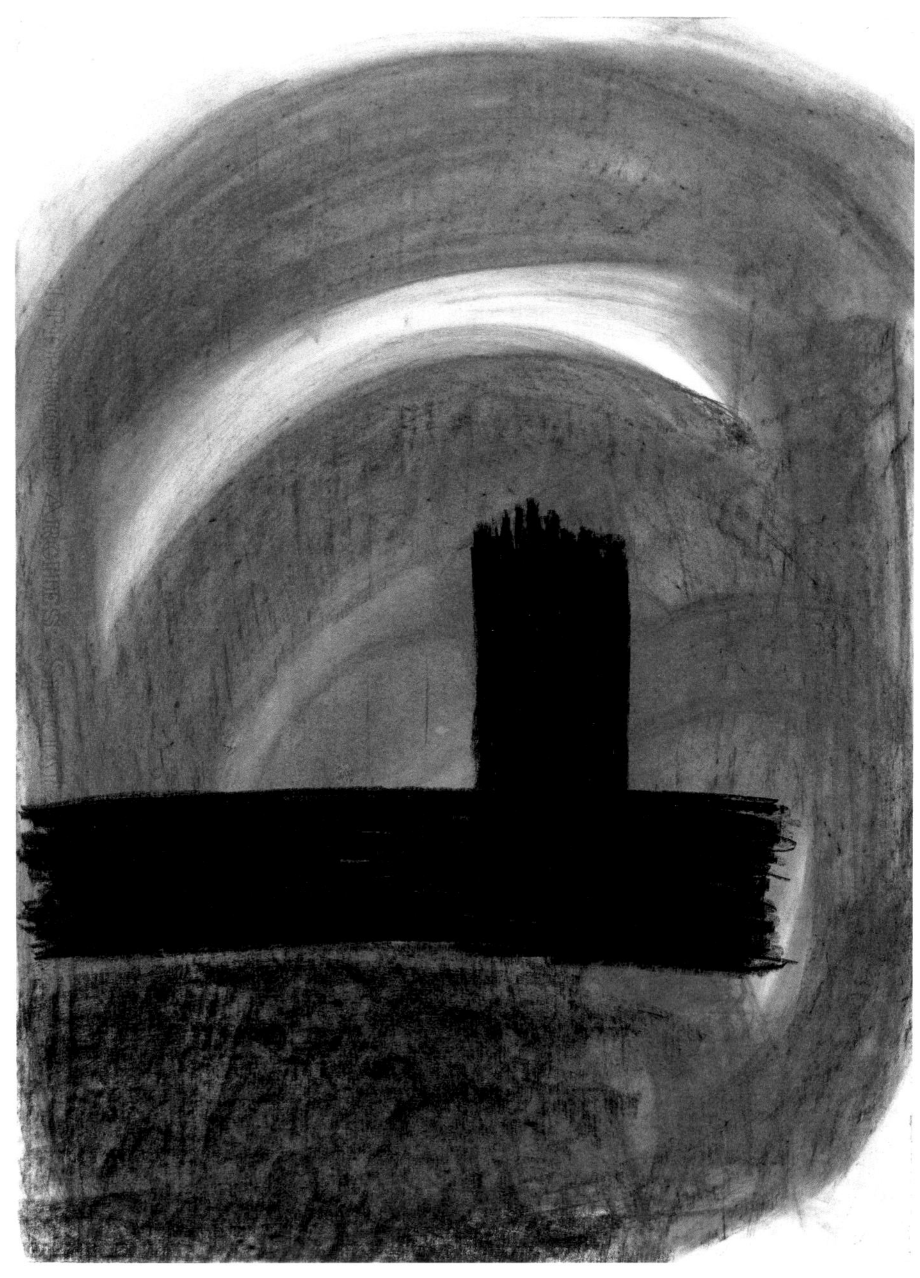

40

Untitled, 1984

Charcoal on paper
30 × 22⅜ inches

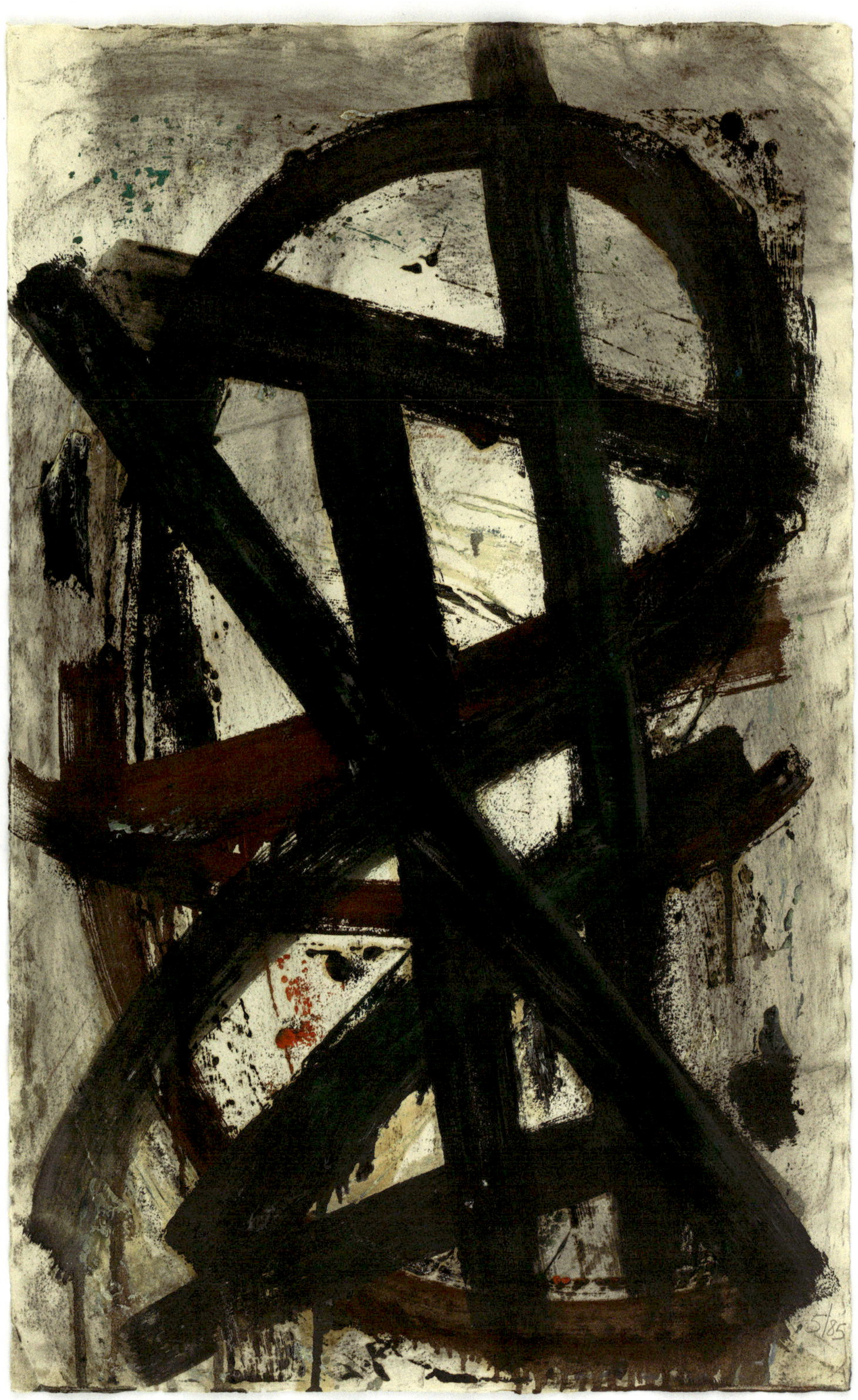

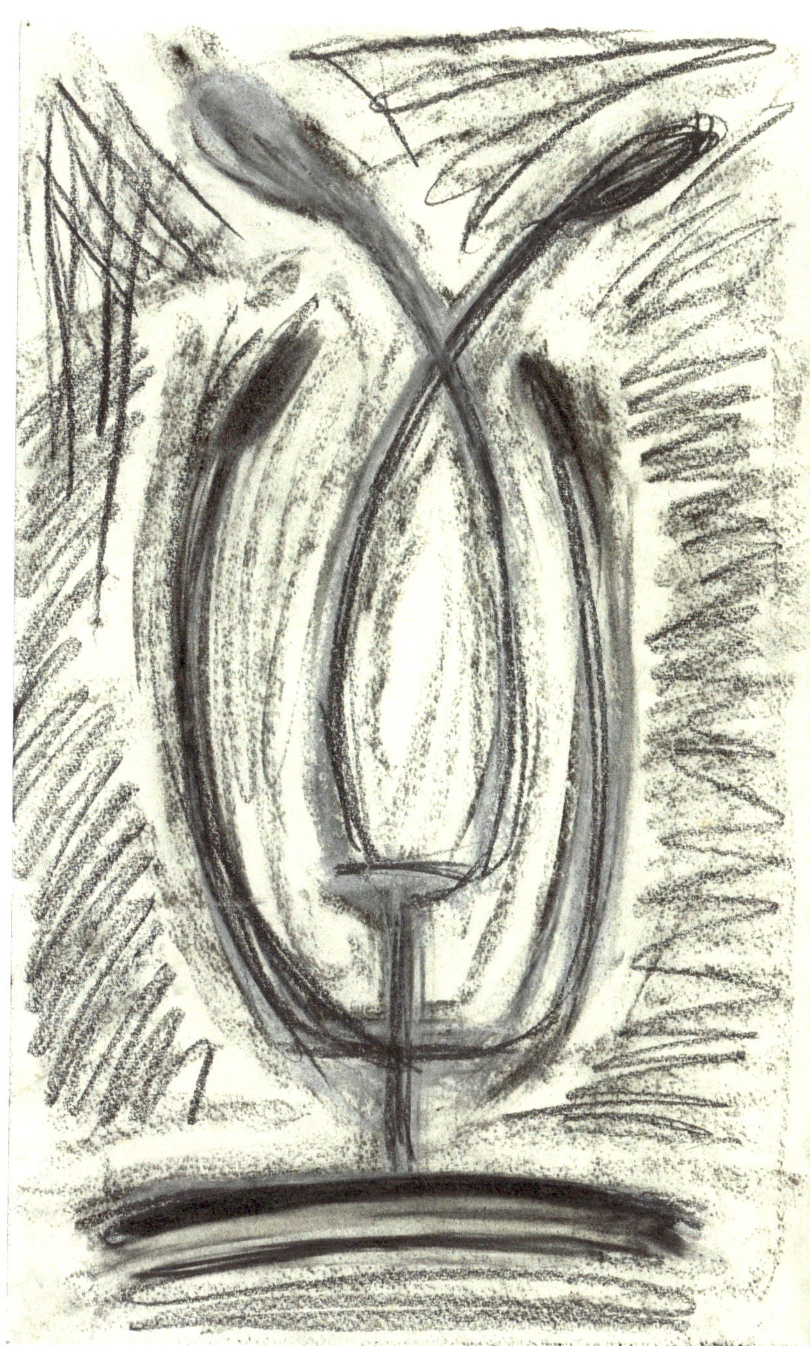

41

Untitled, 1985

Oil and charcoal on paper
34 × 22 inches

42

Untitled, 1984

Charcoal and chalk on paper
19 × 12 inches

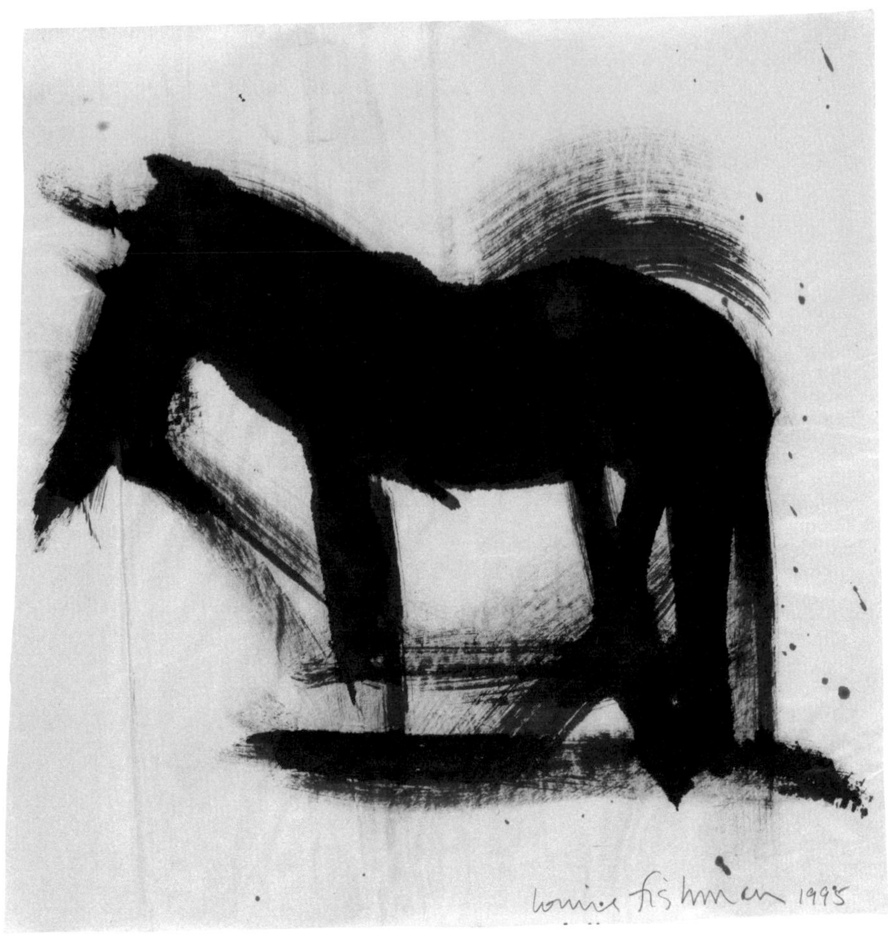

43
Untitled, 1995
Ink on paper
14½ × 13¼ inches

44
Untitled, 1995
Ink on paper
30 × 22¼ inches

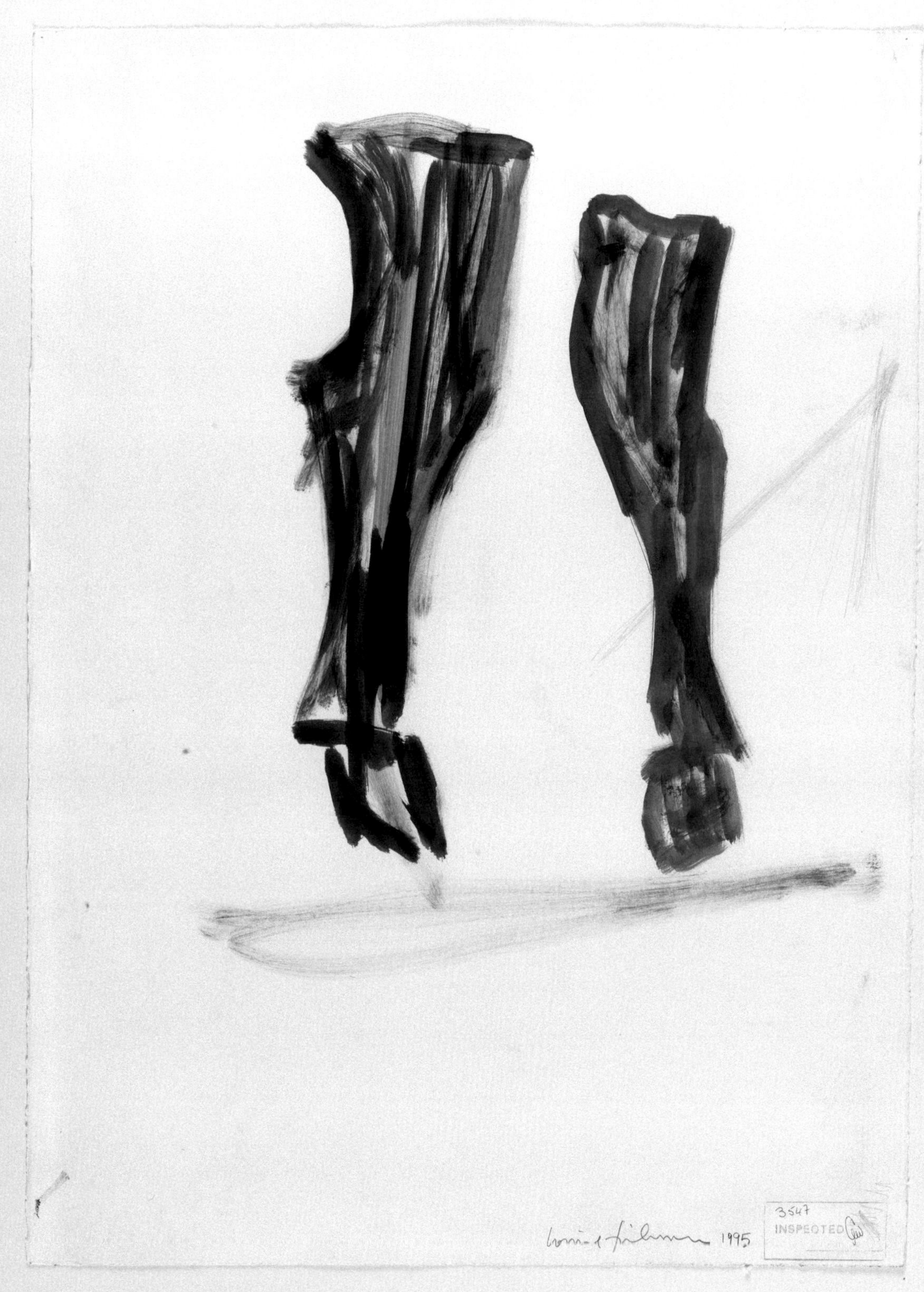

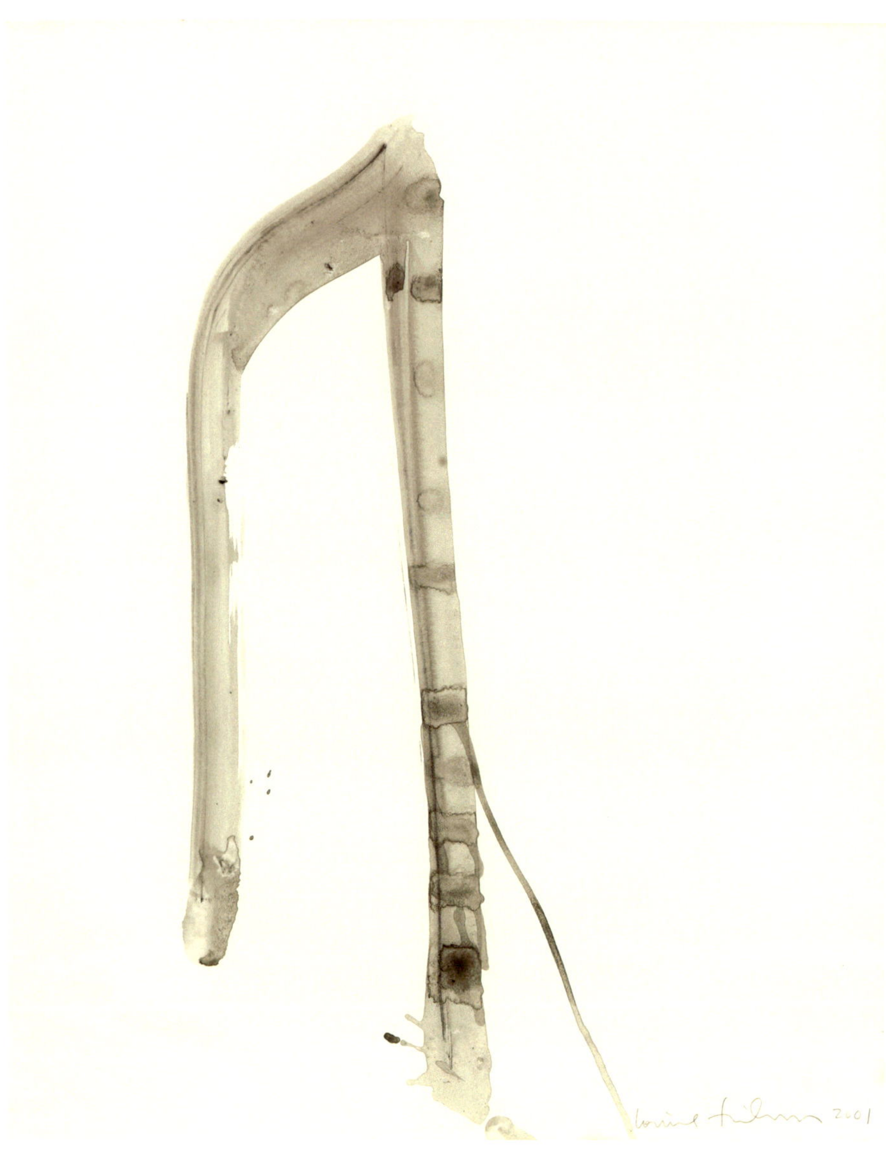

45

Untitled, 2001

Ink on paper
22⅞ × 18⅞ inches

46

Untitled, 2008

Acrylic on paper
30 × 22 inches

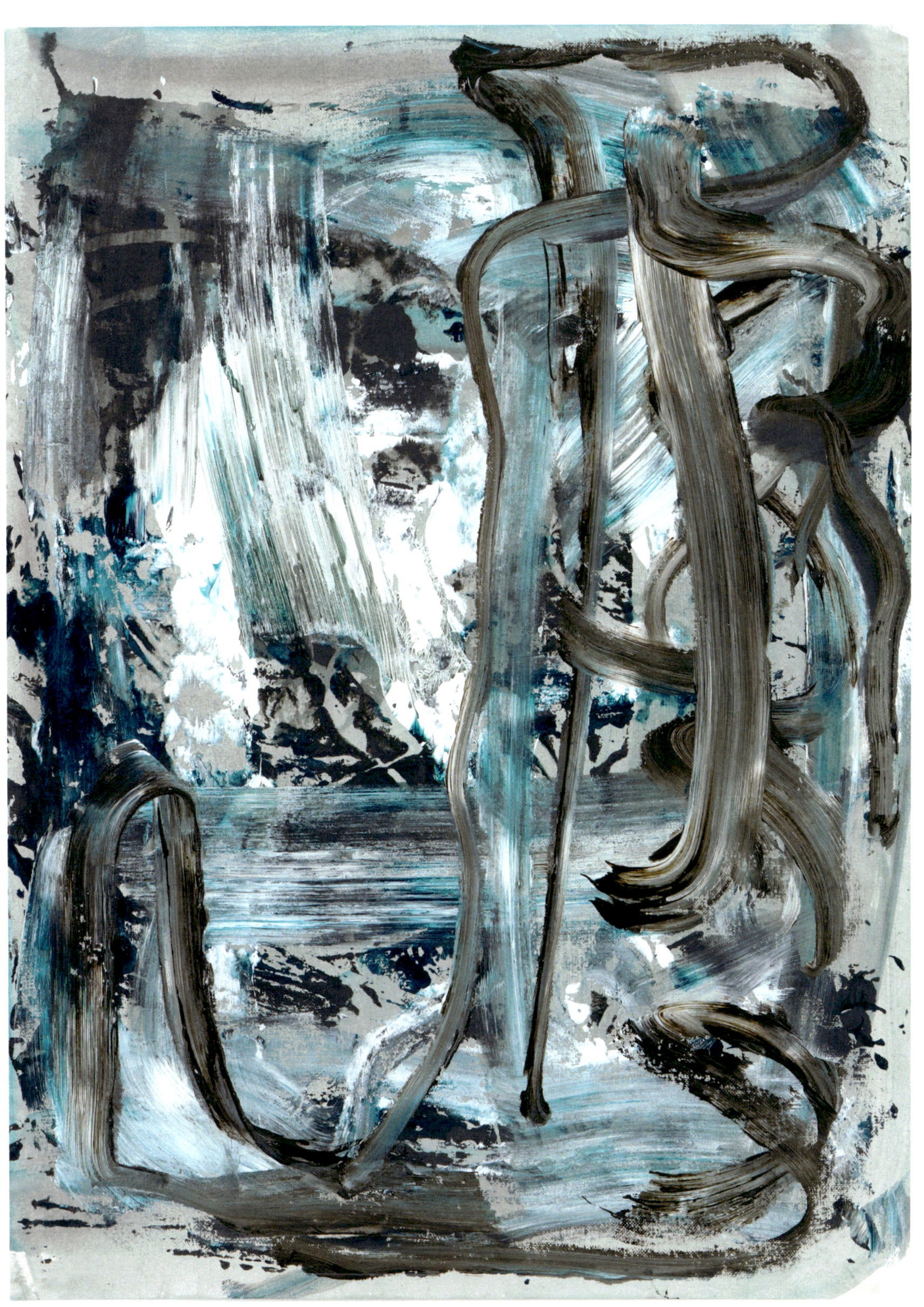

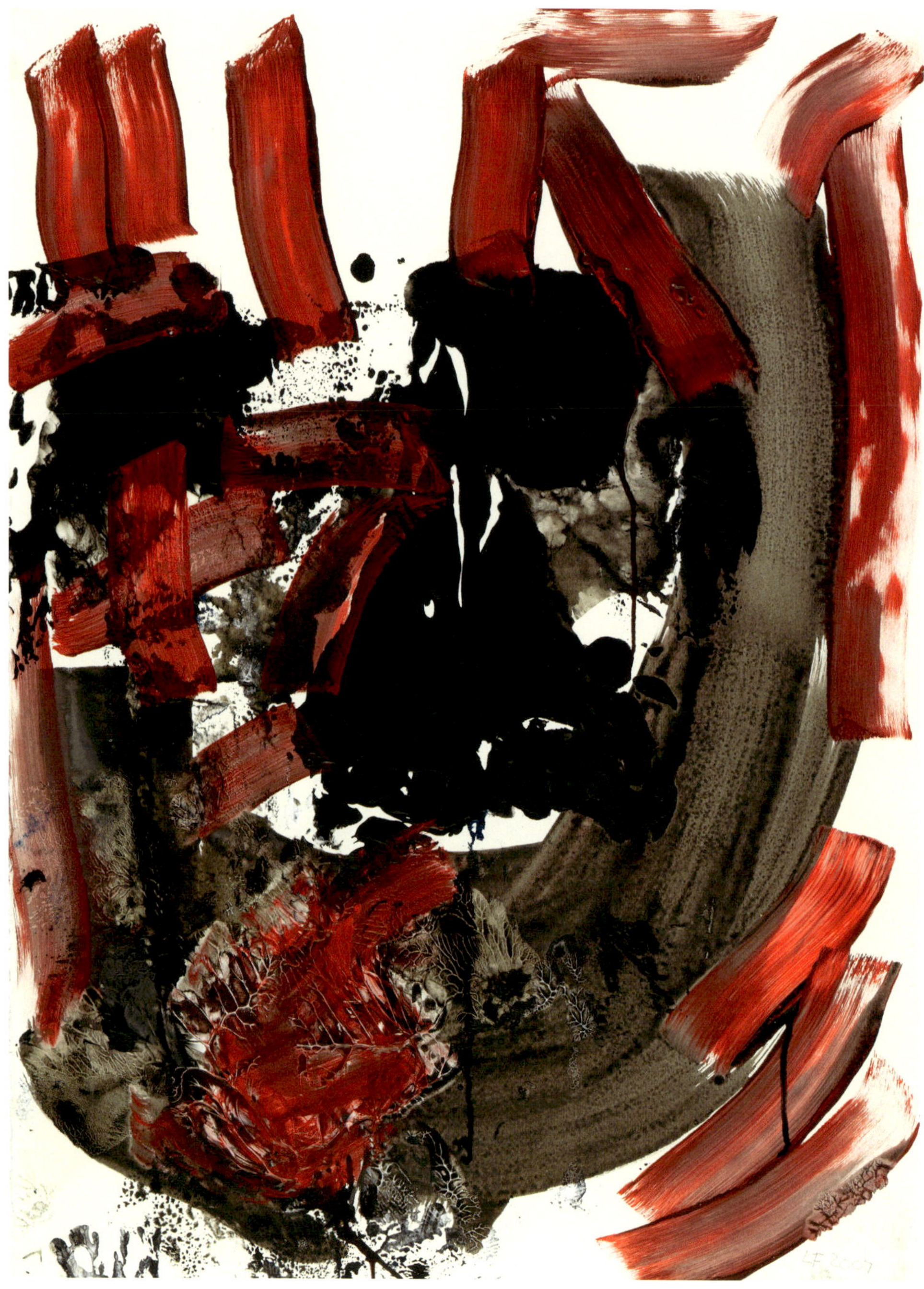

47
Untitled, 2007
Acrylic on paper
30 × 22 inches

48
Untitled, 2007
Acrylic on paper
34 × 23 inches

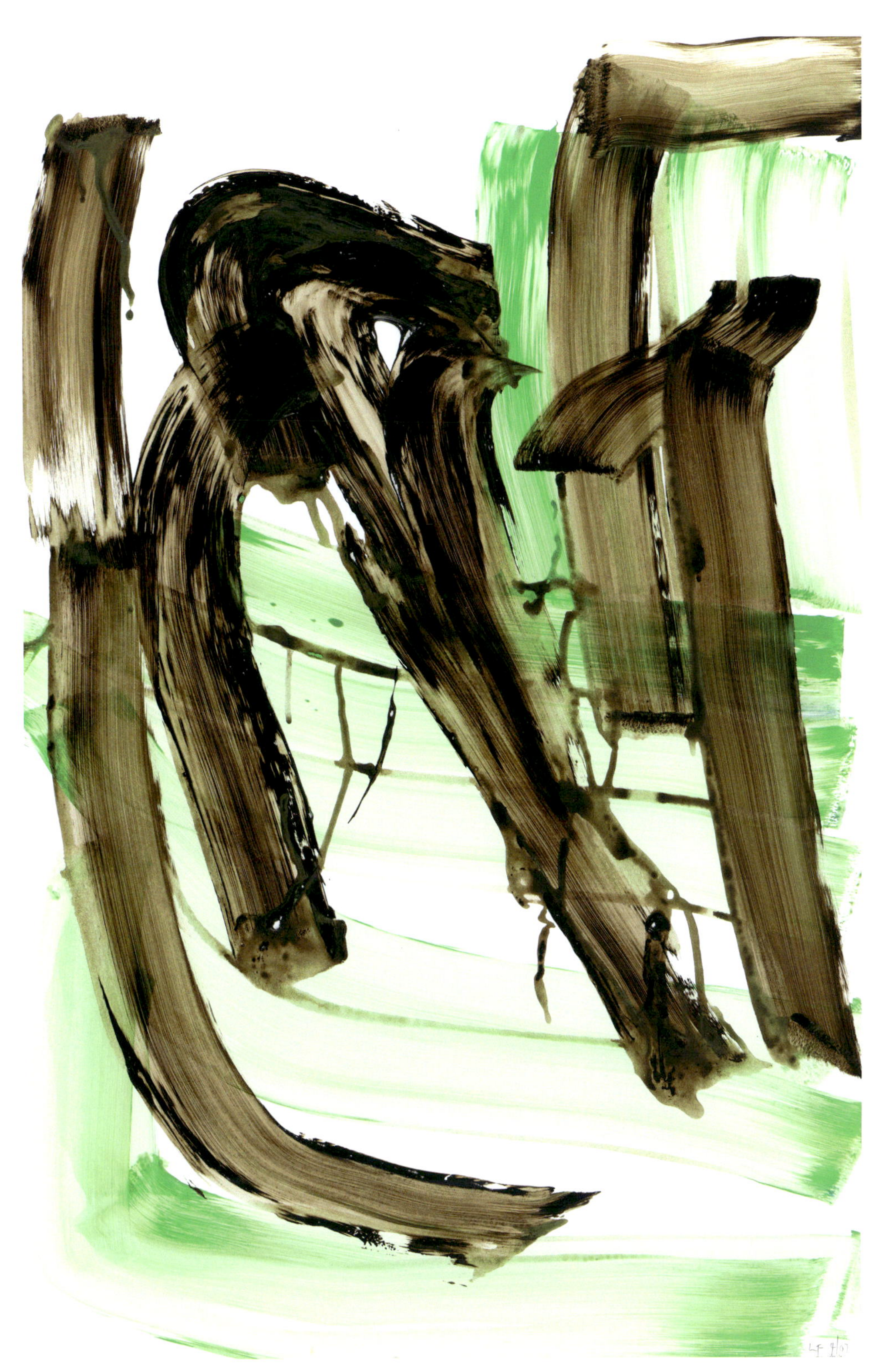

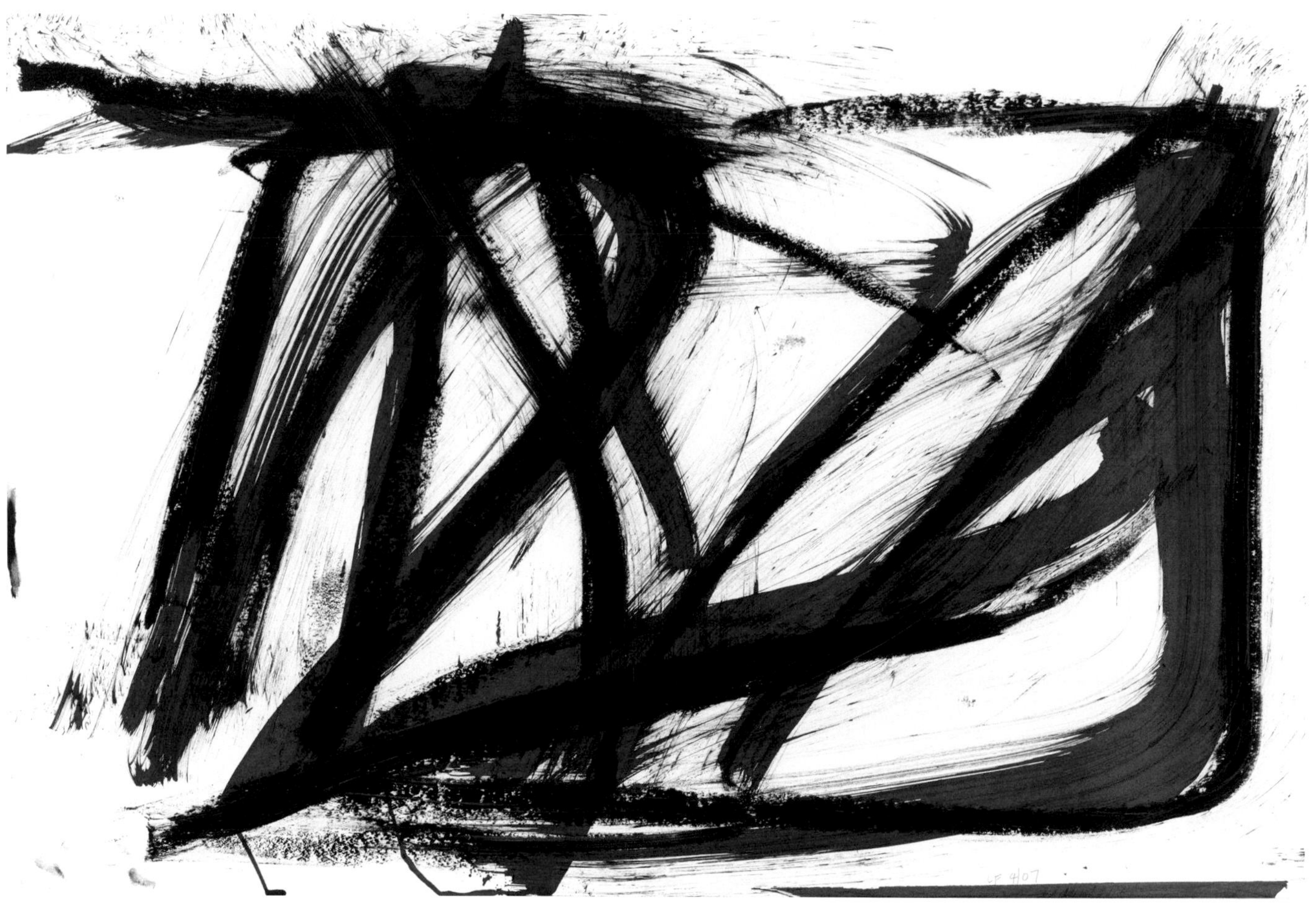

49

Untitled, 2007

Acrylic on paper
23 × 35 inches

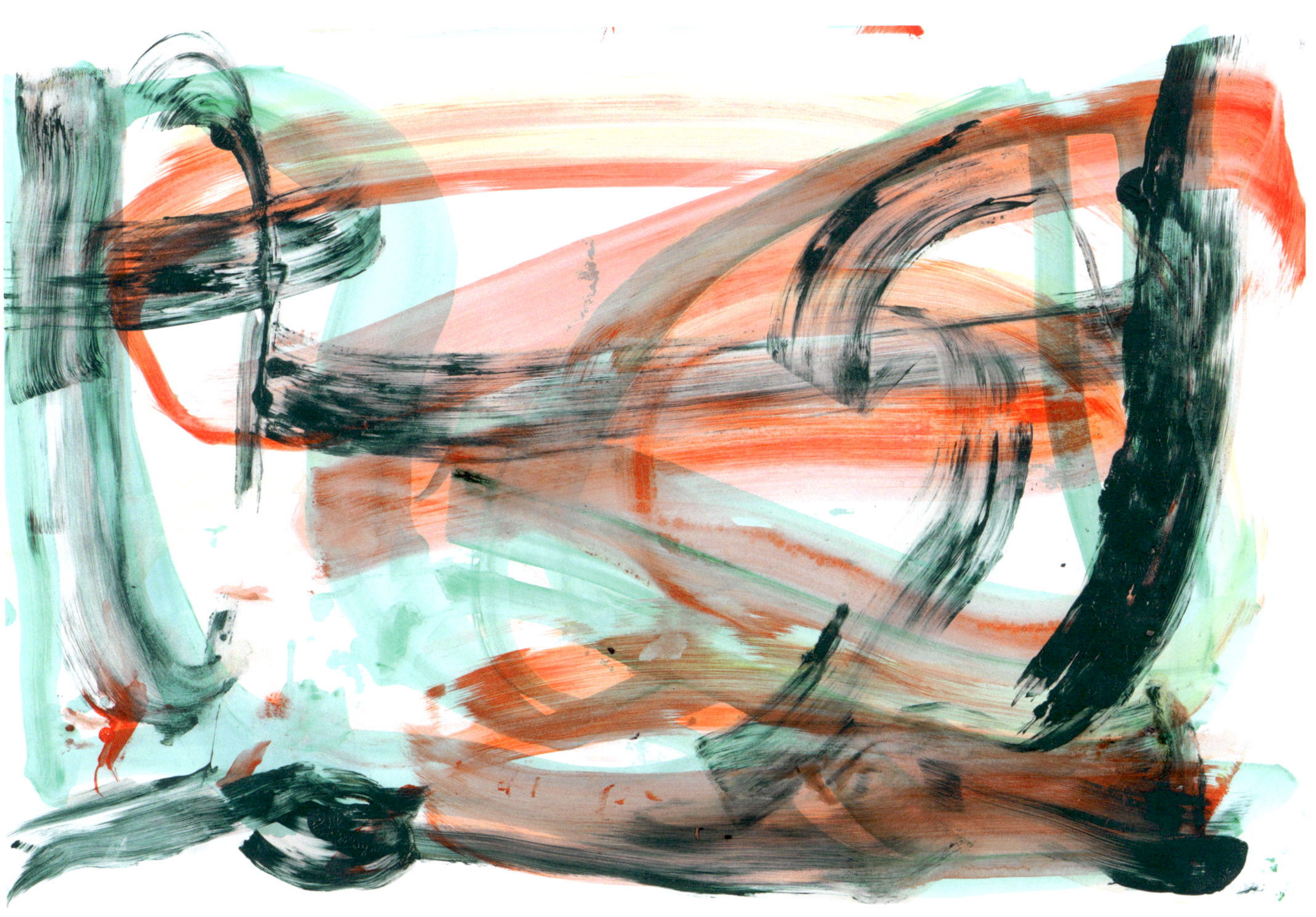

50

Untitled, 2007

Acrylic on paper
23 × 35 inches

51

Drawing, 2015

Oil on linen

50 × 50¾ inches

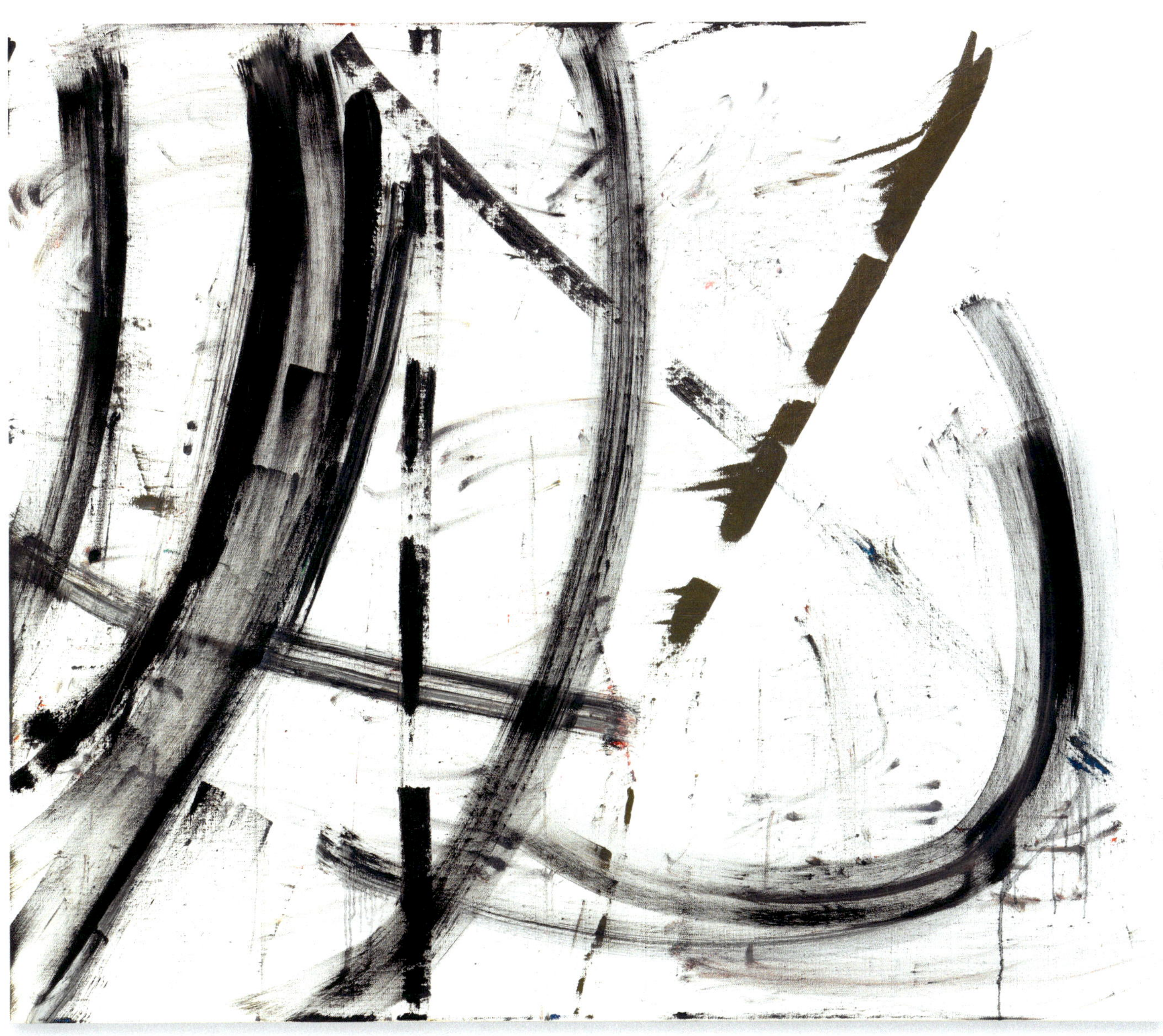

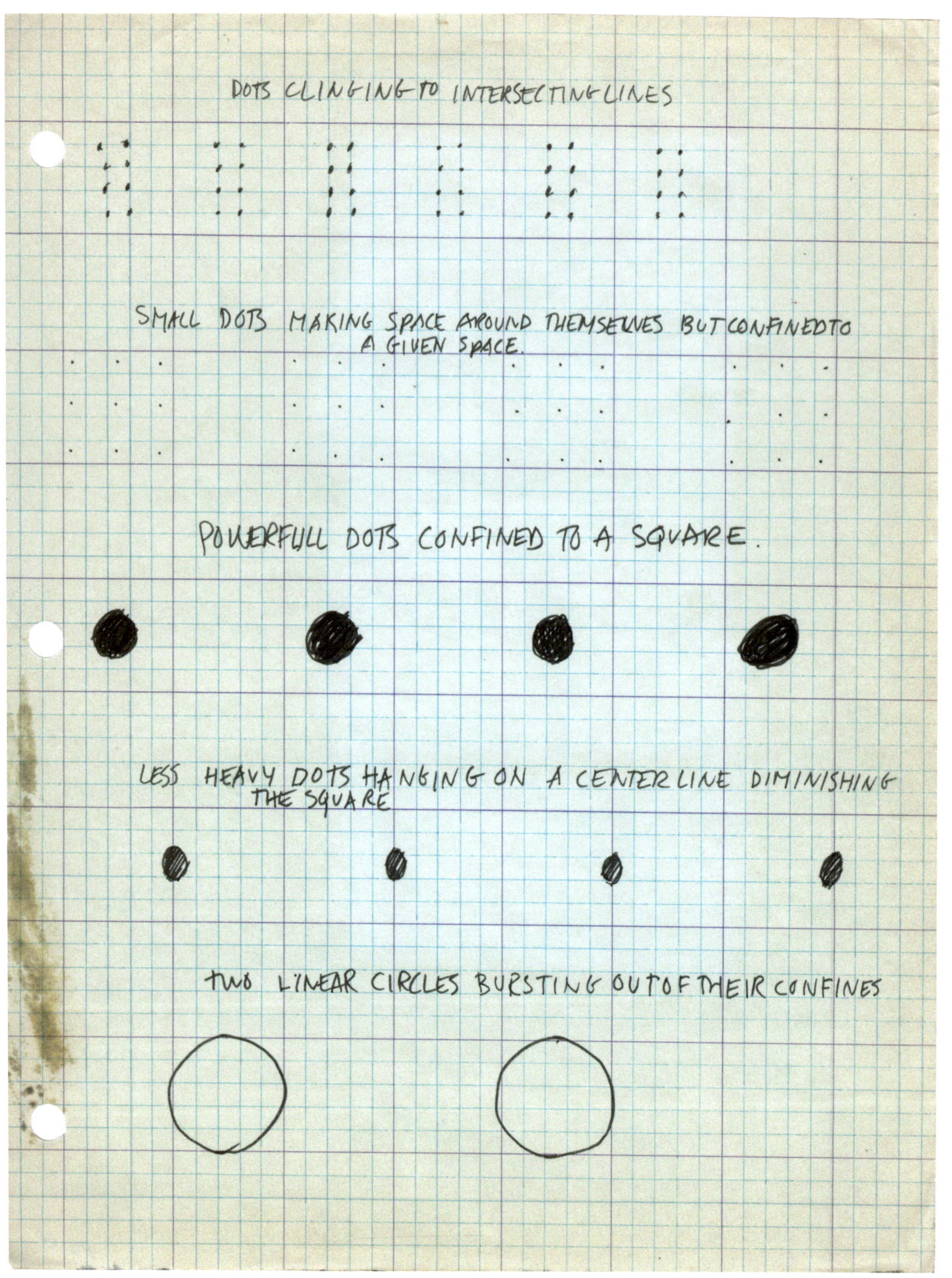
DOTS CLINGING TO INTERSECTING LINES
SMALL DOTS MAKING SPACE AROUND THEMSELVES BUT CONFINED TO A GIVEN SPACE.
POWERFULL DOTS CONFINED TO A SQUARE.
LESS HEAVY DOTS HANGING ON A CENTER LINE DIMINISHING THE SQUARE
TWO LINEAR CIRCLES BURSTING OUT OF THEIR CONFINES

Works on Paper / Works with Paper

Ulrike Müller in Conversation with Louise Fishman

Ulrike Müller: One thing that I've always admired about your work is how you think with and through materials. Your work sets in motion gesture and material alongside bodies and the stuff that surrounds us. What is your relationship to paper in particular, and how has paper been useful to you?

Louise Fishman: That's an interesting question. In art school, I carried a sketchbook with me all the time, and I would pull it out on the subway, in the park, anywhere I was, and draw. I was always drawing. It was like a journal. I think I also kept journals, mainly about what I was looking at. At first, it was a requirement to have a sketchbook, but it became like having a dog. I had a succession of many black-covered sketchbooks.

UM: In the early 1970s, you deliberately stopped working on canvas, in favor of other material supports.

LF: I had been doing these large grid paintings. With the women's group that I organized with Patsy Norvell, among the things we talked about was the male influence on our work. I was living with Esther Newton at the time, the others were all living with men. Esther didn't qualify as a male. Although, had she had an opportunity . . . Anyway, I realized that everything I had done had been informed by a male lineage. My paintings had to do with Sol LeWitt and Ellsworth Kelly, then going back, Paul Cézanne and Chaim Soutine. I decided to cut everything out of my work that's male, including scale, materials, whatever else came up. Of course, it was rather impossible except I did stop using canvas. I worked on whatever I found. I was living on Canal Street, and it was very easy for me to pick up stuff, from the trash and from all kinds of stores.

UM: I'm interested in how recurring elements in your work, like the grid, materialize in different ways and accumulate specific meanings. To my mind, the abstract idea of a grid manifests in a radically different way in, say, the weave of fabric and in graph paper. Let's look at these two untitled drawings on graph paper from 1972 (figs. 4.1 and 4.2). When we first looked at these two drawings together, you —

LF: I hardly remembered them.

UM: You were surprised. I think I was particularly drawn to these because they're like an animation. The grid of the graph paper is the field of action, and then the dots are little characters. Through drawing and writing, two narratives are established, one on each of the two sheets of paper. It seems that you are thinking about how gestural elements move in relation to a grid and how the grid is the —

Fig. 4.1. No title (Dots and circles), 1972. Graphite on paper, 11 × 8½ inches.

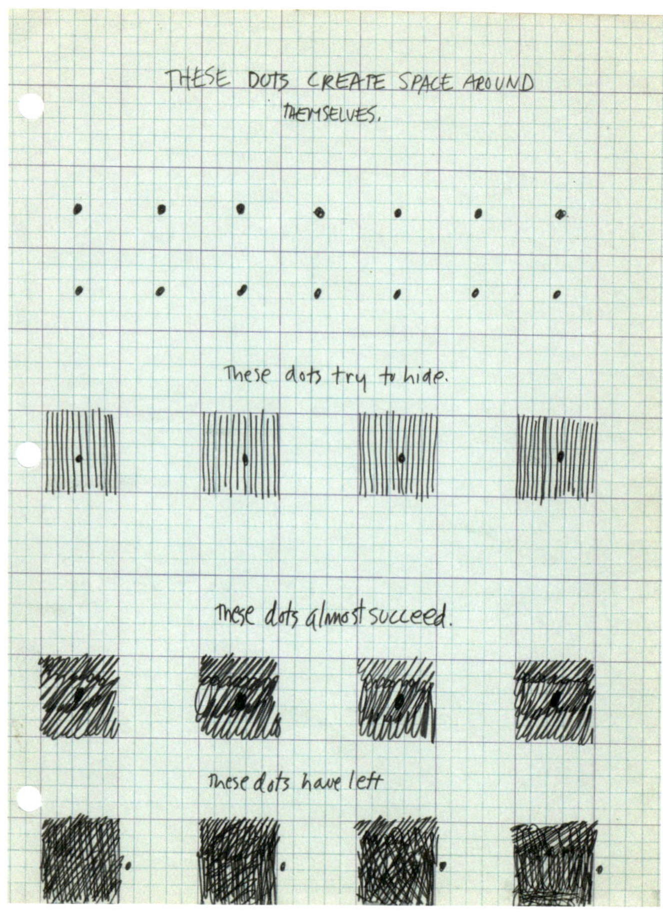

Fig. 4.2. No title (Dots), 1972. Graphite on paper, 11 × 8½ inches.

LF: The rule.

UM: Yes, and they're pushing against that rule. On the second page, it says, "These dots create space around themselves. These dots try to hide. These dots almost succeed. These dots have left."

LF: That was good. It was like I was talking to myself. This is like a journal.

UM: It seems that you're thinking about relationships and composition.

LF: Yeah, it's formal.

UM: It's formal and it's also emotional. It sets up a formal problem, and also a sense of drama.

LF: Well, that's always been the case. The further I got from the emotional, the more restricted the work became. If there wasn't a dialogue that I was in the midst of, then it was a false promise.

UM: I think that makes the works on paper so great: as a viewer, I can enter that dialogue you have with yourself. The back and forth becomes spelled out and legible.

LF: At the time, I worked in the living room of Esther Newton's apartment, and I used whatever I could find. There was a store that had paper and plastic, all kinds of paper things, vellum, stuff I didn't know how to use. I had to figure out how to mark, how to erase and glue and whatever. I had met Eva Hesse and was interested in her work. I started working with liquid rubber, dyeing and dipping materials. Paper was easy to deal with. I coated paper and cardboard with rubber and stitched different materials together. I don't know what I thought I was doing — it was like there were no rules at all. The intention was — and I think it actually happened for me — to follow whatever came up, much like in the consciousness raising we did in the group.

UM: Were you showing your work around that time?

LF: We showed in 1973 as a group at Nancy Hoffman Gallery. I showed my circle paintings, Harmony Hammond her braided rugs, and Jenny Snider did these figures, and Sarah Draney and Patsy were in the show as well. Then, in my first solo show in New York, the following year, at Nancy Hoffman Gallery, I showed cut-wood pieces. After painting on found things, I had started buying four-by-eight-foot sheets of plywood, cutting them up with a jigsaw and putting them together. Then I was invited to teach at the School of the Art Institute of Chicago for two months. They promised me a studio, so I brought my trusty saw and my materials. When I got there, it was an apartment, not a studio that I could do this kind of work in.

UM: So again you were working in an apartment, and using paper?

LF: Exactly. I thought I was making drawings for work I would later execute with wood. As I kept at it, the pieces became more involved, and I continued doing this kind of work after I returned to New York.

UM: When I first saw *Untitled* (1974, plate 53) in reproduction, I thought it was folded. Only when you showed it to me in person I realized that it's actually put together from pieces of paper.

LF: It's collaged. Well, there might be staples as well as glue.

UM: The cut line is striking. The lines are actually edges.

LF: Well, certainly it connects to sculpture and architecture.

UM: It starts making space in a particular kind of way, and it's a lot about what cannot be seen. Even though I can't see it, I know that this piece continues behind that piece. There is sense of something hidden, something not accessible to the eye.

LF: I was concerned with putting it together and overlapping, stapling, making something in space.

UM: You're working on paper, but you're also really working with paper. The paper is not only a surface, it's an object with materiality and depth.

LF: It's not that far from the wood, in a way.

UM: In this group of works on paper from two years later, you're no longer physically building structures but drawing them. They still have the spatial quality that you developed in the collaged pieces, sculptural in crystalline way. They lift off the page and fold.

LF: So interesting. To me, *Al Dente* (1976, plate 56) is sculptural, and *Simple Manners* (1976, plate 60) is architectural. Like a house but it isn't. I was also very consciously painting that white surface or that gray. Initially, I didn't think about the edges of the paper. I was thinking about these wood pieces, objects that I was going to make. And then I gradually started to incorporate more of the rectangle. Around my next show at Nancy Hoffman Gallery (1977), I started moving more and more to the edge, until the paint went all the way to the edge and that shape in the middle was lost by, or incorporated into, a larger scheme.

UM: In *To the Left* (1976, fig. 4.3), I can see how your ideas are building: you are applying the thinking from the diagram drawing with the dots misbehaving, going against the rule of the grid, which here is the edge of the support. And again, you are using the edge of the paper as a line.

LF: These to me are so close to sculpture. I mean, I could have built them. Not that I know *how* to do that, but they could be built out of construction paper or cardboard or metal. I've often been sorry that I didn't become a sculptor, and I think that has a lot to do with what happens in my work. Probably all my work is reaching for that other kind of space.

UM: Interesting! Perhaps your specific painting space is connected to that desire to reach beyond painting — reaching for the page and the kind of space that writing makes, the space of imagination and exploration and ideas. And reaching for the kind of space that sculpture or architecture makes.

LF: Poetry as well, and music. I'm very involved with the formal aspects of music. All of those art forms sort of come together, in my thinking and in my experience.

UM: We're skipping ahead in time, but I would like to also talk about your leporello books (fig. 4.5; plates 2, 4, 14, 19, 20, 29, 30, 37, 68), which made a profound impression on me when I first saw them in the exhibition of your small-scale works and objects that you collect, which Ingrid Schaffner curated at the Institute of Contemporary Art (ICA) in Philadelphia.[1] For me, that exhibition was eye opening: looking at these accordion-folded books, I understood something about the structural thinking and conceptual scaffolding behind the freedom and exuberance of your more recent paintings. In 1992, for *Book I* (plate 13) you used a very particular, prefabricated leporello. Do you remember where you found it?

LF: I got it in Chinatown. The early ones were Chinese. Later, I couldn't find them anymore. These blank leporellos were intended for the pilgrimage along the

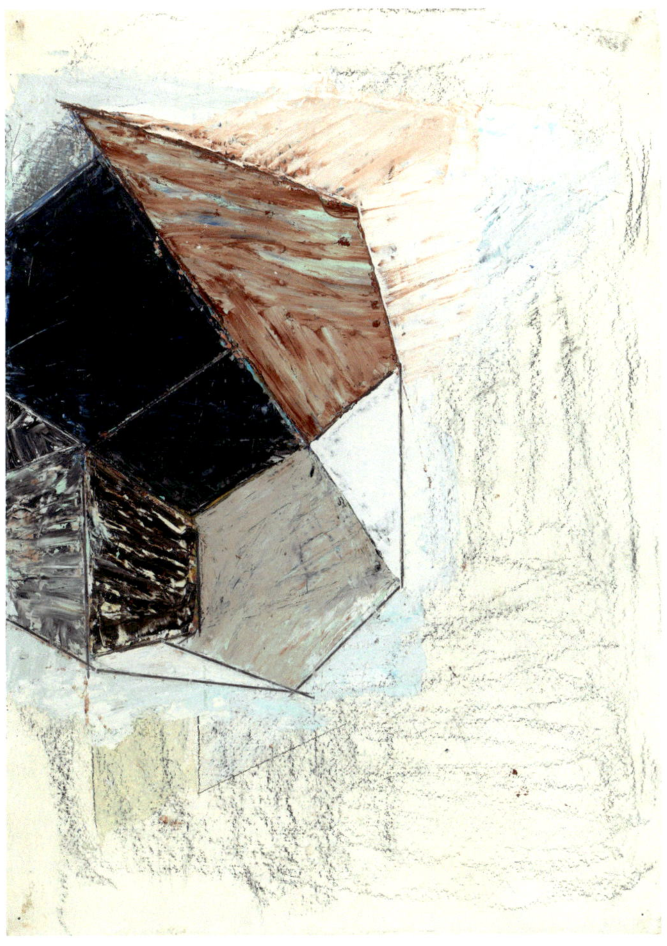

Fig. 4.3. *To the Left*, 1976. Oil and wax on paper, 31 × 22½ inches.

path of the Buddha. I had been studying Buddhism, so this interested me. It was a journey, and each station along the way would be stamped in the book so you had proof that you visited them all, the whole route of the Buddha's enlightenment.

UM: So there is a linearity to the format, a narrative structure. And it is portable.

LF: Now, I told you about the fire in my studio that happened in 1990. It was a very painful time. The ground floor was burned out, the paint tubes and cans burst, and there was paint everywhere, like splattered paint. In the middle was this cross of stretcher bars, all that was left of the last large painting that I had been working on. The odd thing is it was influenced by the black paintings of Goya. I had just been to Spain. After the fire I got very sick, physically, emotionally. I developed chronic fatigue, and I couldn't function. Betsy Crowell was trying to take care of me, and people kept giving me suggestions. Joan Mitchell said, "Get back on the horse, Louise!" And I thought, *What horse am I going to get on now?*

After two years or so of slow recovery, it was suggested that I go and spend two months out in New Mexico. I rented Harmony Hammond's studio. On walks, I would find little pottery shards with grids on them. I became very interested in black-on-black pottery.

UM: And *Book I* is around that same time, about two years after the fire.

LF: During my time in the Southwest, I met Agnes Martin. She showed me her paintings, and also her drawings, very slowly. I thought, *There's that grid. I can do that. I know that grid really well.* Then I started this book, and all the books began with a grid.

UM: It seems to me that there is a consequence to bringing the grid and the book together. I don't know this constellation from Agnes Martin. Putting the grid in the book, we go back maybe to the graph paper, but really also the grid of text. The act of locating the grid inside a book seems to open a whole conceptual and compositional universe. Books and printed texts are gridded spaces. There are columns and rows.

LF: And the letters themselves are based on grids.

UM: In a notebook entry from June 17, 1989 (fig. 4.4) you mention being bothered by what you call an over-reliance on paint, and then you say, "What is the relationship of the structure to the paint?" To me, that resonates with what you're doing in your books. To my mind, the book specifies something about the grid that for you is already structural. In *Book I*, you're using paint on top of a drawn grid, and it follows and doesn't follow the lines. Paint flows and has its own logic; it won't follow the drawn line and builds tension with the structure of the grid.

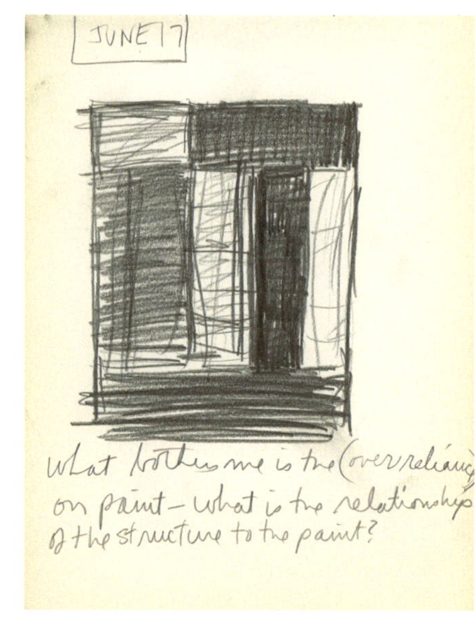

Fig. 4.4. No title (What is the relationship of the structure to the paint?), 1989, from *Journal*, 1986–89. Graphite and ink on paper, $12\frac{5}{8} \times 9\frac{11}{16}$ inches.

LF: This happens in all my paintings, too. I mean, it's very obvious to me. I don't think about the grid anymore. It's so basic, and all my work is connected to the grid, whether it has actual lines in it or not. I just kept making those books, and I was very deliberately introducing those geometries. And the book was a perfect format to work on at a desk, which is what I had. I didn't have a studio; I had a desk.

UM: Throughout *Book I*, it seems like you're moving deeper and deeper into questions of composition. It also strikes me that it's all done with perpendicular lines, and then it ends on a diagonal, which seems dramatic.

LF: Yeah. (laughter)

UM: *Down and Dirty* (1994, plate 29) is the book that you made for Bertha Harris, your then-former girlfriend. There is an increased tension between the cool, found structure of the book and the sense of urgency of your drawings. In a sense, language is also a preexisting structure, and expression runs up against what can and can't be said. I'm interested in how you develop drawing and painting as a kind of language.

LF: As you know, Bertha was a novelist who, unfortunately, drank herself to death and didn't do the work she wanted to do. She was not an easy person, but I adored her. And she also had a lot of respect for my work, and I was her fantasy of the perfect person. I mean, she wrote her novel *Lover* with me in mind, so I was very special to her. Coming from a place where I never felt special, this was hugely important. I did what I could to help her, but I couldn't cross certain lines.

UM: Looking at how you pick up the idea of a written line in your drawings, it seems that you are extending your practice toward her practice.

LF: Her practice, initially, was all handwritten with an ink pen. I talked her into getting an Olivetti typewriter, because she never spent any money. But she always handwrote in addition, and I was always looking at her writing, observing details of her, her hands. I bought her a beautiful pen with gold around it. I mean, at that time, it cost me a lot of money even though it wasn't that expensive. And I got her gold-tipped cigarettes and an ivory cigarette holder. She would do little imitations of David Niven. She was a very bad drunk, and she did a lot of bad things. But she was extraordinary.

UM: You seem to capture two sides in this leporello as well [*Book of Abuse*]. There is a dark page with lots of staples (plate 14).

LF: Well, she had been badly abused, and she had nightmares. It was terrifying to me. These are very tortured pieces. I remember them very well. As you say, the lines have to do with notebooks, and writing. I always had an interest in writing, my friends were writers and academics, and I loved that. I felt excluded because I wasn't a writer.

UM: Later in *Down and Dirty*, the pencil lines reappear. They still are notebook lines, but they have moved out of alignment and are jumbled. It seems important that you are specifically addressing a particular person. And you've done that more than once.

LF: Yeah, despite the fact that my language is abstract and the people I'm involved with are not visual artists. It's an odd thing, because it's a language that a lot of people don't understand. I think in some ways it's a communication with myself, letting me know things that I wouldn't know otherwise. This is the book I made for Ingrid Nyeboe, my partner (plate 30). What a change, huh?

UM: It's completely different in color and tone, but again you are reaching out, building a very specific, intimate conversation with someone you love. In a way, the people that you're close with become your first audience.

LF: Yeah. My audience was not in the art world. It was people I knew, and often they were not artists. The art world was never a place I felt comfortable in. And my community, for the most part, is not connected to the art world.

UM: Knowing whom you're talking to seems to be so important for the work and seems to become really crucial for the kind of autonomy and freedom that you can make for yourself, because you inhabit your work, and you know your audience. I find Ingrid's book to be very touching. It's so intimate and also public.

LF: Well, I don't know that I made it for the public. I think it became public. Ingrid has dealt with my archive and the database of all of my work, and her book became part of that. But my intention was not for it to be shared. I mean, it's okay. It happens to be very beautiful. And it pleases me that it's got all that sexuality in it.

UM: You included hair clippings.

LF: Yep. I swept the floor after Ingrid's hair was cut in our apartment. We used to have this friend, a very nice guy, who would come and cut her hair. And then he would leave. He never cleaned the floor. So I saved her hair. Although, some of it looks not from her head.

UM: Ha.

LF: (Laughter) That I don't remember.

UM: Ingrid mentioned that. She remembers.

LF: Oh, yeah. She would.

UM: There are also instances where you transfer the paint from one page of the leporello onto the next by making contact. So it's a lot about touching, being in touch.

LF: Yeah, being very much in touch. That was such a surprise, meeting her. I mean, I knew her, but what happened when we got together, after Jill Johnston died, it was just remarkable.

UM: This book is from Venice, *Vaporetto Leporello No. 6* (2017, fig. 4.5). It's the city that you and Ingrid have spent time in together. It makes me think of moving through the canals of Venice on a vaporetto, moving laterally through a city that has been painted so much. As seen from the boat, the streets are elevated, and there is a stage-like feeling to city life, which is also reflected in the water . . .

LF: It's also about the walls and the floors. The last time we were there, I started to really look at the floors. The floors in our apartment and the floors in the palaces were a particular earthy red. One man in Venice was responsible for making the solution that went on the floors to give them this special finish and color. Walls also became more and more important to me, and the niches — where sometimes there was nothing and sometimes a beautiful little Madonna — and the doorknobs and other details of the city. I mean, the first time I went, I thought, *I'm walking on these cobblestones that Titian walked on*. How could that have happened? Little me, you know?

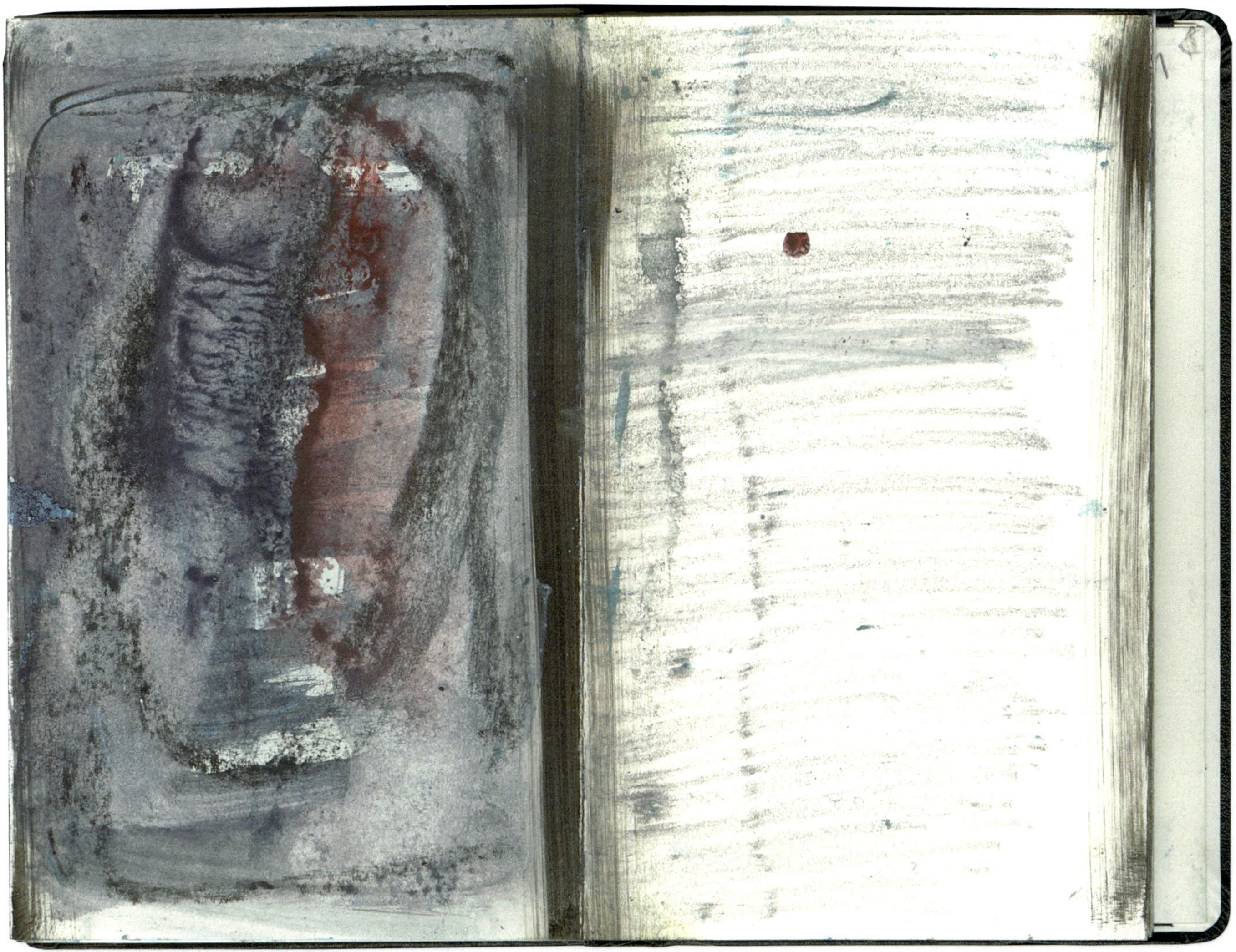

Fig. 4.5. Interior spread from *Vaporetto Leporello No. 6*, 2017. Watercolor and tempera on paper; leporello binding, 5½ × 3½ × ¾ inches (closed).

UM: This here looks like a rubbing, which would be one of the most literal things one could do in relation to the surfaces of a city, touching and transferring them.

LF: Yes, I did rubbings. I've done a lot of rubbings, actually, in my life.

UM: Starting from the earlier books and then arriving at this one, and still having the idea of the grid in mind, and thinking of bodies moving through gridded spaces and how, you know, we said language is a gridded space and, of course, language influences bodies. Architecture is another gridded space that informs bodies. I think it's those terms in relation to each other that operate throughout your work on different scales.

LF: From the time I was in art school, I was interested in architecture. I had a class in architecture when I was a student at Tyler. I think of architecture

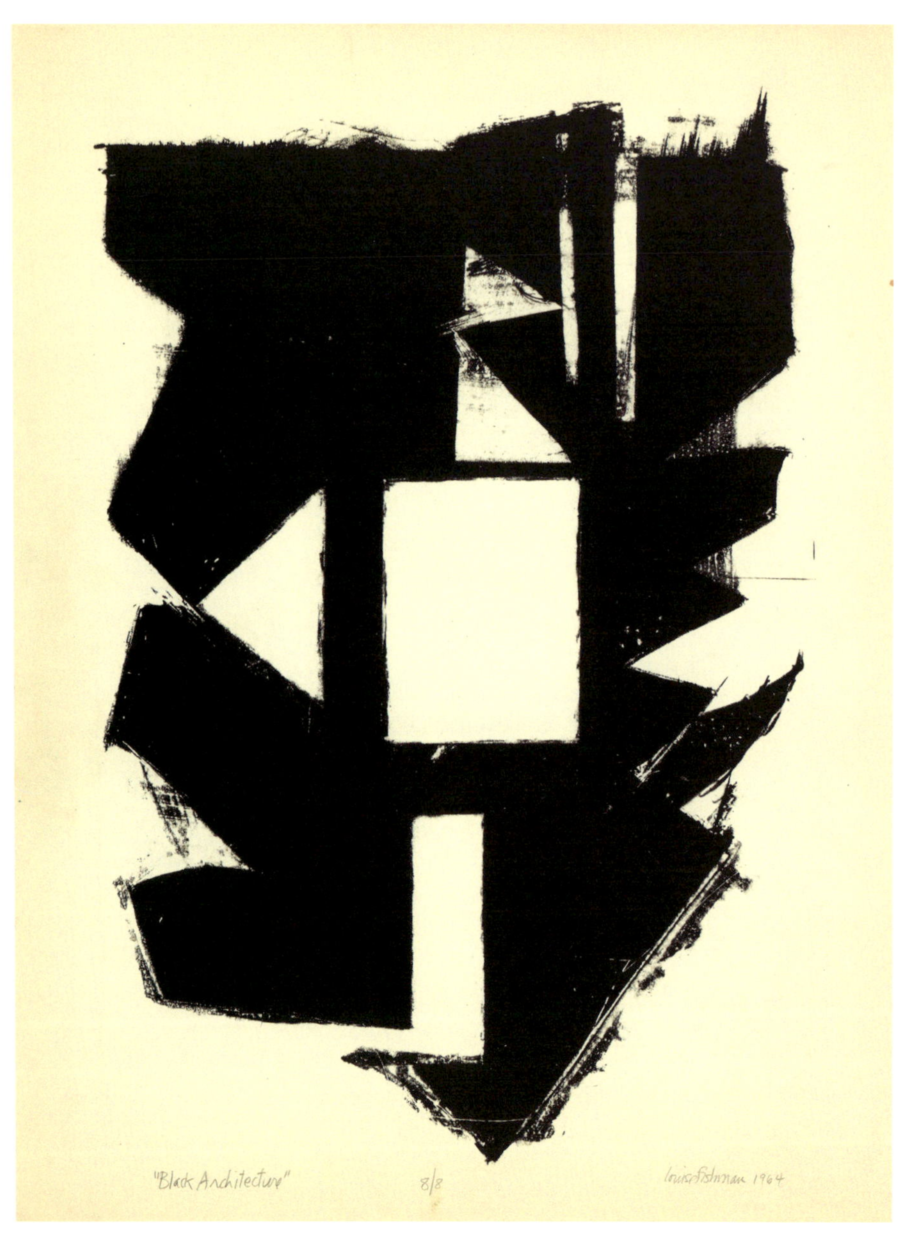

Fig. 4.6. *Black Architecture*, 1964. Lithograph, edition 8/8, 22¼ × 17¼ inches.

as a built grid (fig. 4.6), a grid that one can walk into. The stairs are grids. Everything is a grid. I mean, the armature, all the parts of things, involve a grid.

UM: I think of you as someone continuously scrutinizing your surroundings — the world, objects left behind by others, art history — for their usefulness. In 1977, in a text for the feminist journal *Heresies*, you advised young women painters to "take what you want and leave the dreck."[2] And related to this, when we did a public talk at the ICA in Philadelphia around your show, one of the things you told me is that a painting is a collection.

LF: A collection.

UM: Yes, I will always remember that. And I've been wondering if a self, a person, is also a collection.

LF: Oh, for sure. I mean, I do feel this sense of being miniscule, and my work makes me involved in the external world, although my experience is not external. It's about having a dialogue.

Notes

This interview is edited from a two-hour conversation on January 10, 2020, in Louise Fishman's Chelsea studio in New York.

1. *Paper Louise Tiny Fishman Rock*, Institute of Contemporary Art, University of Pennsylvania, Philadelphia, April 29–August 14, 2016. See Ingrid Schaffner, "Getting Small with Louise Fishman," in *Louise Fishman*, ed. Helaine Posner (Purchase, NY: Neuberger Museum of Art, and Philadelphia: Institute of Contemporary Art, 2016), 185–98.
2. Louise Fishman, "How I Do It: Cautionary Advice from a Lesbian Painter," *Heresies: A Feminist Publication on Art and Politics* 3 (1977): 74.

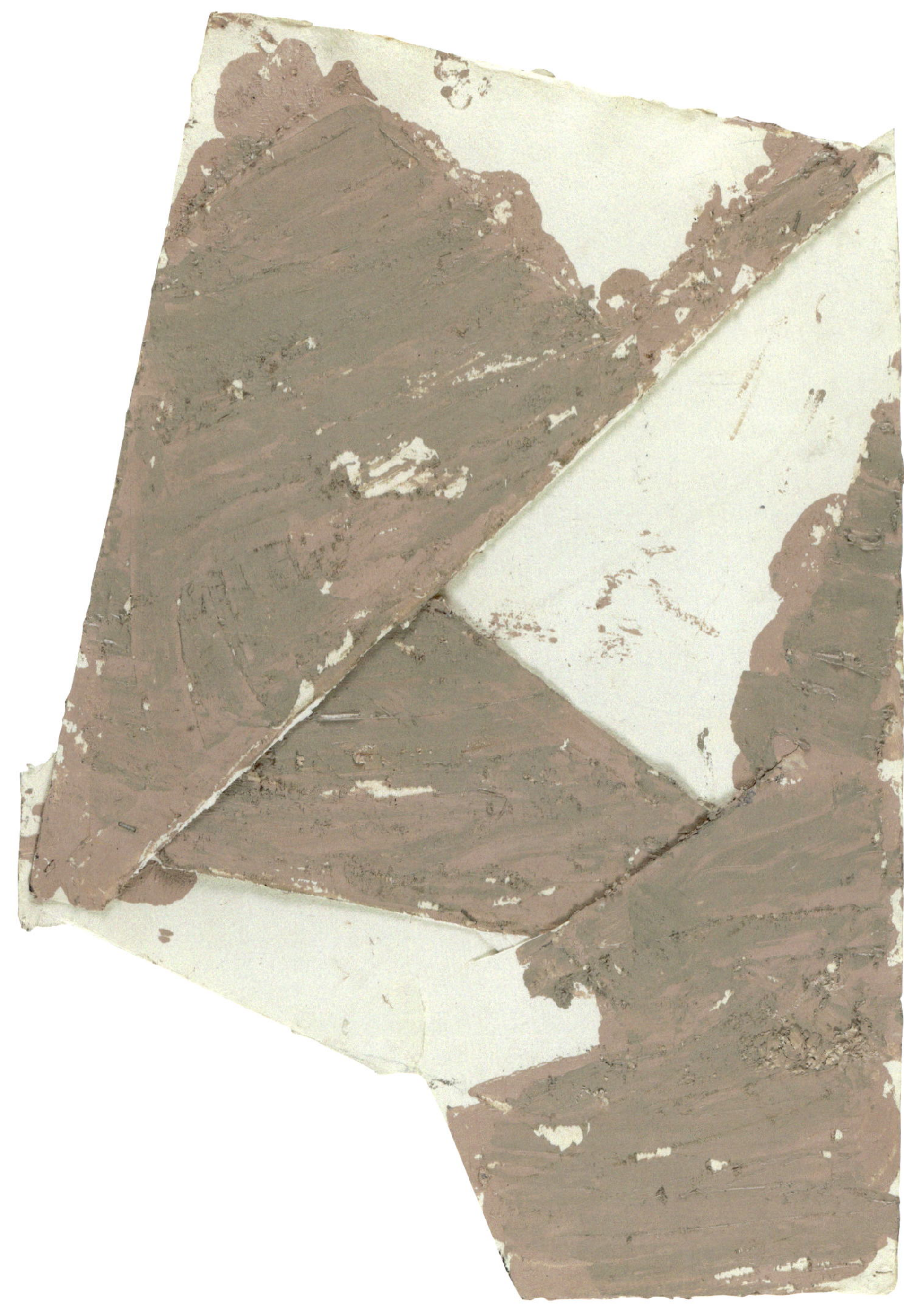

52

Untitled, 1974

Oil, wax, staples, and collage on paper
33 × 23 inches

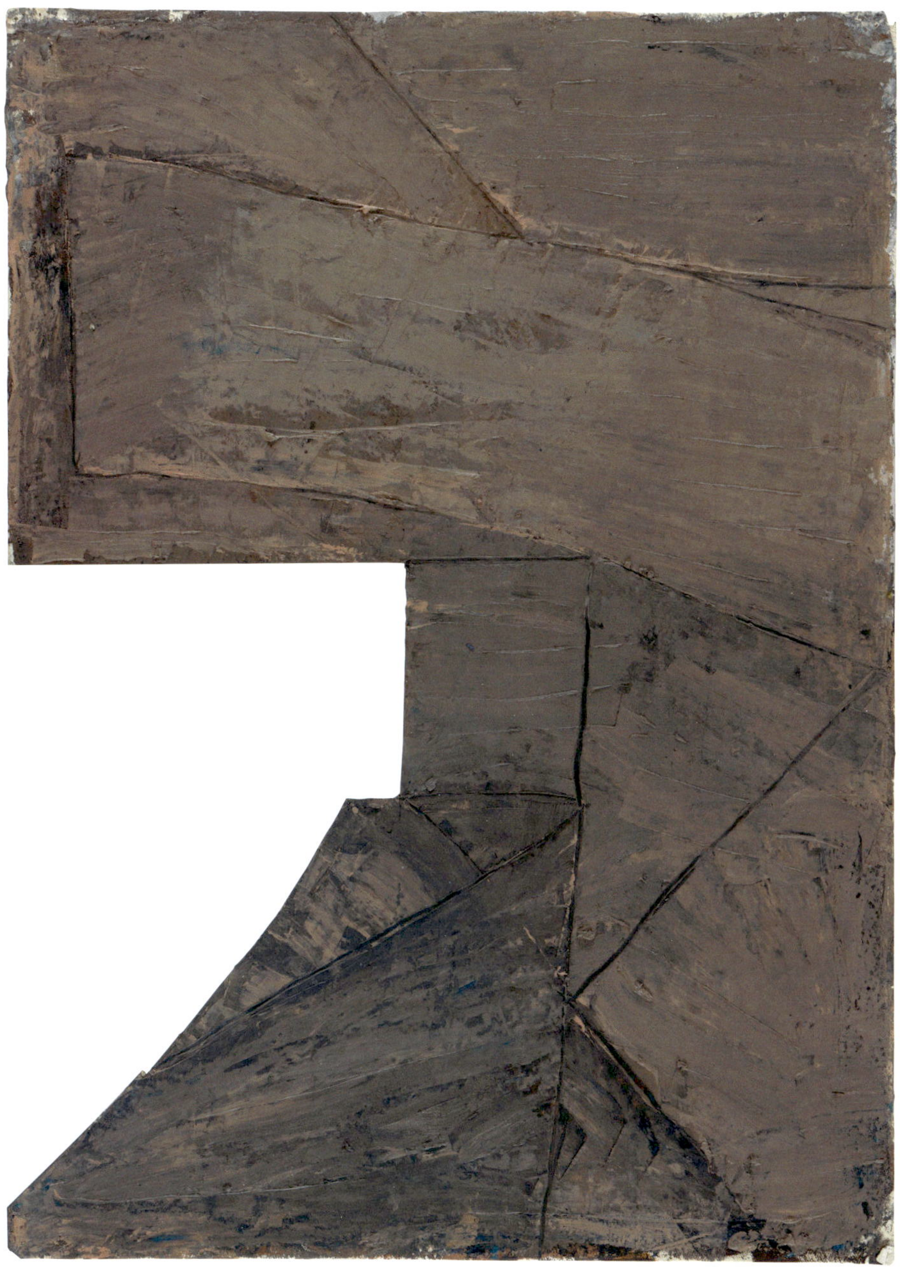

53

Untitled, 1974

Oil on paper
28⅞ × 20 inches

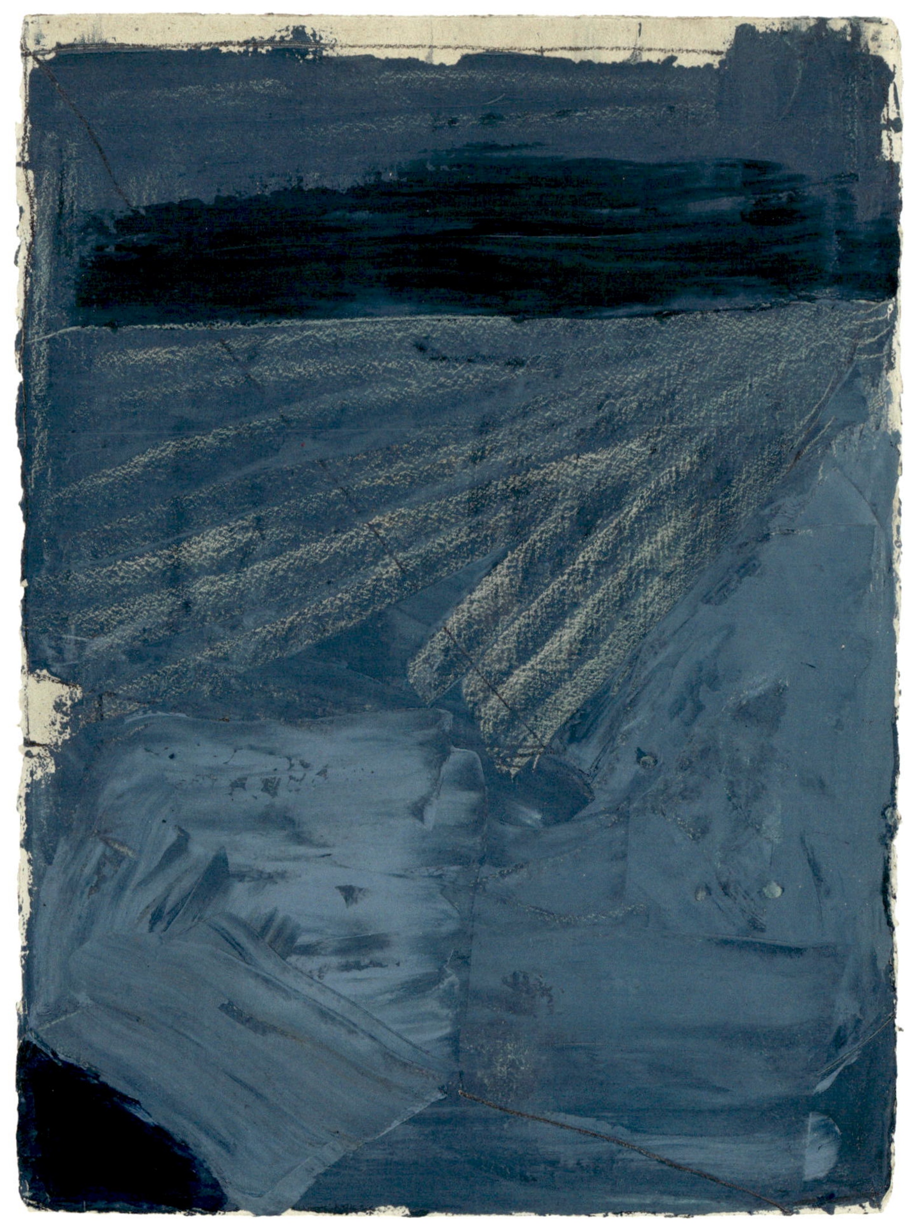

54
Untitled, 1975
Oil on paper
30¼ × 22⅞ inches

55
Untitled, 1975
Oil on paper
31⅛ × 23 inches

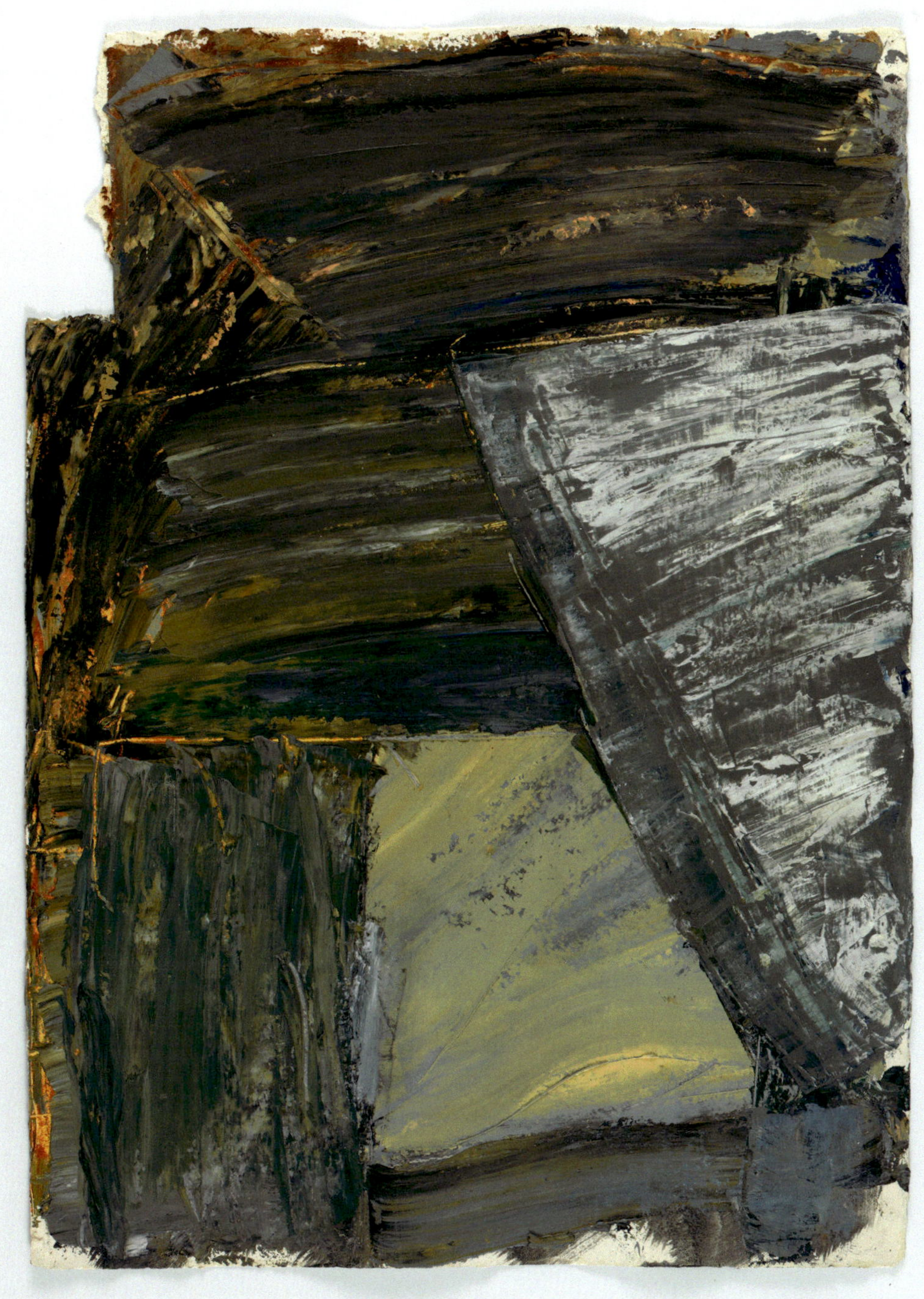

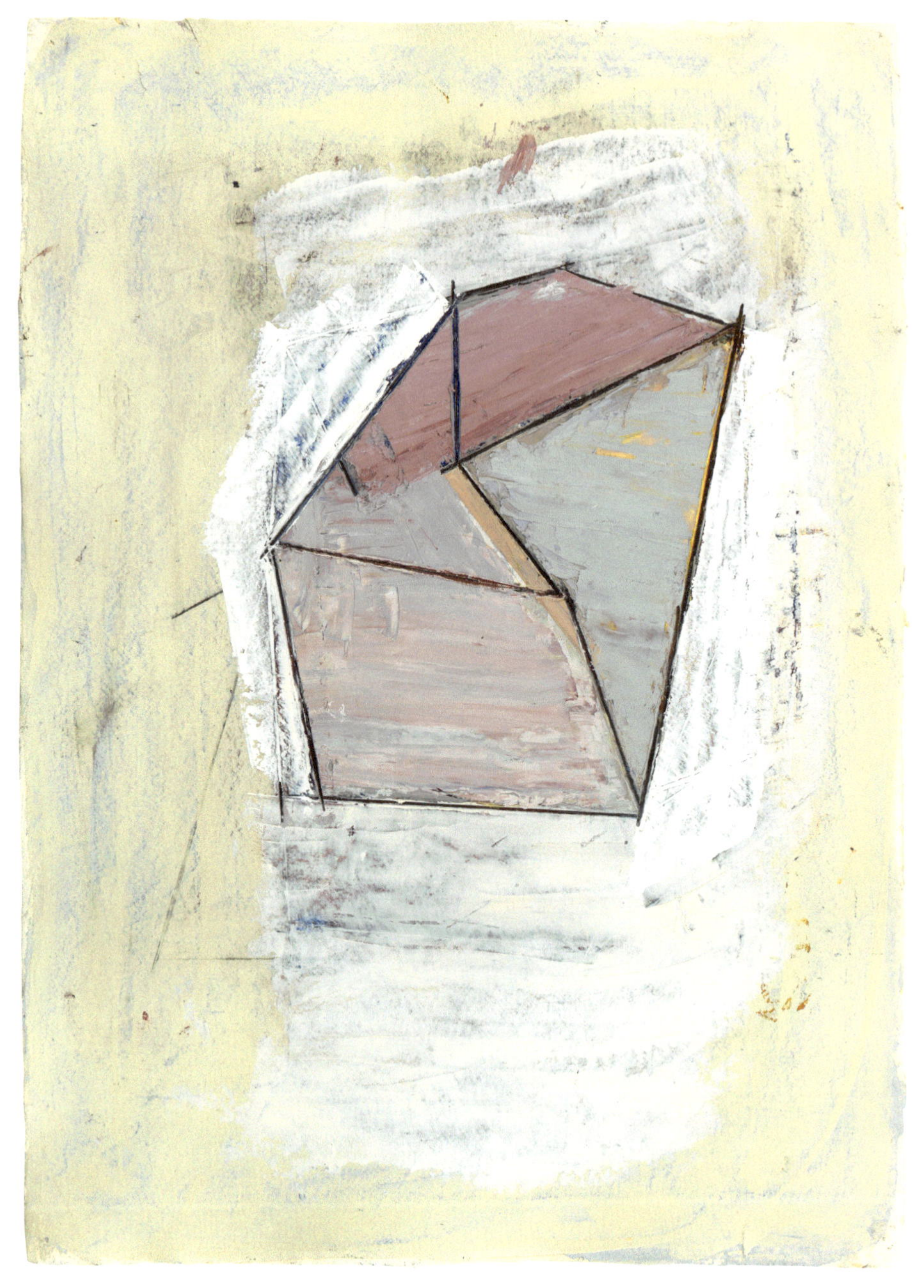

56

Al Dente, 1976

Oil and wax on paper
30 × 22 inches

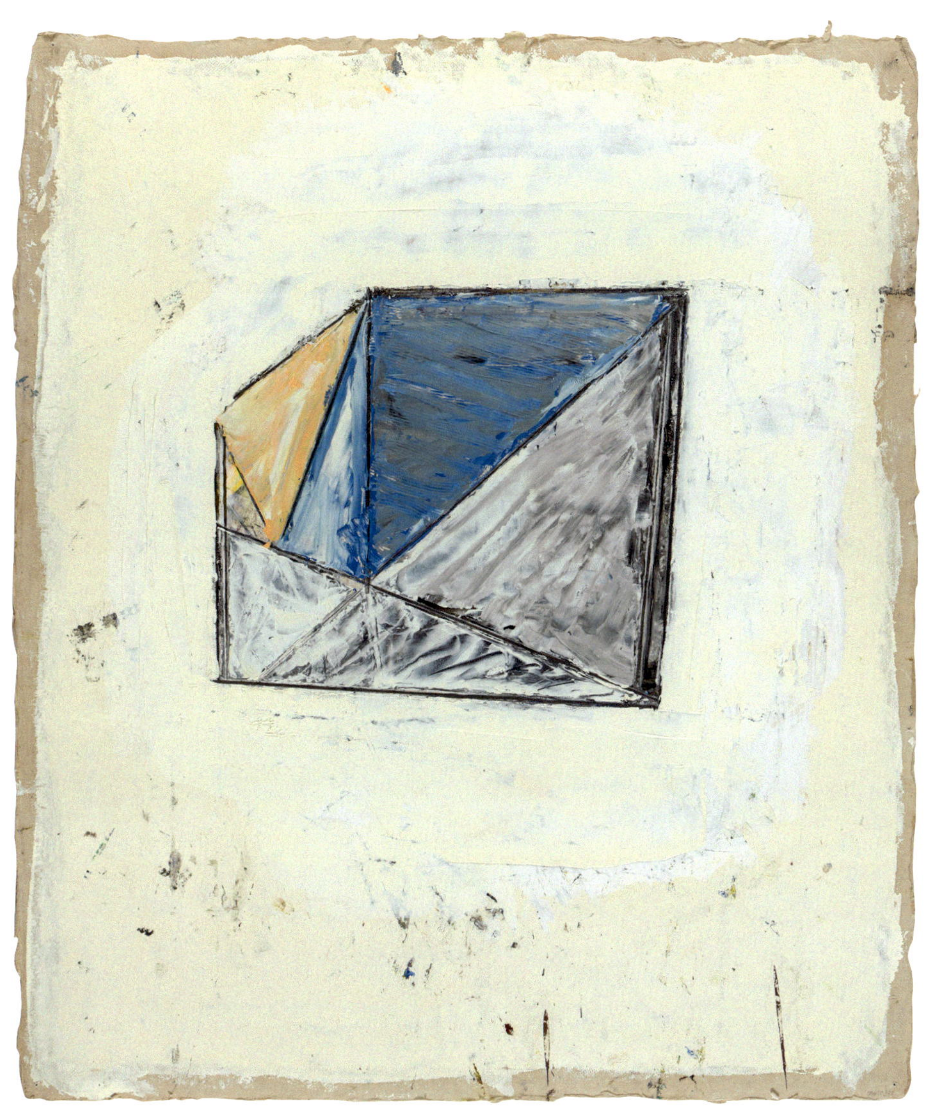

57

Flat Fold, 1976

Oil and wax on paper

28½ × 24½ inches, two sided

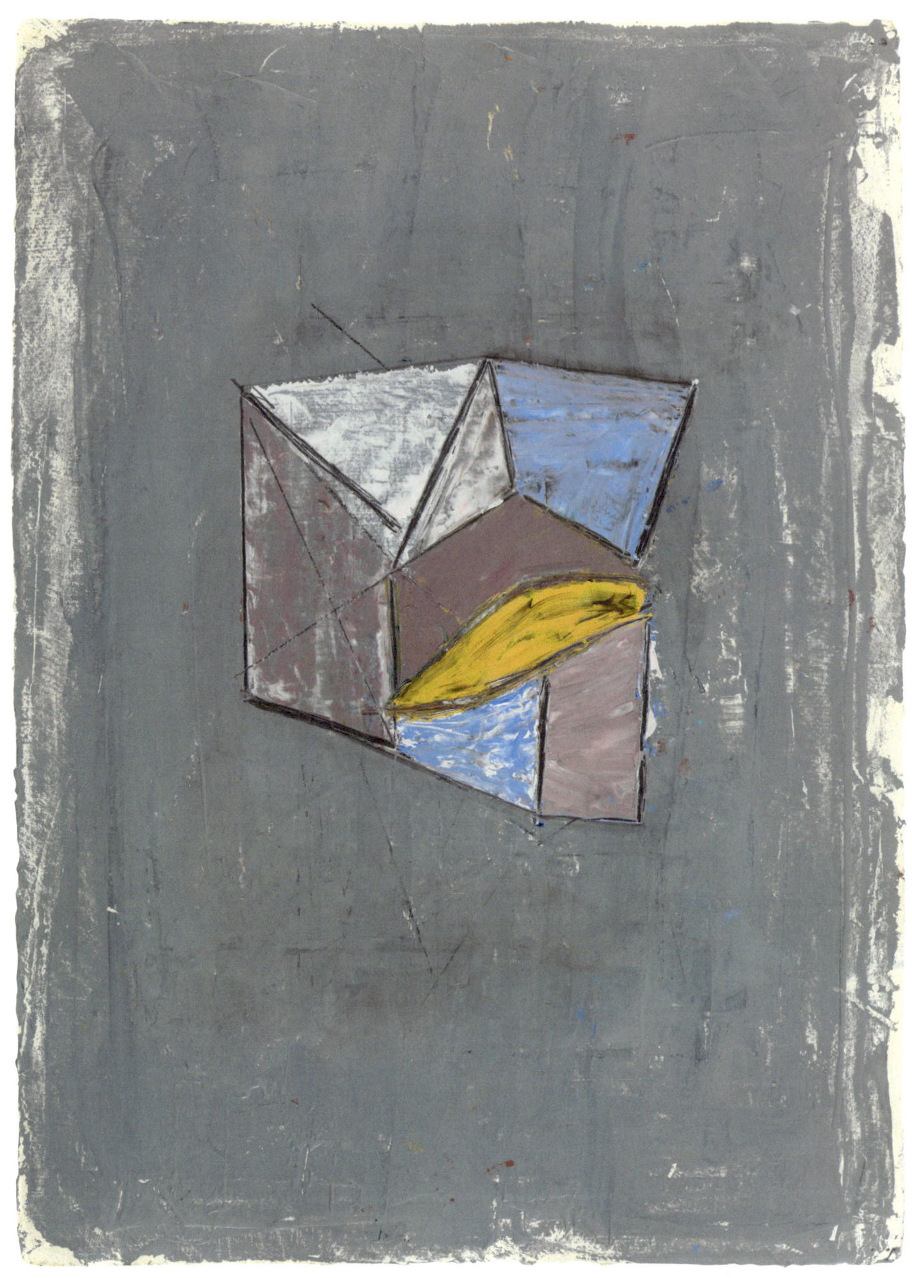

58

Interloper, 1976

Oil and wax on paper
30½ × 22½ inches

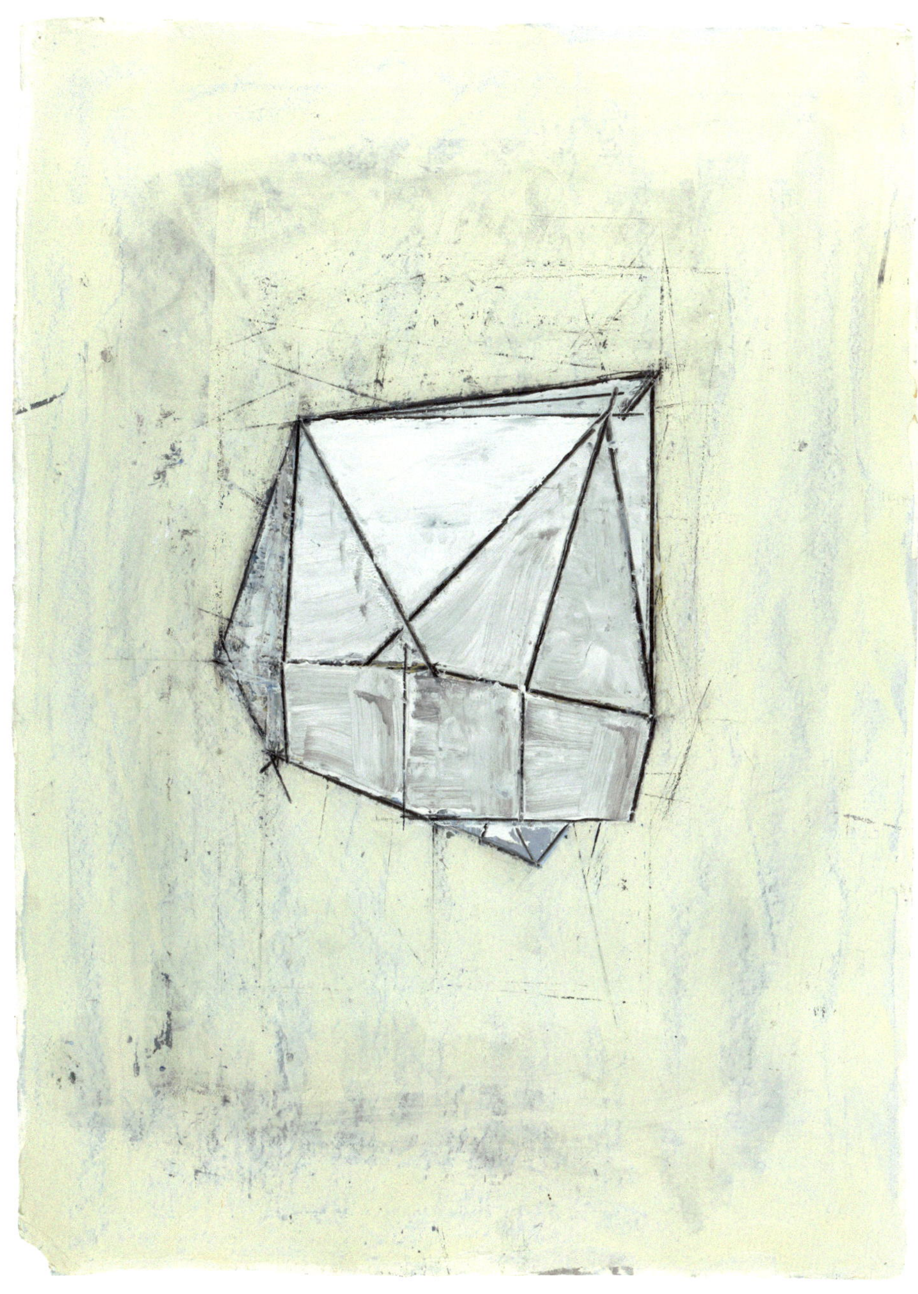

59

My Pigeon, 1976

Oil and wax on paper

30½ × 22½ inches

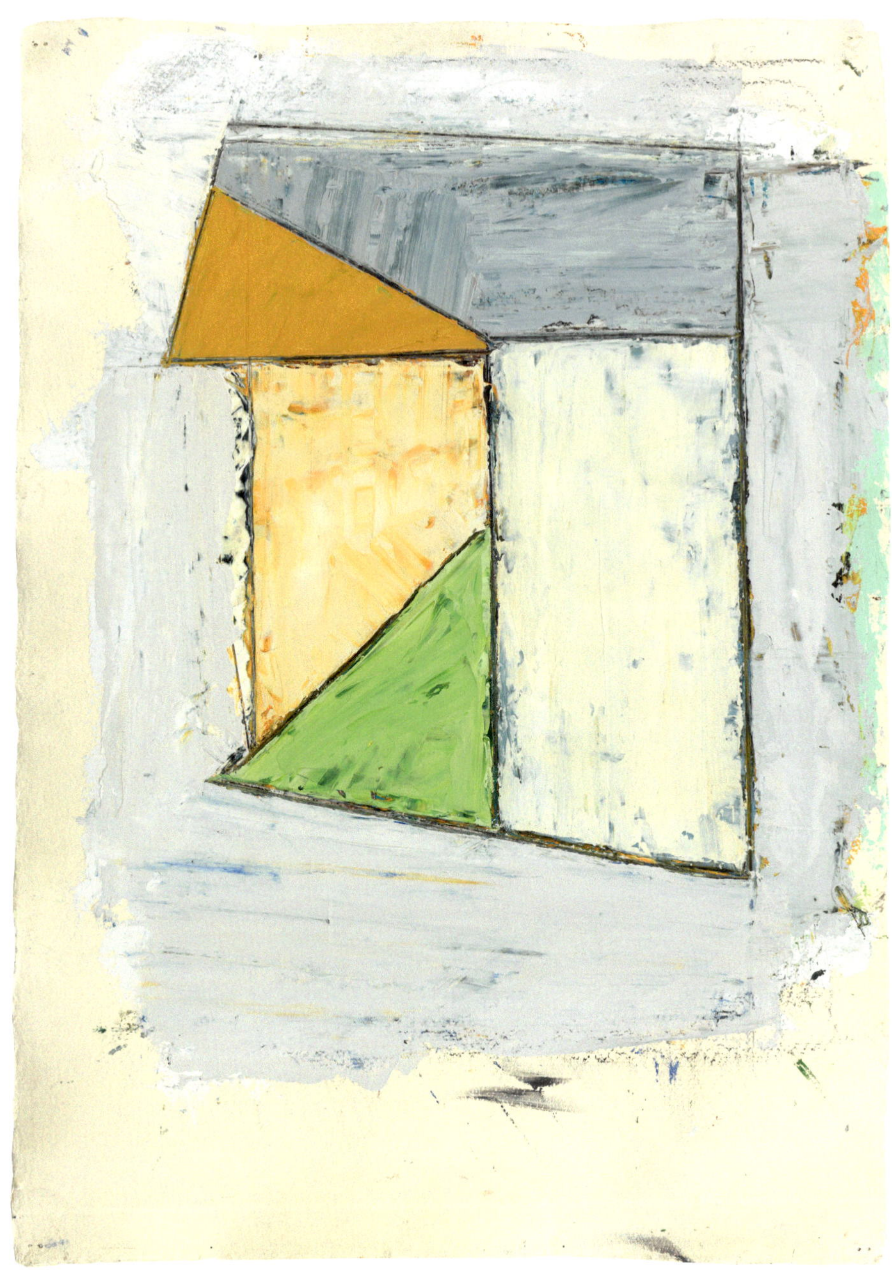

60

Simple Manners, 1976

Oil and wax on paper
31 × 22½ inches

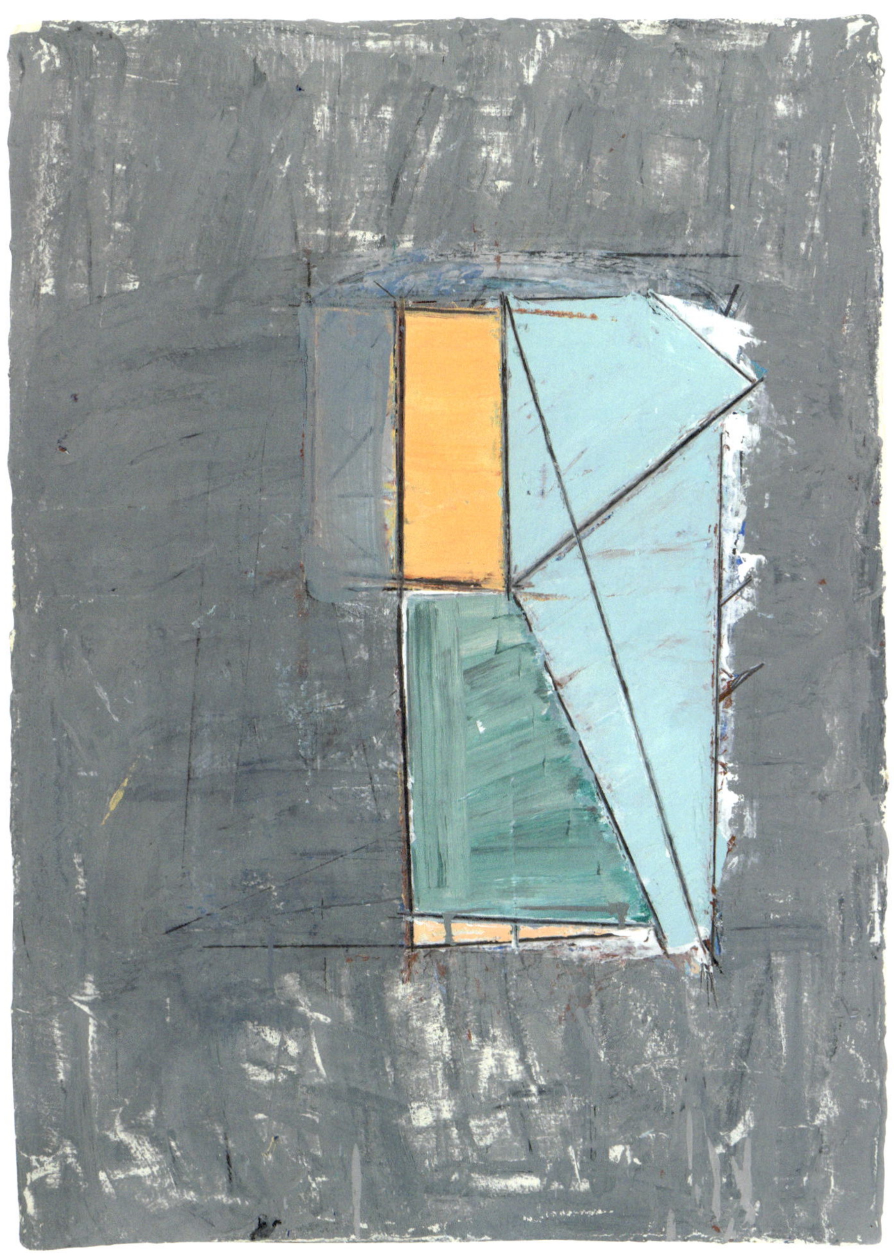

61

To the Right, 1976

Oil and wax on paper
30½ × 22½ inches

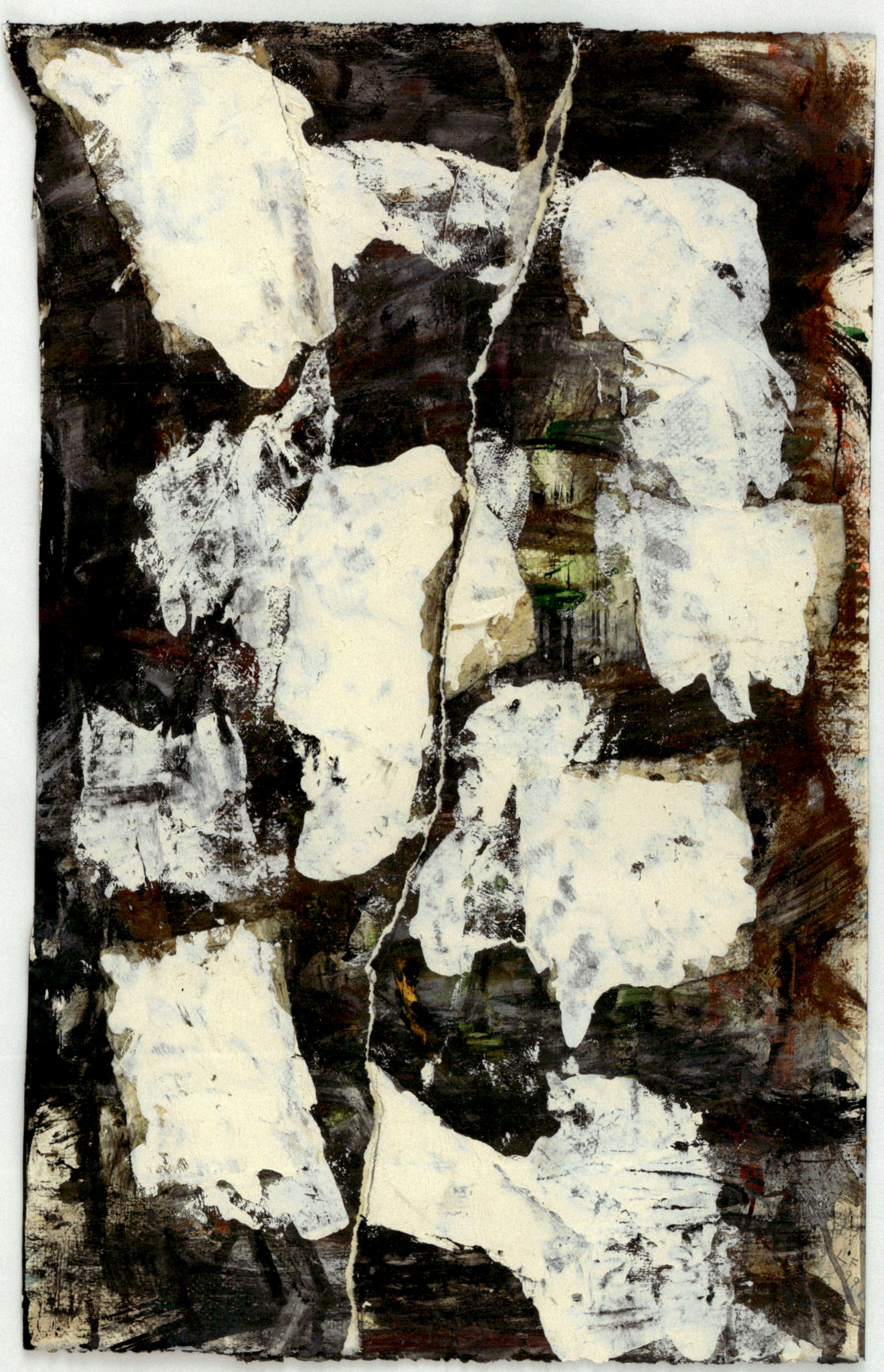

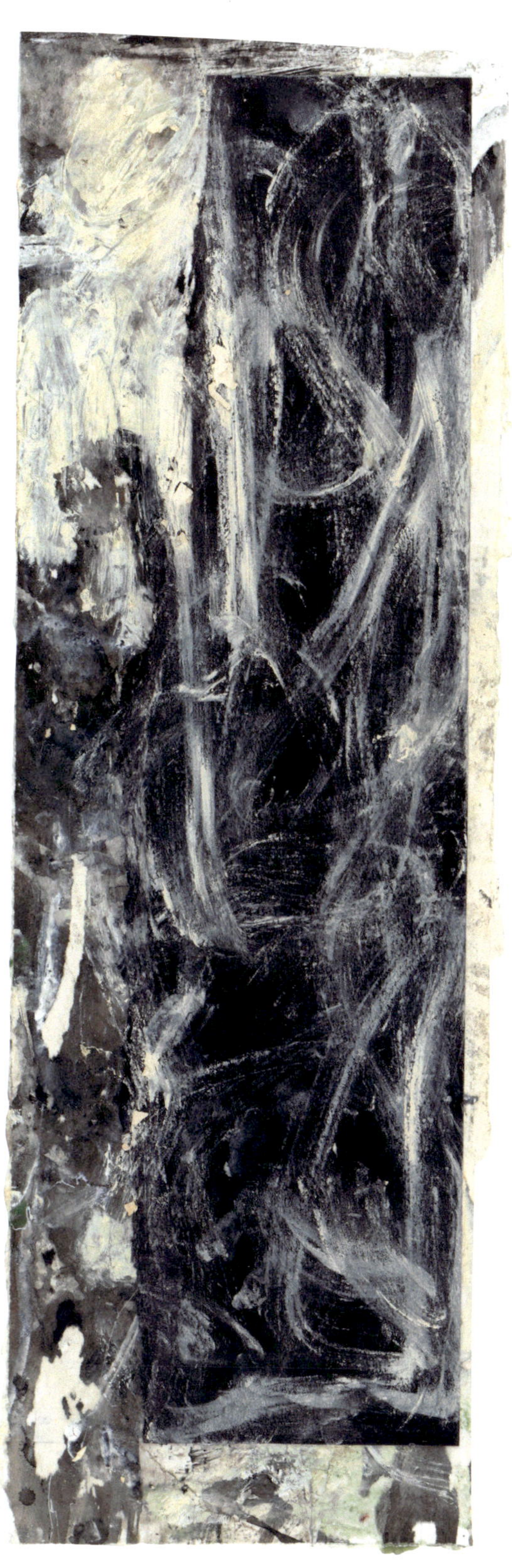

62

Untitled, 1999

Acrylic, ink, and glue on paper
26 × 17 inches

63

Untitled, 1999

Acrylic on paper
22 × 7¼ inches

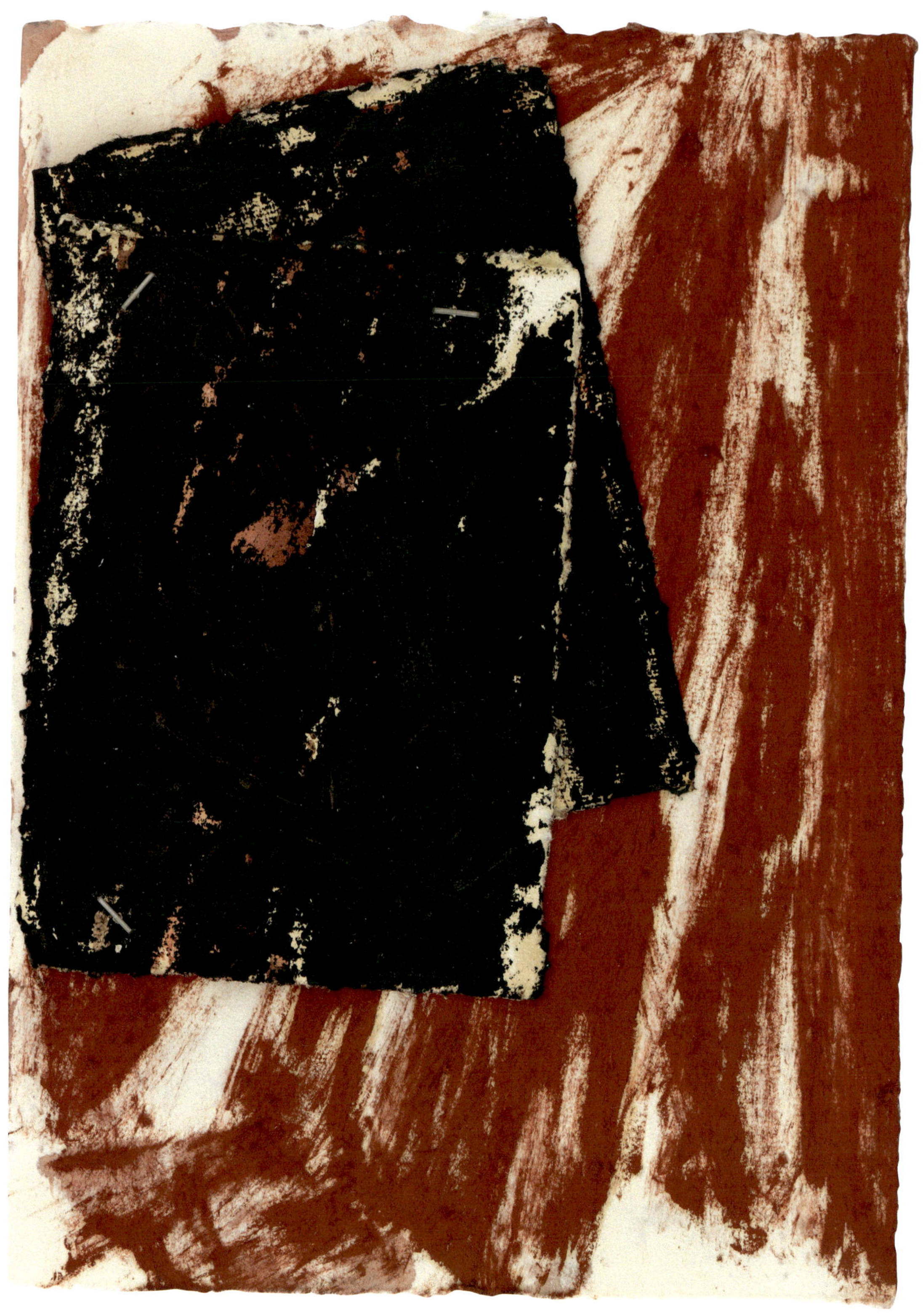

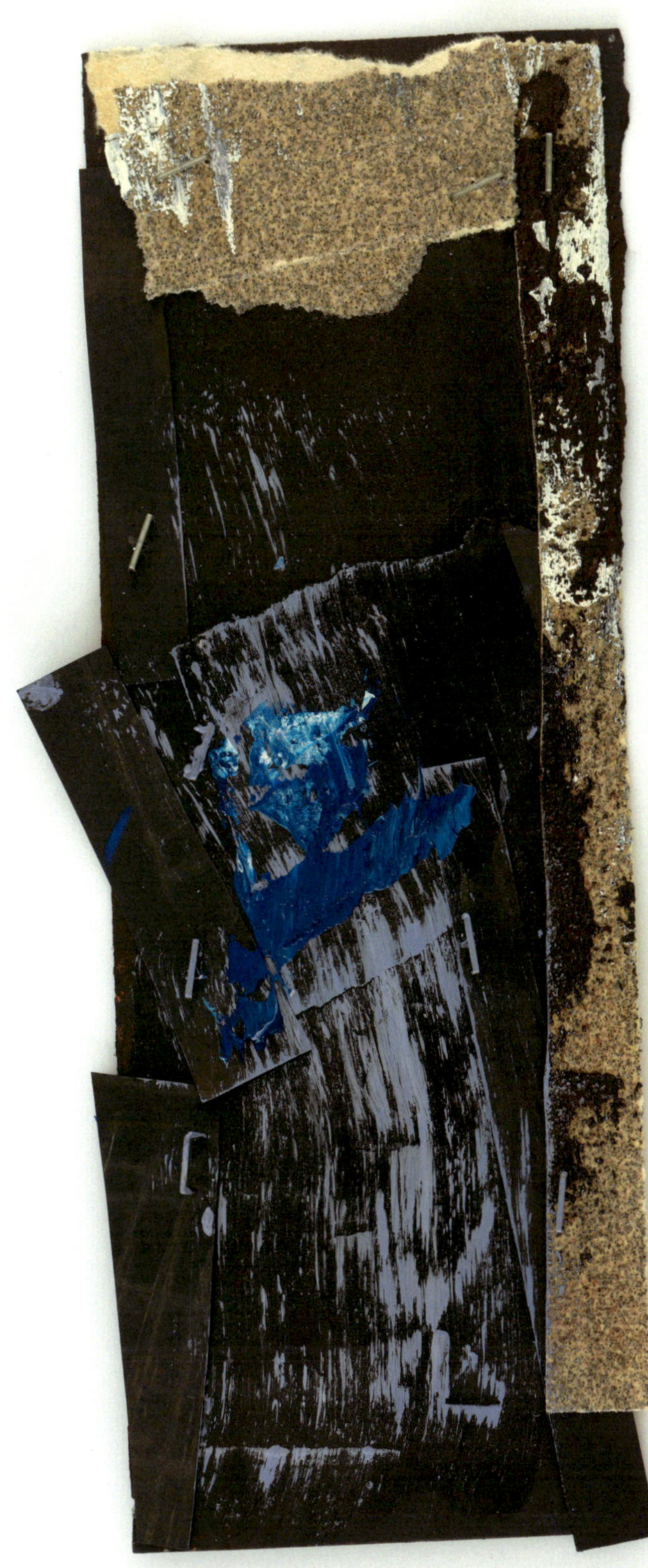

64

Untitled, 2000

Oil, conté crayon, and staples on paper
12⅝ × 9⅛ inches

65

Untitled, 2000

Sandpaper, staples, and oil on construction paper
12⅝ × 5¼ inches

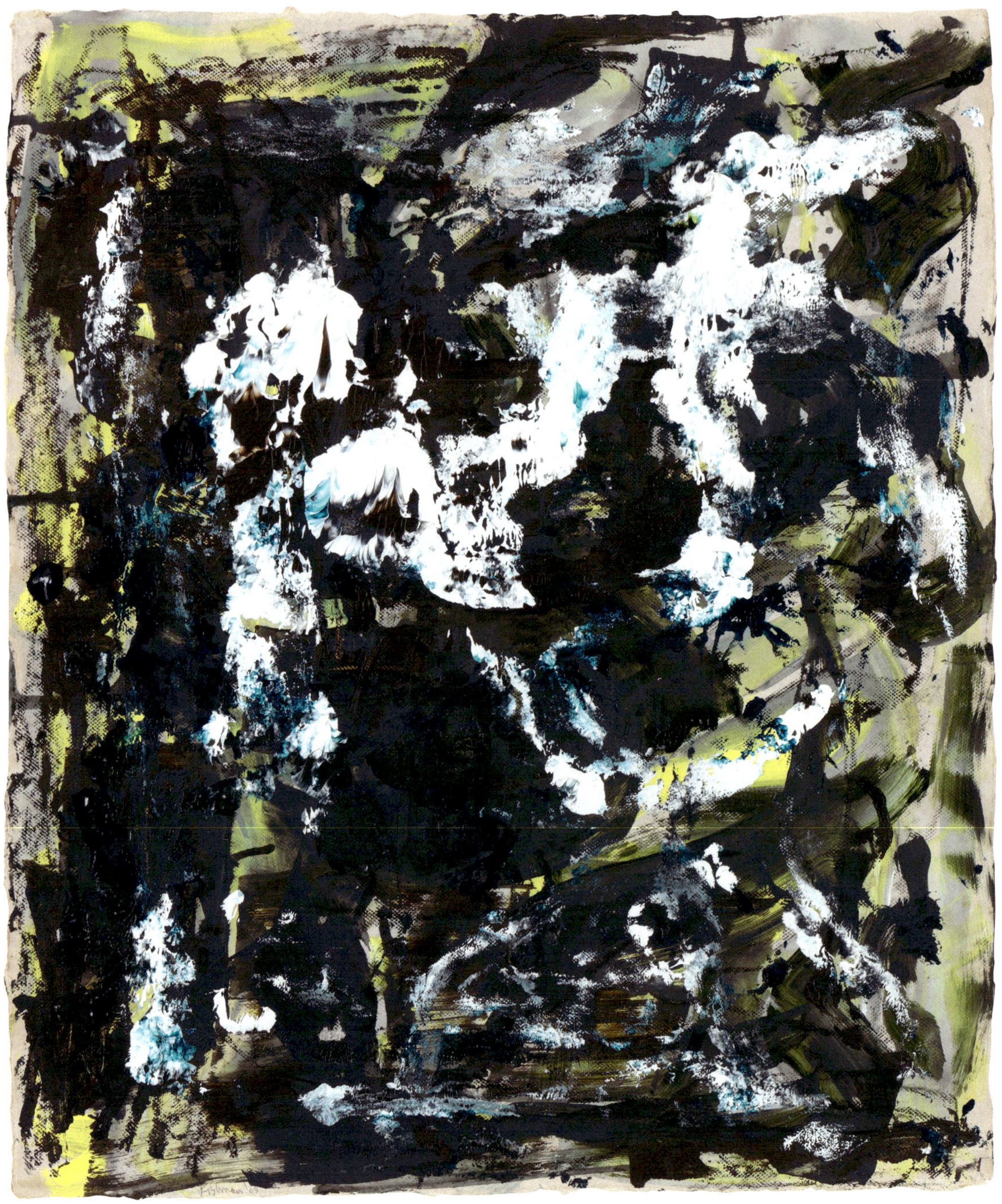

66

Untitled, 2008

Acrylic on paper
28 × 24 inches

Checklist of the Exhibition

Unless otherwise noted, all works are in the collection of the artist. Reference numbers beginning with FS or CM refer to a work's inventory number in the artist's catalog.

1. *Black Architecture*, 1964
Lithograph, edition 8/8
22¼ × 17¼ inches
FS.39267
FIG. 4.6

2. *Untitled*, 1971
Vellum, tracing paper, tape, plastic, canvas, and acrylic
12 × 18 inches (framed)
FS.2027

3. *Untitled*, 1971
Acrylic, chalk, graphite, and thread on canvas
19 × 5¼ inches
FS.16514
FIG. 2.2

4. *Untitled*, 1971
Acrylic on canvas with chalk and string
43¾ × 10¾ inches
Courtesy of Bianca Lanza

5. No title (Dots), 1972
Graphite on paper
11 × 8½ inches
CM#11280
FIG. 4.2

6. No title (Dots and circles), 1972
Graphite on paper
11 × 8½ inches
CM#11279
FIG. 4.1

7. *Angry Joan*, 1973
Acrylic on paper
26 × 40 inches (framed)
FS.11056
PLATE 24

8. *Angry Louise*, 1973
Acrylic on paper
26 × 40 inches (framed)
FS.11043
PLATE 25

9. *Angry Marilyn*, 1973
Acrylic on paper
26 × 40 inches (framed)
FS.11045
PLATE 23

10. *Angry Paula*, 1973
Acrylic on paper
26 × 40 inches (framed)
FS.11039
PLATE 26

11. *Angry Yvonne*, 1973
Acrylic on paper
26 × 40 inches (framed)
FS.11049
PLATE 27

12. No title (This is working class Jewish lesbian art. In case you didn't already know), 1973
Graphite on paper
24 × 18 inches
CM#11278
FIG. 2.1

13. *Leftover Colors*, 1974
Acrylic on paper
18¾ × 20 inches each
"Simple Idea," CM#09960; "New Idea," CM#09968; "Thinking about the Edge of the Circle," CM#09969; "Thinking about Soutine at Barnes," CM#09879; "To Please Jenny and Jeff," CM#09973; "Pencil over 2 Colors," CM#09975; "Pencil from Previous Drawing Thinking about

the Audience," CM#09977; "Painting Turns to Journal," CM#09981
FIG. 1.7

14. *Untitled*, 1974
Oil, wax, staples, and collage on paper
33 × 23 inches
FS.38620
PLATE 52

15. *Untitled*, 1974
Oil on paper
28⅞ × 20 inches
FS.38632
PLATE 53

16. *Dutch Blue*, 1975
Oil and wax on paper
29 × 24¾ inches (framed)
FS.38421

17. *Goodbye Bertha*, 1975
Oil on paper
48 × 30 inches
CM#11286

18. *Untitled*, 1975
Oil on paper
31⅛ × 23 inches
FS.38633
PLATE 55

19. *Untitled*, 1975
Oil on paper
31⅛ × 22⅞ inches
FS.38634
PLATE 10

20. *Untitled*, 1975
Oil and pencil on paper
34½ × 22¾ inches
FS.38510

21. *Untitled*, 1975
Oil on paper
30¼ × 22⅞ inches
FS.38631
PLATE 54

22. *Al Dente*, 1976
Oil and wax on paper
30 × 22 inches
FS.38423
PLATE 56

23. *Flat Fold*, 1976
Oil and wax on paper
28½ × 24½ inches, two sided
FS.38615
PLATE 57

24. *Interloper*, 1976
Oil and wax on paper
30½ × 22½ inches
FS.38424
PLATE 58

25. *My Pigeon*, 1976
Oil and wax on paper
30½ × 22½ inches
FS.38616
PLATE 59

26. *Simple Manners*, 1976
Oil and wax on paper
31 × 22½ inches
FS.38422
PLATE 60

27. *Square Meal*, 1976
Oil and wax on paper
30½ × 22½ inches
FS.38425

28. *To the Right*, 1976
Oil and wax on paper
30½ × 22½ inches
FS.38426
PLATE 61

29. *It's Good to Have Limits*, 1977
Oil and wax on paper
31 × 23 inches
JP Morgan Chase Art Collection

30. Lyn Blumenthal and Kate Horsfield
Louise Fishman: An Interview, 1977
½-inch open-reel video, sound (black & white, mono, 4:3)
55:13 minutes
Courtesy of Video Data Bank
FIG. 1.6

31. *Untitled*, 1980
Charcoal on paper
25¼ × 19 inches
FS.38505
PLATE 38

32. No title (Self-portrait), 1981
Graphite on paper
16¼ × 13 inches
CM#10662
FIG. 3.4

33. *Untitled*, 1981
Charcoal on paper
11½ × 15 inches
LF#32

34. *Untitled*, 1982
Charcoal on paper
30 × 22 inches
FS.38506
PLATE 39

35. *Untitled*, 1983
Charcoal, conté crayon, and graphite on paper
16⅞ × 13⅞ inches
FS.38663

36. *Untitled*, 1983
Charcoal on paper
30 × 22¾ inches
FS.38772

37. *Untitled*, 1984
Charcoal on paper
20 × 26 inches (framed)
CM#0234

38. *Untitled*, 1984
Charcoal and chalk on paper
19 × 12 inches
FS.38504
PLATE 42

39. *Untitled*, 1984
Charcoal on paper
30 × 22⅜ inches
FS.38769
PLATE 40

40. *Untitled*, 1985
Oil and charcoal on paper
49 × 38 inches, two sided
FS.38435
PLATE 67

41. *Untitled*, 1985
Graphite, charcoal, and pastel on paper
23¾ × 19 inches
FS.38494
PLATE 11

42. *Untitled*, 1985
Oil and charcoal on paper
34 × 22 inches
FS.38509
PLATE 41

43. *Untitled*, 1985
Charcoal on paper
22½ × 30¼ inches (framed)
CM#06134

44. No title (Knots), 1986
Graphite on paper
13⅞ × 17 inches
CM#10663
FIG. 2.4

45. No title (Knots), 1986
Graphite on paper
13¾ × 16¾ inches
CM#10664
FIG. 2.5

46. No title (What is the relationship of the structure to the paint?), 1989, from *Journal*, 1986–89
Graphite and ink on paper
12⅝ × 9$^{11}/_{16}$ inches
CM#11284
FIG. 4.4

47. *Untitled*, 1990
Oil on paper
31 × 22¾ inches
FS.34828
PLATE 15

48. *Pin Up*, 1991
Graphite on paper
5½ × 7½ inches, two sided
FS.39268
PLATE 3

49. *Untitled*, 1991
Watercolor, charcoal, and graphite on paper
8 × 10⅜ inches
FS.39269
PLATE 1

50. *Book I*, 1992
Gouache and pencil on paper; Japanese leporello binding
4⅞ × 3⅝ × 1¼ inches (closed)
FS.35384
PLATE 13

51. *A Grogger for Eva and Agnes*, 1992
Watercolor and graphite on paper
10 × 10 inches
The Jewish Museum, Gift of the artist, 1992-32
FIG. 1.1

52. *Grogger from Mesa Verde*, 1992
Watercolor and graphite on paper
5½ × 5½ inches
The Jewish Museum, Gift of the artist, 1992-58
FIG. 1.5

53. *Untitled*, 1992
Graphite and ink on paper
5⅜ × 7⅛ inches
FS.39303

54. *Untitled*, 1992
Charcoal and oil on tracing paper
20½ × 18½ inches
FS.38464
PLATE 12

55. *Untitled*, 1992
Ink and acrylic on paper
52¾ × 42¼ inches
FS.38436
PLATE 28

56. *Book of Abuse*, 1993–94
Acrylic, oil, oil stick, graphite, staples, and wire with aluminum and paper collage on paper; Japanese leporello binding
6⅜ × 3⅝ × 1⅝ inches (closed)
FS.35386
PLATE 14

57. *Untitled*, 1993
Charcoal and sumi ink on paper
24 × 19 inches, two sided
FS.38472
PLATE 6

58. *Down and Dirty (A Book for Bertha Harris)*, 1994
Oil, gouache, graphite, staples, and paper collage on paper; Japanese leporello binding
4⅞ × 3⅝ × 2 inches (closed)
FS.35378
PLATE 29

59. No title (Red notebook [horse]), July 25, 1994–January 1997
Sumi ink
6¼ × 4⅝ × ¾ inches (closed)
CM#10386

60. *Untitled*, 1994
Ink on cotton fabric
26 × 15 inches
FS.38630
PLATE 7

61. *Blonde Ambition*, 1995
Oil on linen
90 × 65 inches
Krannert Art Museum, Museum Purchase through the John N. Chester Fund and the Richard M. and Rosann Gelvin Noel Fund, 2019-1-1
PLATE 17

62. *Knots and Burls*, 1995
Intaglio, proof A3
20¼ × 20 inches
CM#11277

63. No title (Wood veneer monoprint), 1995
Ink on paper
12½ × 12¾ inches
FS.38621

64. *Untitled*, 1995
Watercolor, ink, and collage on paper
9⅜ × 6¼ inches, two sided
FS.39275

65. *Untitled*, 1995
Ink on paper
6¼ × 9⅜ inches
FS.39274

66. *Untitled*, 1995
Watercolor and ink on paper
9⅜ × 6⅜ inches
FS.39272
PLATE 16

67. *Untitled*, 1995
Ink on paper
14½ × 13¼ inches
FS.38627
PLATE 43

68. *Untitled*, 1995
Ink on paper
18½ × 22⅞ inches
FS.38629

69. *Untitled*, 1995
Ink on paper
30 × 22¼ inches
FS.38623
PLATE 44

70. *Untitled*, 1997
Oil and ink on paper
30 × 18 inches (framed)
FS.34829
PLATE 18

71. *Untitled*, 1998
Sumi ink on paper
17¾ × 13½ inches
FS.38586

72. *Untitled*, 1999
Acrylic on paper
22 × 7¼ inches
FS.38646
PLATE 63

73. *Untitled*, 1999
Acrylic on paper
22½ × 15⅞ inches
FS.38767

74. *Untitled*, 1999
Acrylic, ink, and glue on paper
26 × 17 inches
FS.38640
PLATE 62

75. *Untitled*, 2000
Sandpaper, staples, and oil on construction paper
12⅝ × 5¼ inches
FS.39280
PLATE 65

76. *Untitled*, 2000
Oil, conté crayon, and staples on paper
12⅝ × 9⅛ inches
FS.39279
PLATE 64

77. *Untitled*, 2000
Ink on paper
19 × 26⅛ inches
FS.4772

78. *Untitled*, 2001
Charcoal and gouache on paper
30⅞ × 22⅞ inches
FS.39116
PLATE 33

79. *Untitled*, 2001
Oil on paper
30 × 22¼ inches
Weatherspoon Art Museum, University of North Carolina at Greensboro, Museum purchase with funds from the Lynn Richardson Prickett Acquisition Endowment and the Weatherspoon Guild Acquisition Endowment, 2017

80. *Untitled*, 2001
Acrylic on paper
26¼ × 19 inches
FS.39122

81. *Untitled*, 2001
Acrylic and charcoal on paper
30⅛ × 22¼ inches
FS.39119
PLATE 32

82. *Untitled*, 2001
Acrylic on paper
27⅝ × 19¾ inches
FS.39127
PLATE 34

83. *Untitled*, 2001
Acrylic and watercolor on paper
30 × 22¼ inches
FS.39120

84. *Untitled*, 2001
Acrylic on paper
30 × 22¼ inches
FS.39130
PLATE 8

85. *Untitled*, 2001
Oil and oil stick on paper
20¾ × 29¾ inches
FS.39128
PLATE 69

86. *Untitled*, 2001
Ink on paper
22⅞ × 18⅞ inches
FS.39133
PLATE 45

87. *Untitled*, 2001
Oil on paper
30 × 22¼ inches
FS.39125
PLATE 31

88. *Untitled*, 2004
Sumi ink on paper
22 × 30 inches
FS.38479

89. *Untitled*, 2004
Sumi ink on paper
22 × 30 inches
FS.38482

90. *Untitled*, 2004
Sumi ink on paper
22 × 30 inches
FS.38485
PLATE 35

91. *Untitled*, 2004
Sumi ink on paper
22 × 30 inches
FS.38486

92. *Untitled*, 2005
Acrylic on paper
30⅜ × 38 inches
FS.11801

93. *Untitled*, 2005
Acrylic on paper
30⅜ × 38 inches
FS.11803

94. *Gertie and Louise*, 2005
Monotype on collagraph plate on paper
15 × 17 inches (framed)
FS.31105

95. *Gertie and Louise*, 2005
Monotype on collagraph plate on paper
15 × 19¾ inches (framed)
FS.31106

96. *Untitled*, 2007
Acrylic on paper
30 × 22 inches
FS.39291

97. *Untitled*, 2007
Acrylic on paper
23 × 35 inches
FS.39290
PLATE 49

98. *Untitled*, 2007
Acrylic on paper
23 × 35 inches
FS.39289

99. *Untitled*, 2007
Acrylic on paper
23 × 35 inches
FS.39299
PLATE 50

100. *Untitled*, 2007
Acrylic on paper
34 × 23 inches
FS.39287
PLATE 48

101. *Untitled*, 2007
Acrylic on paper
30 × 22 inches
FS.39286
PLATE 47

102. *Untitled*, 2008
Acrylic on rice paper
16¾ × 12½ inches (framed)
FS.15316

103. *Untitled*, 2008
Acrylic on paper
28 × 24 inches
FS.39301
PLATE 66

104. *Untitled*, 2008
Acrylic on paper
30 × 22 inches
FS.39302
PLATE 46

105. *Untitled* (Cartiera Magnani notebook), 2011
Watercolor on paper
12 × 12 × 3/4 inches (closed)
CM#10271

106. *Untitled*, 2012
Oil on tracing paper
41 7/8 × 49 1/2 inches
FS.38437
PLATE 5

107. *Ingrid*, 2013
Watercolor and hair on paper; leporello binding
5 1/2 × 3 3/4 × 3/4 inches (closed)
FS.38438
PLATE 30

108. *Untitled*, 2013
Tempera, ink, and watercolor on paper
24 × 18 inches
FS.38061
PLATE 9

109. *Untitled*, 2013
Watercolor and pencil on paper
7 1/16 × 6 3/4 inches
Courtesy of Beth Rudin DeWoody

110. *Bel Canto*, 2014
Oil on linen
74 × 88 inches
FS.33555
FIG. 1.4

111. *Drawing*, 2015
Oil on linen
50 × 50 3/4 inches
FS.36129
PLATE 51

112. *Untitled*, 2016
Acrylic on paper
18 × 24 inches
FS.38071
PLATE 36

113. *Untitled*, 2016
Watercolor on paper
12 5/8 × 17 5/8 inches
FS.38079
PLATE 22

114. *Untitled*, 2016
Watercolor on paper
15 1/2 × 11 1/4 inches
FS.38077
PLATE 21

115. *Untitled*, 2016
Watercolor and ink on paper
8 1/4 × 5 3/4 inches
FS.38112

116. *Vaporetto Leporello No. 1*, 2016
Watercolor and tempera on paper; leporello binding
8 1/4 × 5 × 3/4 inches (closed)
CM#10833
PLATE 19

117. *Vaporetto Leporello No. 2*, 2016
Watercolor and tempera on paper; leporello binding
5 × 8 1/4 × 3/4 inches (closed)
CM#10834
PLATE 2

118. *Vaporetto Leporello No. 3*, 2016
Watercolor and tempera on paper; leporello binding
8 1/4 × 5 × 3/4 inches (closed)
CM#10835
PLATE 20

119. *Vaporetto Leporello No. 4*, 2017
Watercolor and tempera on paper; leporello binding
8 1/4 × 5 × 3/4 inches (closed)
CM#10836
PLATE 4

120. *Vaporetto Leporello No. 5*, 2017
Watercolor and tempera on paper; leporello binding
5 1/2 × 3 1/2 × 3/4 inches (closed)
CM#10837
PLATE 37

121. *Vaporetto Leporello No. 6*, 2017
Watercolor and tempera on paper; leporello binding
5 1/2 × 3 1/2 × 3/4 inches (closed)
CM#10838
FIG. 4.5

122. *Vaporetto Leporello No. 7*, 2017
Watercolor and tempera on paper; leporello binding
5 1/2 × 3 1/2 × 3/4 inches (closed)
CM#10839
PLATE 68

123. *Untitled*, 2018
Oil on paper
30 1/4 × 22 1/2 inches
CM#11271

124. No title (Notebook), undated
Notebook
8 1/2 × 10 1/4 × 1/2 inches (closed)
CM#11283

Selected Works on Paper Exhibition History and Bibliography

This selected exhibition history and bibliography focuses on Louise Fishman's works on paper, noting the inclusion of specific works from *A Question of Emphasis*, where known.

Solo Exhibitions

2020
Louise Fishman: Ballin' the Jack, KARMA, New York

2019
Cut Pieced Painted Stapled: Sculptural Paintings from the '70s, Frameless Gallery at Frieze New York

Louise Fishman: My City, Locks Gallery, Philadelphia

2017
Louise Fishman, Cheim & Read, New York
CAT. 115

2016
Louise Fishman: A Retrospective, Neuberger Museum of Art, Purchase College, State University of New York, Purchase. Traveled to Weatherspoon Art Museum, University of North Carolina, Greensboro
CATS. 8–10, 47, 61, 70, 79

Paper Louise Tiny Fishman Rock, Institute of Contemporary Art, University of Pennsylvania, Philadelphia
CATS. 50, 56, 58

2015
Louise Fishman, Cheim & Read, New York
CATS. 109, 110

2014
Louise Fishman: Venice Watercolours, 2011–2013, Frameless Gallery and Gallery Nosco, London

2013
Louise Fishman: It's Here-Elsewhere, Goya Contemporary Gallery, Baltimore

2012
Louise Fishman: Paintings, Drawings and Prints, John Davis Gallery, Hudson, New York

Louise Fishman: Five Decades, Jack Tilton Gallery, New York
CATS. 4, 8–11, 61

2010
Louise Fishman, Gallery Paule Anglim, San Francisco

2007
Louise Fishman, the Tenacity of Painting: Paintings from 1970 to 2005, Hood Museum of Art, Dartmouth College, Hanover, New Hampshire
CAT. 61

2004
Louise Fishman: Recent Work, Manny Silverman Gallery, Los Angeles

2003
Louise Fishman, Cheim & Read, New York

2002
Louise Fishman, Manny Silverman Gallery, Los Angeles

1996
Louise Fishman: Recent Paintings, Robert Miller Gallery, New York
CAT. 61

1992
Louise Fishman: Drawings and Experimental Work, 1971–1992, Tyler Galleries, Tyler School of Art, Temple University, Elkins Park, Pennsylvania
CATS. 7–11

1978
Louise Fishman, Diplomat's Lobby, United States Department of State, Washington, DC

1977
Louise Fishman, Nancy Hoffman Gallery, New York
CAT. 29

Group Exhibitions

2019
Art after Stonewall, 1969–1989, Columbus Museum of Art. Traveled to Grey Art Gallery and Leslie-Lohman Museum, New York; and the Patricia and Phillip Frost Art Museum, Miami
CAT. 8

2018
Carry the Bend, Brennan & Griffin, New York

The Humble Black Line, Frameless Gallery, London

2017
Black on White / Black on Bone, Weber Fine Art, Greenwich, Connecticut

2016
#Pussypower, David & Schweitzer Contemporary, Brooklyn

Leporelli Veneziani, Archivio Emily Harvey Foundation, Venice, Italy

2015
Painting 2.0: Expression in the Information Age, Museum Brandhorst, Munich. Traveled to the Museum Moderner Kunst Stiftung Ludwig Wien, Vienna
CATS. 7, 11

2012
Generations: Louise Fishman, Gertrude Fisher-Fishman, and Razel Kapustin, Woodmere Art Museum, Philadelphia
CATS. 94, 95

2011
Dance/Draw, Institute of Contemporary Art, Boston. Traveled to Grey Art Gallery, New York University, New York; and the Frances Young Tang Teaching Museum and Art Gallery, Skidmore College, Saratoga Springs, New York

Seeing Gertrude Stein: Five Stories, Contemporary Jewish Museum, San Francisco. Traveled to the National Portrait Gallery, Washington, DC

The Women in Our Life: A Fifteen-Year Anniversary Exhibition, Cheim & Read, New York

2009
Propose: Works on Paper from the 1970s, Alexander Gray Associates, New York
CAT. 2

2007
WACK! Art and the Feminist Revolution, Museum of Contemporary Art, Los Angeles. Traveled to the National Museum of Women in the Arts, Washington, DC; MoMA P.S.1, Long Island City, New York; and Vancouver Art Gallery, Vancouver, Canada
CATS. 7–11

2006
High Times, Hard Times: New York Painting 1967–1975, organized by Independent Curators International, New York. Circulated to Weatherspoon Art Museum, University of North Carolina at Greensboro; American University Museum at the Katzen Arts Center, Washington, DC; National Academy Museum, New York; Museo Tamayo Arte Contemporaneo, Mexico City; Neue Galerie Graz, Austria; and ZKM Center for Art and Media Karlsruhe, Germany

2005
Looking at Words: The Formal Presence of Text in Modern and Contemporary Works on Paper, Andrea Rosen Gallery, New York

2004
Drawing Exhibition, Galerie S 65, Cologne, Germany

2002
Personal and Political: The Women's Art Movement, 1969–1975, Guild Hall Museum, East Hampton, New York

1999
Drawing in the Present Tense, Parsons, the New School for Design, New York

1996
Women's Work, Greene Naftali, New York
CAT. 61

1994
Abstract Works on Paper, Robert Miller Gallery, New York

1993
30th Anniversary Exhibition of Drawings, to Benefit the Foundation for Contemporary Performance Arts, Inc., Castelli Gallery, New York

The Linear Image II, Marisa del Re Gallery, New York

Drawing the Line against AIDS, under the aegis of the 45th Venice Biennale, Peggy Guggenheim Collection, Venice, Italy. Reinstalled at the Guggenheim Museum, New York

1992
The Jewish Museum's Masked Ball in Celebration of Purim, The Jewish Museum, New York
CATS. 51, 52

1989
A Decade of American Drawing 1980–1989, Daniel Weinberg Gallery, Los Angeles

Works on Paper, Lennon, Weinberg, Inc., New York

1986
Spirit Tracks — Big Abstract Drawings, Pratt Manhattan Center Gallery, New York, and Pratt Institute Gallery, Brooklyn

1985
Drawings 1975–1985, Barbara Toll Fine Arts, New York

1984
New Prints Since 1980, Philip Johnson Center, Muhlenberg College, Allentown, Pennsylvania

Relief Prints Since 1980, Summit Art Center, Summit, New Jersey

Second Nature: Abstract Drawings and Paintings, Procter Art Center, Bard College, Annandale-on-Hudson, New York

1983
Drawing It Out, Baskerville & Watson Gallery, New York

1980
Work on Paper, Mary Boone Gallery, New York

1977
Preparatory Notes — Thinking Drawings, Part II, 80 Washington Square East Galleries, New York University, New York

1973
A Woman's Group, Nancy Hoffman Gallery, New York

1972
Open A.I.R., A.I.R. Gallery, New York

1963
National Watercolor and Drawing Exhibition, Pennsylvania Academy of the Fine Arts, Philadelphia

Selected Bibliography

Ammer, Manuela, Achim Hochdörfer, and David Joselit, eds. *Painting 2.0: Expression in the Information Age*. Exh. cat. New York: DelMonico, 2015.
CATS. 7–9, 11

Broude, Norma, and Mary D. Garrard, eds. *The Power of Feminist Art: The American Movement of the 1970s, History and Impact*. New York: H. N. Abrams, 1994.

Burk, Tara. "In Pursuit of the Unspeakable: *Heresies*' 'Lesbian Art and Artists' Issue, 1977." *Women's Studies Quarterly* 41, nos. 3/4 (Fall/Winter 2013): 63–78.
CAT. 29

Butler, Sharon L. "Art in Conversation: Louise Fishman with Sharon Butler," *The Brooklyn Rail*, October 2012, 19–21.
CATS. 116–22

Cheim, John. *Drawing the Line against AIDS*. Exh. cat. New York: AMFAR International, 1993.

Cheim & Read. *Louise Fishman*. Exh. cat. New York: Cheim & Read, 2017
CAT. 115

Cheim & Read. *Louise Fishman*. Exh. cat. New York: Cheim & Read, 2012.
CAT. 106

Cohen, Cora. "Social Volition." *Bomb* 37 (Fall 1991): 58–65.

Cotter, Holland. "Art after Stonewall: 12 Artists Interviewed." *Art in America* 82, no. 6 (June 1994): 56, 59–60.

Desmett, Don. *Louise Fishman*. Exh. cat. Elkins Park, PA: Tyler Galleries, Tyler School of Art, 1993.
CATS. 8, 10

Feinberg, Jean E. "Louise Fishman: New Paintings," *Arts Magazine* 54, nos. 1–2 (1979): 105–7.

Fishman, Louise. "Simultaneous Diaries," *Texte zur Kunst* 86 (June 2012): 165–71.

Frameless Gallery. *Cut Pieced Painted Stapled: Sculptural Paintings from the '70s*. Exh. cat. New York: Frameless Gallery, 2019.

Gallery Nosco and Frameless Gallery. *Louise Fishman: Venice Watercolours 2011–2013*. Exh. cat. London: Gallery Nosco and Frameless Gallery, 2014.

Gotthardt, Alexxa. "On Louise Fishman's Hard-Won Task: Making Feminism and Abstract Expressionism Play Nice." *Artsy*, November 9, 2015, http://www.artsy.net/article/artsy-editorial-louise-fishman-on-making-abstract-painting-a-feminist-pursuit.
CATS. 8, 9, 11, 110

Hammond, Harmony. *Lesbian Art in America: A Contemporary History*. New York: Rizzoli, 2000.

Hirsch, Faye. *Louise Fishman: The Tenacity of Painting, Paintings from 1970 to 2005*. Exh. cat. Hanover, NH: Dartmouth College, Studio Art Exhibition Program, 2007.
CATS. 9, 10, 61

Karma Gallery. *Louise Fishman*. Exh. cat. New York: Karma Books, 2020.
CATS. 7–11, 14, 15, 18, 21, 61

Lord, Catherine. "Their Memory Is Playing Tricks on Her: Notes Toward a Calligraphy of Rage." In *WACK! Art and the Feminist Revolution*. Edited by Cornelia Butler. Exh. cat. Los Angeles: Museum of Contemporary Art, and Cambridge, MA: MIT Press, 2007, 440–57.
CATS. 7–11

Lord, Catherine, and Richard Meyer. *Art and Queer Culture*. New York: Phaidon, 2013.

Molesworth, Helen, ed. *Dance/Draw*. Boston: Institute of Contemporary Art, and Osfildern, Germany: Hatje Cantz, 2011.

Moyer, Carrie. "Zero at the Bone: Louise Fishman Speaks with Carrie Moyer." *Art Journal* 71, no. 4 (Winter 2012): 36–53.

Olin Gallery. *Louise Fishman: Small Paintings*. Exh. cat. Gambier, OH: Olin Gallery Kenyon College, 1992.

"Portfolio on Work," *Heresies: A Feminist Publication on Art and Politics* 1, no. 3 (Fall 1977): 72.
CAT. 29

Posner, Helaine, ed. *Louise Fishman*. Exh. cat. Purchase, NY: Neuberger Museum of Art, and Philadelphia: Institute of Contemporary Art, 2016.
CATS. 8–10, 47, 50, 56, 58, 61, 70, 79

Seidel, Miriam. "Material Imperatives," *Art in America* 81, no. 9 (September 1993): 95–98.

Siegel, Katy, ed. *High Times, Hard Times: New York Painting 1967–1975*. Exh. cat. New York: Independent Curators International and D.A.P., 2006.

Simmons, William J. "Louise Fishman's Abstract Activism," *Interview Magazine*, May 2, 2016, http://www.interviewmagazine.com/art/louise-fishman.
CAT. 31

Suggs, Andrew. "Louise Fishman: Returning." In *Louise Fishman: My City*. Locks Gallery. Philadelphia: Locks Art Publications, 2019.
CATS. 9, 10

Taylor, Simon, and Natalie Ng, *Personal and Political: The Women's Art Movement, 1969–1975*. East Hampton, NY: Guild Hall, 2002.

Thompson, Margo Hobbs. "Agreeable Objects and Angry Paintings: Female Imagery in Art by Hannah Wilke and Louise Fishman, 1970–1973." *Genders* 43 (April 1, 2006), http://www.colorado.edu/gendersarchive1998-2013/2006/04/01/agreeable-objects-and-angry-paintings-female-imagery-art-hannah-wilke-and-louise-fishman.

Vida, Ginny, ed. *Our Right to Love: A Lesbian Resource Book*. Englewood Cliffs, NJ: Prentice-Hall, 1978.
CAT. 30

Weinberg, Jonathan, ed. *Art after Stonewall, 1969–1989*. Exh. cat. Columbus, OH: Columbus Museum of Art, and New York: Rizzoli Electa, 2019.
CAT. 8

Whitworth, Sarah. "Angry Louise Fishman (Serious)." *Amazon Quarterly* 1, no. 4 (October 1973): 57–59.

Woodmere Art Museum. *Generations: Louise Fishman, Gertrude Fisher-Fishman, and Razel Kapustin*. Exh. cat. Philadelphia: Woodmere Art Museum, 2012.
CATS. 7–11, 94, 95

Yau, John. "Drawing a New Line," *Art on Paper* 8, no. 3 (January/February 2004): 56–61.

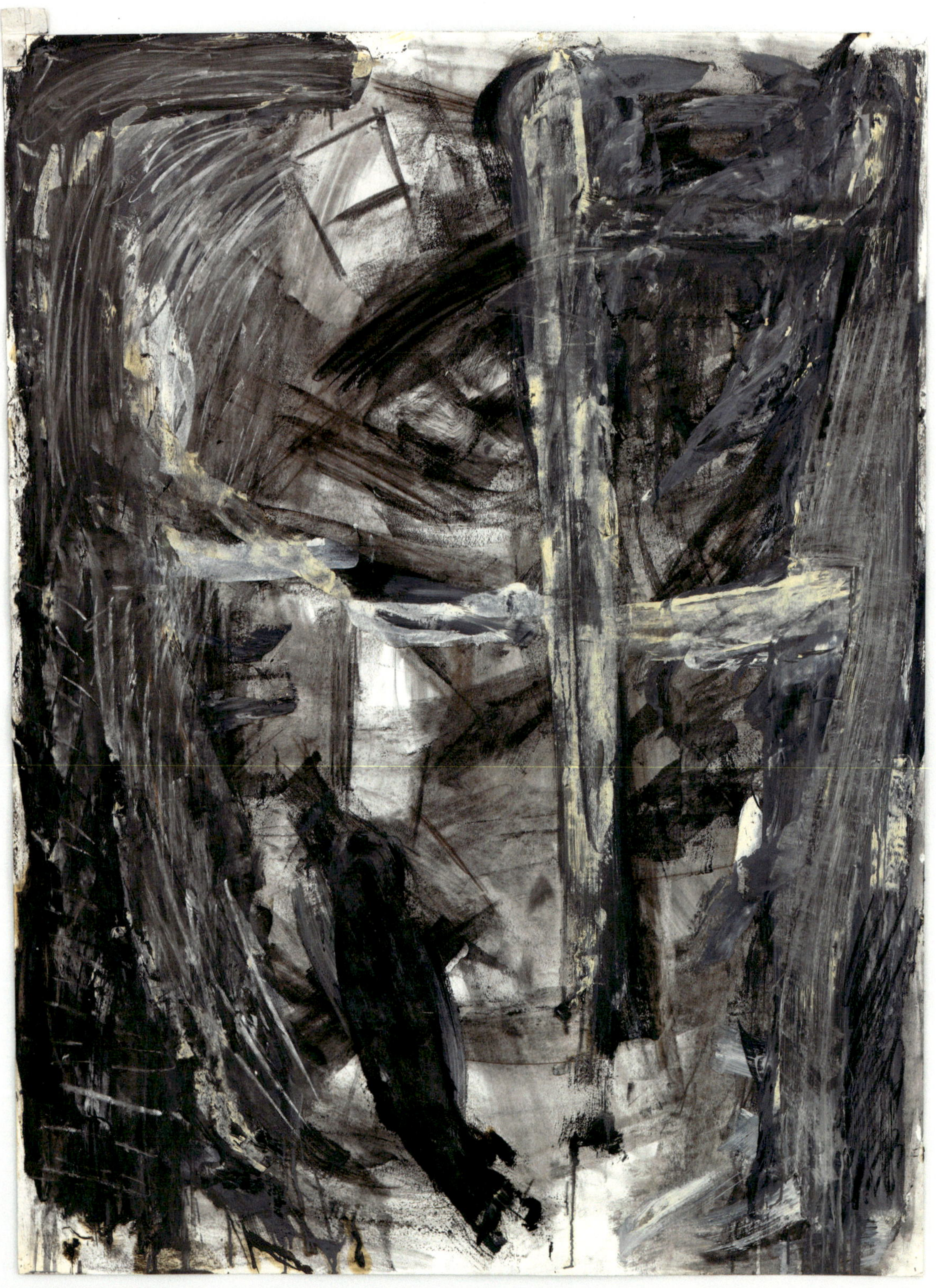

Acknowledgments

Being a curator at the University of Illinois has brought me endless fascination with the intellectual, material, and alumni resources at hand. Krannert Art Museum (KAM) Senior Director of Advancement Brenda Nardi introduced me to Louise Fishman (MFA 1960) in 2017, just as I began searching for my first in-depth project on painting. I could not have predicted what would follow, and this book reflects the joint efforts of many dedicated colleagues and supporters. At KAM, I am especially grateful to Director Jon Seydl and Senior Curator Allyson Purpura for their consistent encouragement and collective imagination. Assistant Curator and Publications Specialist Kathryn Koca Polite, Museum Registrar and Exhibitions Director Christine Saniat, Collection Manager Kim Sissons, and Design and Installation Specialists Tim Fox and Walter Wilson make any KAM undertaking possible, and their professionalism and good humor is reason to come to work every day. Enormous thanks to Associate Director Claudia Corlett-Stahl and Office Administrator Chris Schaede for navigating all of the administrative and budgetary details of this exhibition and publication. It is a pleasure to work with our education team: Anne Sautman, Kamila Glowacki, and Liza Sylvestre, along with Assistant Director for Marketing and Communications Julia Nucci Kelly. Thanks also to Alyssa Bralower, who helped gather research materials in the early stages of this project, to my curatorial intern Grace Parker, and to Curator of European and American Art Maureen Warren.

A Question of Emphasis: Louise Fishman Drawing developed in large part due to Helaine Posner's excellent 2016 paintings retrospective, which I saw when it traveled to the Weatherspoon Art Museum in 2017. Enormous thanks to Helaine for her steady support, as well as to Ingrid Schaffner and Judith Stein. The full staff at Cheim & Read were indispensable when I developed the checklist for this exhibition. Special thanks to Maria Bueno, Stephen Truax, Karen Polack, Ellen Robinson, and John Cheim. Locks Gallery, Vielmetter Los Angeles, and Karma, New York, have been a curator's dream to work with. I thank Sueyun Locks, Erin Batson, Liz Griffin, Susanne Vielmetter, Michael Smoler, Olivia Gauthier, Ariel Pittman, Brendan Dugan, and Anna Blum for their unwavering support and belief in Louise's work. I remain profoundly grateful to the University of Illinois System President Timothy L. Killeen and to Richard M. and Rosann Gelvin Noel for ensuring that Louise's remarkable painting *Blonde Ambition* would find its home in KAM's permanent collection. The Henry Luce Foundation provided lead support for this project, with special thanks to Terry Carbone and Lorraine Morales. The College of Fine and Applied Arts at the University of Illinois Urbana-Champaign has been a stalwart supporter, and I am grateful for their matching grant support for this project, with special thanks to Dean Kevin Hamilton.

Conversations with a number of colleagues and friends have shaped my perspective on Louise's work. Sincere thanks to Jill H. Casid, Emma Chubb, Nancy Davidson, Patrick Earl Hammie, Sharon Irish, Allyson Purpura, and Sandra Ruiz. Beth Rudin DeWoody and Bianca Lanza loaned spectacular works from their

67

Untitled, 1985

Oil and charcoal on paper
49 × 38 inches, two sided

personal collections, and I am likewise grateful to the Jewish Museum, the JP Morgan Chase Collection, and the Weatherspoon Art Museum for lending their works on paper. Thanks to Stephen Brown, Katherine Danalakis, Charlotte Eyerman, Jessica Iannuzzi Garcia, Elaine Gustafson, and Kimberly Terbush for ensuring these institutional loans. Video Data Bank at the School of the Art Institute of Chicago is an invaluable resource, and I extend my thanks to Melanie Emerson and Zach Vanes for facilitating both images from Lynn Blumenthal and Kate Horsfield's 1977 video interview with Louise and their institution's loan to the exhibition.

I am beyond fortunate for this to be the first book published by KAM while working with Lucia | Marquand, and my enormous thanks goes to Adrian Lucia, Kestrel Rundle, Melissa Duffes, Leah Finger, Kim Kent, and Meghann Ney for their professionalism and expertise. Tom Eykemans's design beautifully illuminates Louise's work: thank you. My thanks as well to Kristin Swan for her sharp editing prowess and to Kathryn Koca Polite for managing all aspects of production so smoothly. Jill H. Casid, Catherine Lord, and Ulrike Müller not only contributed dynamite texts to this book, their thinking about Louise's work is of such consequence for painting, art history, and kinship that I cannot adequately communicate how honored I am to publish their work. Deep thanks especially to Jill for instilling the hows and whys of imagining possibilities and making them real.

In Louise's studio, I thank Cristina Miranda and Annelie McGavin. Ingrid Nyeboe deserves a category all her own as Louise's archivist, spouse, and greatest advocate. Ingrid and Louise brought me into the fold from our very first meeting. Our conversations about painting, politics, and personalities have shaped my worldview and helped me to make sense of the genealogies among women that have always been at the center of my life. Such are the gifts between artist and curator, and for this my greatest thanks is reserved for Louise: for your tremendous and fearless work, your storytelling, and your care.

Amy L. Powell
CURATOR OF MODERN AND CONTEMPORARY ART

I am fortunate to have had a number of people support me in examining and passing on my work on paper.

I would like to thank Helaine Posner, who was the first to point out the necessity for a retrospective of my work on paper. Her curatorial approach to my painting retrospective at the Neuberger Museum of Art in 2016 gave me new insights into my work that I will forever treasure.

I also thank Brenda Nardi, senior director of advancement, Krannert Art Museum | School of Art and Design | Japan House, and Alan T. Mette, professor and director of the School of Art and Design, both at the University of Illinois. They came, they saw, and were conquered; thus, they were quick to encourage Amy Powell, the curator of modern and contemporary art at Krannert Art Museum to pay me a visit in my studio and also to visit Cheim & Read, which represented me at the time.

Amy Powell is the force behind the entire enterprise, soup to nuts. She quickly recognized and selected these hundred-plus works from among thousands in my archive. Her imagination, her sensitivity, and intelligence are manifest in her choices of my work. She is generous and brilliant. I thank her, again and again.

I am grateful to Jon Seydl, director of the Krannert Art Museum, for his enormous support and confidence in my work.

I thank the staff at Cheim & Read, where I was represented from 1998 until 2018, for their generous work on my behalf.

I would like to thank my former archivist, Cristina Miranda, whose dedication to preserving my work is much appreciated. And a special thank-you to Annelie McGavin for creating a condition report of the works in this exhibition, and for her superior knowledge of my work.

Finally, I thank my beloved spouse, Ingrid Nyeboe, for trusting my work and my history as an artist, and for uncountable hours doing the grunt work required to prepare the work on paper (and me) for examination and presentation.

Louise Fishman

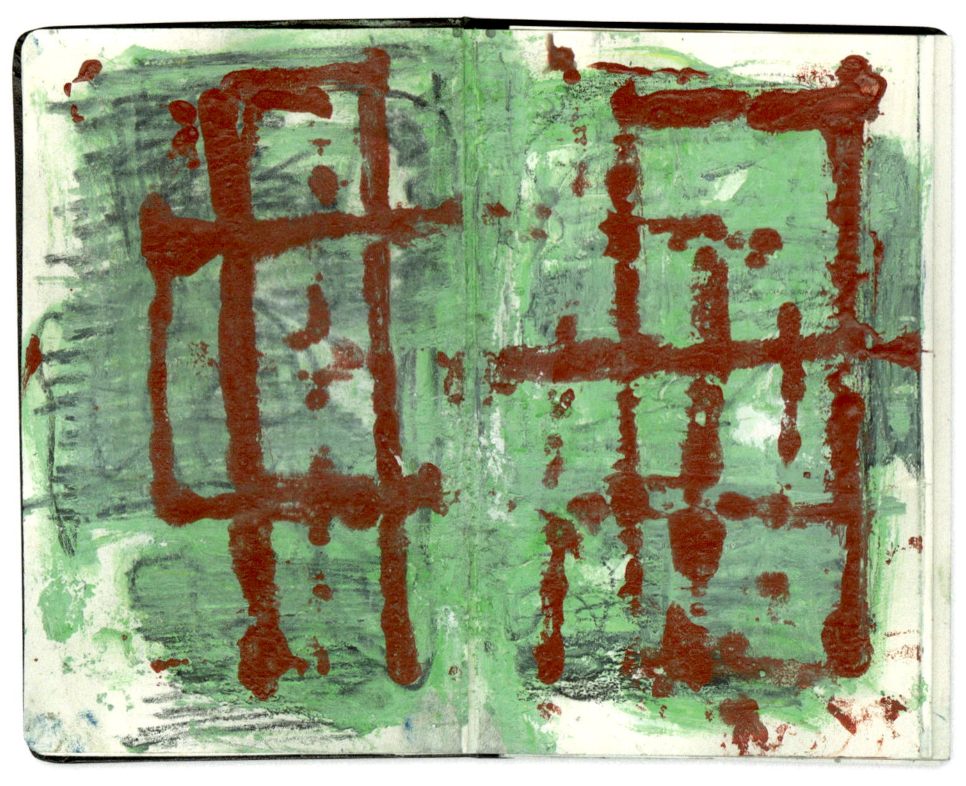

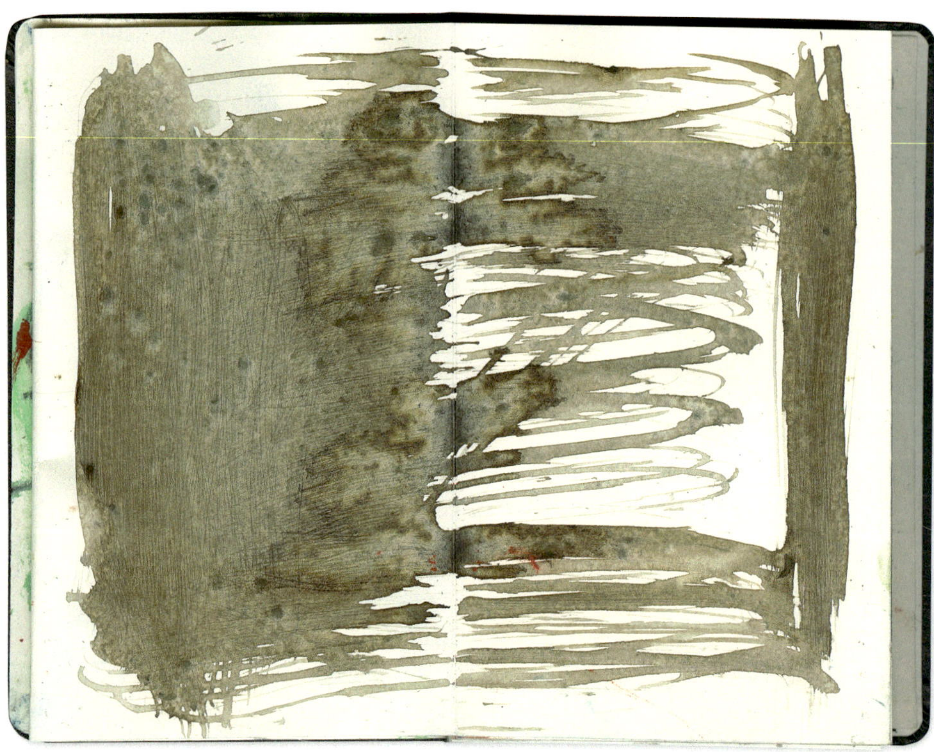

Contributors

Jill H. Casid is a theorist, historian, practicing artist, and professor of visual studies in the Departments of Art History and Gender and Women's Studies at the University of Wisconsin-Madison, where she founded and served as the first director of the Center for Visual Cultures. Casid is currently at work on a two-book project titled *Form at the Edges of Life*. Since the publication of *Sowing Empire: Landscape and Colonization* (University of Minnesota Press, 2005), which received the College Art Association's Millard Meiss award, she has continued to write on approaches to landscape while pursuing work on the history and theory of photography, queer and trans art practices, and the materializing effects of imaging with *Scenes of Projection: Recasting the Enlightenment Subject* (University of Minnesota Press, 2015) and on approaches to the global with *Art History in the Wake of the Global Turn* (coedited with Aruna D'Souza; Yale University Press, 2014).

Catherine Lord, an artist and writer, divides her time between Hudson and Manhattan, New York. Professor emerita of art at the University of California, Irvine, she is the author of *The Summer of Her Baldness: A Cancer Improvisation* (University of Texas Press, 2004) and *Art and Queer Culture* (with Richard Meyer; Phaidon Press, 2013).

Ulrike Müller is a painter based in New York City and Vienna, Austria. Müller shifts her formal vocabulary between material and affective states and makes use of a variety of materials and techniques. Alongside small-scale paintings in vitreous enamel on steel, she produces expansive wall paintings, publications, prints, and textiles. Müller was a coeditor of the queer feminist journal *LTTR* and organized *Herstory Inventory: 100 Feminist Drawings by 100 Artists*. Recent solo exhibitions appeared at Mumok (Vienna, 2015) and Kunstverein für die Rheinlande und Westfahlen (Düsseldorf, 2018). At Mumok, Müller, with Manuela Ammer, co-curated the collection exhibition *Always, Always, Others: Non-Classical Forays into Modernism* (2015). Her work was included in the 2017 Whitney Biennial, the 57th Carnegie International (2018), and the 58th international art exhibition of the Biennale di Venezia (2019).

Amy L. Powell is curator of modern and contemporary art at Krannert Art Museum (KAM) at the University of Illinois Urbana-Champaign. Her research engages contemporary art with a commitment to university art museums as sites for knowledge production and experimentation. Her exhibitions at KAM have included solo presentations with Kennedy Browne, Basel Abbas and Ruanne Abou-Rahme, Autumn Knight, and Zina Saro-Wiwa; group exhibitions *Time/Image* and *Attachment*; and a permanent collections installation titled *Art Since 1948*. Her work has been supported by the Andy Warhol Foundation for the Visual Arts, the Smithsonian Institution, and the Institute for Research in the Humanities at the University of Wisconsin-Madison, where she earned a PhD in art history in 2012.

68

From **Vaporetto Leporello No. 7**, 2017

Watercolor and tempera on paper; leporello binding
5½ × 3½ × ¾ inches (closed)

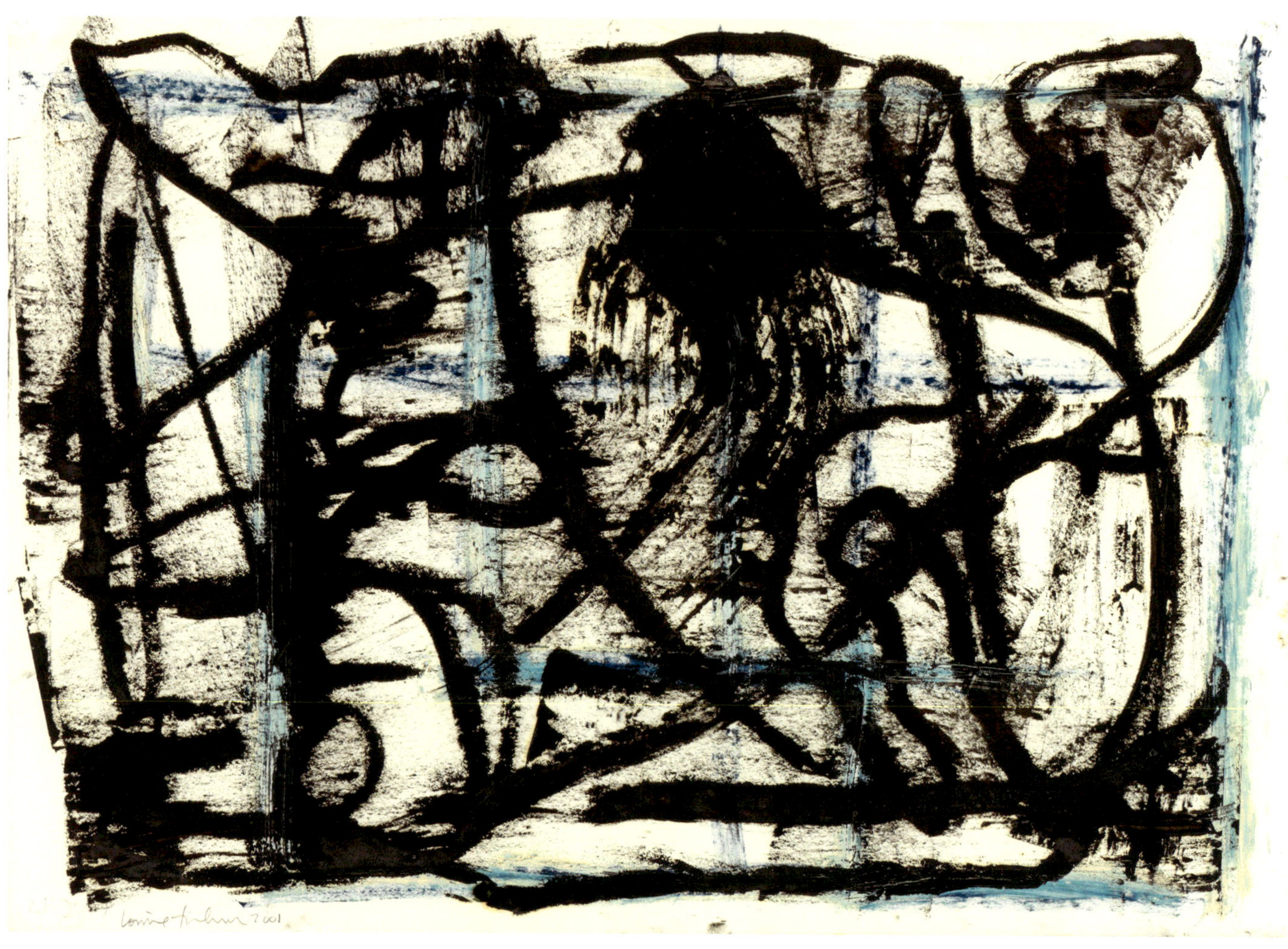

69

Untitled, 2001

Oil and oil stick on paper
20¾ × 29¾ inches